From the Gestapo
to the Gulags

One Jewish Life

From the Gestapo to the Gulags

One Jewish Life

ZEV KATZ

Foreword
Yehuda Bauer

To Felix Posen
with warm regards
Zev Katz

Jerusalem
15-2-05

VALLENTINE MITCHELL
LONDON • PORTLAND, OR

First published in 2004 in Great Britain by
VALLENTINE MITCHELL
Crown House, 47 Chase Side
London N14 5BP

and in the United States of America by
VALLENTINE MITCHELL
c/o ISBS, 920 NE 58th Avenue, Suite 300
Portland, Oregon 97213-3786

Website: www.vmbooks.com

Copyright © 2004 Zev Katz

British Library Cataloguing in Publication Data

Katz, Zev
From the Gestapo to the Gulags: One Jewish life
1. Katz, Zev 2. Katz (family) 3. Holocaust, Jewish (1939–1945)
– Personal narratives 4. Jews – Poland – Yaroslav –
Biography 5. Jews – Soviet Union – Biography
I. Title
940.5'318'092

ISBN 0-85303-474-5 (paper)

Library of Congress Cataloging-in-Publication Data

Katz, Zev
From the Gestapo to the Gulags: One Jewish life
Zev Katz; foreword by Yehuda Bauer.
p. cm.
ISBN 0-85303-474-5 (pbk.)
1. Katz family. 2. Jews – Poland – Biography. 3. Refugees,
Jewish – Soviet Union – Biography. 4. Jews, Polish – Soviet
Union – Biography. 5. World War, 1939–1945 – Jews – Soviet
Union – Biography. 6. Holocaust, Jewish (1939–1945) – Poland.
I. Title. II. Series.

DS135.P63K285 2003
940.53'18'0922438 – dc21
[B]   2003051001

Typeset in 11/13pt Zapf Calligraphica by Vallentine Mitchell
Printed in Great Britain by MPG Books Ltd, Victoria Square, Bodmin, Cornwall

I dedicate this book to the memory of
my mother, Batia,
and
my father, Arieh.

Contents

List of Illustrations and Maps

Acknowledgements

This memoir is largely a result of prompting by my family and friends. On each occasion, when the various stories of my life were told, my daughters Nina and Odette, my grandchildren and other members of my family, in particular my nieces and nephews, pressured me by saying: 'You must write it down! This is quite a saga!' They persuaded me at last – and here is the book.

It was my good fortune, during my teaching at the Spiro Institute in London some years ago, to get to know Frank Cass, one of the foremost publishers in London. I am most grateful to him for his advice and encouragement, which lead to the publication of this book.

I am extremely grateful to Yehuda Bauer, one of the world's foremost Holocaust scholars, for writing such an encouraging preface to this book.

Judy Fatal in Jerusalem and Georgina Clark-Mazo in London have done invaluable work in preparing this book for publication.

Finally, I owe a permanent bouquet of flowers and heart-felt thanks to my wife, Doris, for her wise advice, editing and – yes – criticism, as well as prompting me to complete this work.

As the reader will see, I am dedicating this book to the memory of my parents who kept our family alive and united through all those perilous years.

Foreword

Many hundreds of memoirs, if not more than that, have been written and published by Holocaust survivors, relating their experiences during those tragic times. On the other hand, not many Jews who fled or were deported to the Soviet Union wrote memoirs. There were basically two kinds of Jewish refugees from Poland who spent the war years in Soviet Central Asia or the Siberian tundra and taiga: those who fled to the Soviet Union as the Nazis advanced into Poland in the autumn of 1939 or the summer of 1941 and after; and those who were deported to Siberia by the Soviet authorities as 'capitalists', 'bourgeois counter-revolutionaries', 'enemies of the people', refugees and the like. These deportations took place from Soviet-occupied Eastern Poland (today Western Belarus and Western Ukraine) between the end of 1939 and right up until a week before the German invasion took place on 22 June 1941. Zev Katz and his family belonged to this latter group. There are very few accounts available to the reader of Western European languages – and this one surely belongs to the very best of this rare breed.

The Katz family lived in Jaroslaw [Yaroslav], a smallish town in Southeastern Poland, and were reasonably well to do. When the Germans invaded Poland in September 1939, they became, as did all Jews, an endangered species. They were expelled by the Gestapo from Yaroslav into the eastern part of Poland, which had just been occupied by the Soviets. As experienced traders, they maintained themselves for a while partly by hard physical labour, partly – and mainly – by illicit trading. Young Zev attended a Soviet school where, among other things, he studied the so-called 'Stalin Constitution of the

Soviet Union', a marvellous piece of mass deception, which promised the most liberal kind of personal and collective liberties; and which, of course, was completely ignored in practice. In the end the Soviet secret police caught up with the Katzes and deported them to 'the white bears', as the saying went then – to Siberia. There, they were brought into a slave labour camp, where their main occupation was to be gathering sap from trees and felling them, which was not exactly what they had been used to back in Yaroslav. Food was scarce, and rationed according to the amount of wood produced by back-breaking work. Medicine and clothing were even scarcer, and the attitude of the guards ranged from indifference to worse. Zev remembered the Constitution and its promise to accord free education to all youngsters in the land. He was of high school age, so he wrote a letter of complaint to Comrade Stalin, saying he wanted to attend school. This was unheard of – an inmate of a Gulag, in the middle of exactly nowhere, having the cheek to write to the Sun of the Nations himself with a petty complaint. But, lo and behold, in due time he got an answer which was a first step towards the release of the whole family from the camp and their move to a fairly large town, Semipalatinsk, in Northern Kazahkstan. The family then had to find some kind of employment, and they tried all kinds of things, but their two sons then began working at a major government store, which enabled them to get more food, and to exchange articles they acquired by not very legal means for food and other items. Katz tells his story with some gentle irony, and through it we get a glimpse of what life was like in the USSR during wartime, from Eastern Poland to Siberia, and with different kinds of Soviet people. In the end, after the war, the Katzes made their way back to Poland; and from there, via illegal immigration to Palestine, right into the Israeli War of Independence. After that war, Zev Katz had a successful career as a well-known journalist in Israel's leading intellectual daily, *Ha'aretz*, and as a university lecturer with a British degree. In Israel today, Katz works with immigrants from the Soviet Union, in the framework of a secular Jewish college teaching Jewish culture.

The Katz story is both unusual and characteristic of Jewish fate. It is not just a personal story but also the story of a tightly knit family. The real hero of the story is, I think, Mother Katz. She is the one who holds the family together, whose authority carries the day, though she listens carefully to the others. Life centres around her. The story is often touching, sometimes tragic, sometimes almost hilarious. Thus, in newly established Israel, the children decide to establish a kiosk for their parents in Jerusalem so they can earn their keep; nothing unusual there, except they decide to set up the kiosk at a central crossroads in Jerusalem – it has to be Jerusalem, because of the father's health problems. They run into the justly maligned Israeli bureaucracy; but no bureaucracy will defeat the Katzes – they had outwitted Soviet officials, and the Israeli ones were child's play by comparison. The boys set up the kiosk, of course.

On the serious – very serious – side is the story of their deportation to Siberia: the fact of the matter is that had they not first been expelled by the Gestapo and then deported by the Soviets, they most likely would not have survived, because they would have come under German rule, and would have died together with the Jews of Eastern Poland. At the time, deportation was a terrible tragedy. It turned out to be their luck.

Zev Katz has written a gripping account of a family story on the margins of the Holocaust. For a vast majority of readers it will be something new and unheard of. From the point of view of Jewish history, it is a chapter that should be remembered, and the book presented here is a good way of doing so.

Yehuda Bauer
Academic Advisor, Yad Vashem
Professor Emeritus, Hebrew University of Jerusalem

Introduction

This book is about one largely unknown aspect of Jewish life, or the life of a Polish-Jewish family mainly during the Second World War and several years after (1939–49). During that period the world was drawn into a vortex of unpredictable and unimaginable events – often in paradoxical ways.

Much has been published about the Holocaust and the death camps. Very little was written about other developments resulting from the Holocaust and profoundly affecting Jewish life in Eastern Europe. My family – parents and four children – did not perish in the Holocaust. But we were exiled by the Gestapo and uprooted from the town in which my family had lived for generations. We were cut off from the rest of our family, from friends and neighbours. We lost our home and all our belongings and were left penniless refugees. The Nazis endeavoured to destroy the Jewish people. The Soviets exiled us, in turn, to Siberia and Kazakhstan. For years, by day and night, they endlessly hammered Soviet ideology into us. They relentlessly attacked Judaism and Zionism. The upshot of all this was paradoxically not what was intended both by the Nazis and Soviets. I, myself, and my family, were only strengthened in our determination to go to Israel and settle there. This is what we eventually did.

'A Jew found in this town after 3 p.m. today will be shot', said a Gestapo man to us.

It was 10 a.m. of that day at the end of September 1939. Until then, our family of six lived in the city of Yaroslav in Southern Poland.

'Where shall we go?' – we asked

'Eastwards' – was the answer.

So, within a few hours, we turned from a well-to-do family with a thriving grocery shop and some export business into hapless refugees. Our family owned two houses and was living in a well-furnished villa. What we had worked for, and saved and built, for many years had disappeared in smoke.

We went 'east', where we found ourselves under the Soviet Army which then occupied Eastern Poland. We briefly lived in a village nearby until, one night in June 1940, we were taken by the Soviet Secret Police to a railway station, put in cattle trucks and exiled to Siberia. We found ourselves in a Labour Camp in the forests of the Altay Region close to the Mongolian and Chinese border. After the German attack on the Soviet Union in June 1941, we were recognized as 'former Polish citizens', released from the camps and allowed to settle in the city of Semipalatinsk in Northern Kazakhstan. In May 1946, we were 'repatriated' to Poland. However, due to the rampant anti-Semitism there, we left Poland semi-illegally and, finally, found ourselves in a DP Camp in the town of Wetzlar near Frankfurt in West Germany. Our intention was to go to Israel. I was the first of my family to go there, as a volunteer in the Israeli Army in the War of Independence. The rest of our family arrived in the spring of 1949. So our family was reunited after a ten years' Odyssey – a rare, almost miraculous event for those years.

In the Epilogue of this book I describe developments after 1949 until almost the present day.

Unpredictable and unfathomable are the paths of history. Why, out of so many Jewish families, were we saved though we were in the hands of the Gestapo, in a Soviet Labour Camp, a DP Camp and all the wars of Israel?...

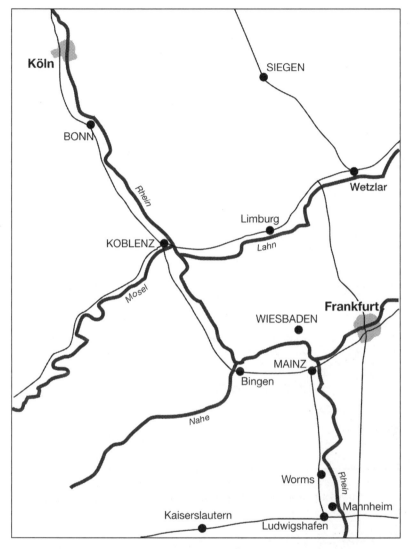

1. The Altay area of Siberia, where Zev Katz was imprisoned.
It is located between Mongolia and China. The city of Semei
in Kazakhstan, where the Katz's lived in 1941–46, was then
known as Semipalatinsk.

2. The city of Wetzlar, where the DP camp was
located, 1946–48, was to the north of Frankfurt-am-Main.

1 • Under the Germans in Our Town

'We direct our attention mainly to Germany, since in Germany there are the most progressive conditions of the European civilisation.'

Karl Marx and Friedrich Engels,
The Communist Manifesto (1848)

'German soldiers! In front of our house' – we peered through a crack in the shutters of a front window in sheer horror. It looked like a surrealistic picture from some horror film …

It was a sunny September morning in 1939. On the first of that fateful month the German army attacked Poland. It took them only ten days to arrive in our small town of Yaroslav in the south of Poland, halfway between Cracow and Lvov. Event followed on event. At first we had general mobilization and huge, ultra-patriotic demonstrations. The swift advance of the German forces sent an endless stream of civilian refugees through our town, including some members of our family from western Poland who came to live with us, crowding our apartment. They were soon followed by columns of the retreating Polish Army. The railway station and other strategic points in our town were bombed. The bridge over the River San – a tributary of the central Polish river, the Vistula – was blown up. Our house was situated on a road leading to the east, so we could see the endless columns marching nearby, day and night. Then the road became ominously empty. We heard some shooting during the night and some artillery bombardment, and then – silence. We slept behind bolted doors and shuttered windows. In the morning we peeped through the shutters and could not believe our eyes: there they were!

What was so surprising was that this, our first encounter with the 'Germans', was so 'idyllic'. In front of our house adjoining the road, there was a small square with a mechanical well in the centre. There was no running water in our house, much like the other houses in our town. There was a huge iron wheel on the well with a handle; when it was turned water came from the spout over the well.

A detachment of German motorized infantry with several armoured cars chose the square in front of our house for their morning toilette and breakfast.

What a contrast they were compared to the retreating Polish army! But for the officers, who donned smart uniforms and shining boots, the ordinary Polish soldiers were poorly dressed. During the rapid retreat they were unshaven and often unwashed. They had few motorcars. Even many of the guns and ammunition supplies were horse drawn. Most of the army marched on foot. The orderly retreat soon turned into chaos, discipline collapsed. Supplies often did not keep up, so the soldiers begged for food or 'sequestered' whatever they could lay their hands on.

In comparison, the Germans looked like some kind of super-men – in our inexperienced eyes at least. Even their ordinary soldiers were dressed in bluish uniforms of fine cloth. All of them were 'motorized' – we rarely saw a German soldier on foot. Some of them fought their war with elegant slippers on their feet. They were remarkably orderly and clean. After some time, a field kitchen mounted on a truck arrived and hot food was served in gleaming clean dishes. In turn, several of them came to the well, stripped their shirts, washed and shaved. Many had elegant toilette bags of a kind we had not seen before. Altogether, they looked more as if they were on a jolly picnic than in the midst of a war.

Moreover, their attitude was not at all menacing; initially it was correct and then friendly. Slowly some children approached them, then some younths and older people. Soon a conversation developed using sign language and through some neighbours who knew a little German. Some of the soldiers offered sweets and tidbits of their food to the children. Soon some women came to the well for water and were not above a little flirting with the handsome young soldiers.

One specific incident made a deep impression on me. Further to the east, our road swung round to the right. Straight on, a small road led to a cul-de-sac in front of a church. When the Polish army was retreating, their columns almost inevitably made a mistake and entered the cul-de-sac. The result was chaos and pandemonium: it was very difficult to turn around in the narrow sideroad, the main road became blocked, provoking shouts, curses, threats and sometimes blows. When the Germans arrived, the first thing they did was to put out clear road signs and post traffic wardens on motorcycles. The motorized military columns rolled smoothly on, without ever entering the hapless cul-de-sac.

After several hours this German column left – and soon the idyllic interlude was over. Following the army, the Gestapo arrived in our area and all to soon fear and terror gripped us. They invited the elders of the Jewish community for a 'meeting' and put them in jail. Then they demanded a 'ransom' of valuables, and when this was delivered they doubled the amount. My father, a relatively successful businessman, went into hiding, in case they came to arrest him as well. The Germans made widespread arrests among the Polish officials and community leaders. People were forcibly drafted into work gangs for the German military.

The situation in our town was relatively mild in comparison with some others. In a city not far from us, the Germans arrested 70 local Jewish community leaders, put them on trucks and took them out of town. For days it was impossible to find out what happened to them. Then women came from a nearby village and said to the Jews of that town: 'Why do you leave the bodies of your people lying in the wood without a decent burial?' The entire Jewish population walked to that wood where they identified the bodies of members of their families and friends. In another small town, the birthplace of my sister-in-law, Ruzhan, the Germans gathered all the Jews into the local synagogue, locked its gates and set fire to it. Miraculously, a high-ranking German Army officer happened to be passing by. He ordered the soldiers to open the gates just as the Jews were on the brink of being burned alive.

Days of fear and terror ensued. The Germans arrested the Polish policemen and appointed self-declared Volksdeutsche and rabble collaborators as auxiliary police. Along with the German soldiers, they took to making rounds in the houses in search of wine, valuables and women. One day a German soldier forced his way into our house. 'We heard that you are hiding some weapons in your attic', he said. He ordered my mother to go with him to search the attic. When they were there alone he accosted her. Luckily, my mother knew German well. She persuaded him that she was old enough to be his mother, and showed him her legs, which were permanently swollen with varicose veins, upon which the soldier beat a hasty retreat.

A cousin of mine, a lovely and delicate girl, was not so lucky. Two drunken German soldiers came to their house one evening and took her away with them. At dawn the next morning she was found half naked and semi-conscious on a side road several miles away, where the rapists had thrown her out of their car. Her tribulations did not end there. They must have liked her, because they came again several evenings after that. All the pleadings, crying and screaming by her mother and father were to no avail. After returning next morning, she left home, for fear they would come again. It is not surprising that girls and young women were kept constantly at home; at the appearance of a German soldier in the vicinity, they went into hiding.

From time to time, the German-appointed police would come to our house, hammer loudly on the bolted front door and demand: 'Three (four) people from this house to work – immediately!' On several occasions I went together with my younger brother. We were both in our early teens. My brother was a 'typical Aryan': blond straight hair, blue eyes, milky white complexion. We used to call him 'Moishe the Catholic'. It was because of his appearance that we sent him to work for the Germans – perhaps they would let him go. Our first 'job' was cleaning the City Hall in the town centre. As we formed a single line in front of the City Hall , a rotund member of the Gestapo stepped out of the building. He started to berate us and jeer at us. But when he came to Moshe he stopped, obviously puzzled: *'Bist du ein Jude? Sicher?'* (Are you a Jew? For sure?)

The same happened the next time when we 'worked' for the Germans, inside a local army encampment which was turned into a field hospital for wounded soldiers. Two young SS officers walked around him and looked at him shaking their heads as if they could not believe their eyes. Later, there were rumours that in their quest to enlarge the 'Aryan' race, the Nazis kidnapped children with a suitable appearance in order to raise them as Germans; from then on we kept Moshe at home.

Our first experience with the Germans at City Hall was grim enough; yet it turned out to be a relatively mild affair compared to another time at the 'hospital'. We witnessed morbid scenes. The Germans took particular pleasure in tormenting Jews of a religious appearance. They pulled and tore their beards and sidelocks, and set them impossible tasks. When these poor Jews could not execute the tasks, the Germans screamed at them, cursed them and beat them. In one corner of the central court, a detail of six, mainly religious, Jews were ordered to carry a huge iron basin full of building debris out through the gate. The basin was extremely heavy and the Jews were either old or weak youngsters. Forced by the screams and beatings of the Germans, they put their hands beneath the basin and tried to lift it and move it. After a step or two, they were not able to keep it up – down it fell on their hands breaking their fingers. Under severe beatings and shouts of 'You Yiddish lazybones, you will be shot if you refuse to move the basin', they tried again with bleeding hands to raise it. But after a few steps it fell again and practically severed the arm of an elderly, bearded Jew. He fell to the ground screaming with pain, but the German soldier, a young boy, continued mercilessly beating him with his rifle. In another corner, several officers were tearing the sidelocks off a young Hassid; then they stood him against a wall. While laughing, they took out their pistols and said: 'Quick, say your prayers *verfluchte Jude* (bloody Kike)! We are going to shoot you.' The Hassid did not fully understand, but seeing them directing their weapons towards him started loudly to intone prayers,   his face whiter than the wall and his whole body shaking to his chanting rhythm. This amused the Germans greatly and they continued to shout at him 'Louder you Jew pig! Louder!' They talked about it as 'a fine shooting practice' and argued among themselves as to who would shoot first.

A sharp command from 'our' German tore us away from the place and we never knew what happened to the Hassidic boy in the end. We worked several hours more inside a building full of wounded and ailing German soldiers until we came to a long corridor with a door at the end. Our German supervisor was not with us and nobody was around. We peered through the door – it lead to the street outside! We did not hesitate, though we could be shot if caught. Quickly we stepped outside, past the nearby opening and found ourselves in the street. Slowly, nonchalantly, we walked on as if we were taking a casual stroll. Within half an hour we were hammering at the main door of our house. Not surprisingly, we were received with exclamations of joy by our family. When someone was taken away to 'work' for the Germans, one never knew whether they would ever return.

Meantime, under German occupation came the season of the High Jewish Holidays. In some respects, our own little town of Yaroslav was still very much like part of the 'old times'. In its Jewish part, which actually included the City Hall and main market square, it was almost totally closed on the Jewish Sabbath.

On the High Holidays even the non-Jewish businesses closed down. From all corners of town, people – many in white robes and prayer shawls, with medieval fur hats on their heads – hurried to the synagogues. The town came practically to a standstill, with the loud chanting of prayers audible all over. At the end of the Yom Kippur fast and prayers, everyone in town shook hands, even with strangers, and women kissed each other.

How different things were under the Germans! A hush fell on our town, not a soul could be seen in the empty streets. In our house, we gathered behind shuttered windows in a large room, put on prayer shawls and started our prayers. Some of the older people were crying, tears running down their cheeks. Outside some youngsters were posted as lookouts. In the middle of the silent, most solemn, prayer, we heard a signal from the lookout – a German soldier had been seen nearby. In panic, we hid our prayer books and shawls and dispersed. In our minds we screamed to God: 'Why?! Why are we not even allowed to pray on Yom Kippur?'

2 • My Shtetl Yaroslav

'Belz, mine shtetl Belz.
Mine heimele wu ich hob
mine kinder yourn verbracht.'*

Yaroslav, the town of my birth, is situated halfway between Cracow and Lvov in southern Poland. It was a clean city in which much of the previous Austrian influence was felt; from the late eighteenth century until 1918 it had been part of the Habsburg Empire. There were few cars to be seen – it still lived in the era of horse and carriage. Within the population of some 25,000, some 7,000 were Jewish and lived mostly in a specific part of the town. Almost all of them were religious, with some of them deeply Hassidic. My own family was of Belz Hassidic persuasion. Deeply orthodox at first, our family moved slowly to a modern orthodox orientation, mainly under the influence of our mother. She lived during the First World War in Bohemia, knew German well and had received some 'secular' education. She was also from a deeply orthodox family, yet she used to read books, quote from the poetry of Goethe, Schiller and Heine, and even hum the occasional aria from the then popular operettas of Kalman. Altogether, she was a remarkable woman and had high ambitions, especially for the education of her children. It was in this field that the change was particularly discernible.

According to the ancient tradition, I was put in the charge of a Hebrew teacher (*melamed*) at the age of 4, as soon as I was able to walk to the *Heder* (Hebrew religious school). Again in line with tradition, this famous establishment was simply a large window-less room adjoining the house of the *melamed*. It contained a long wooden table and some benches. Our teacher, a middle-aged

*'Belz, my little town Belz. My little home where I have my childhood years spent.'

man, his *tsitsit* (prayer shawl) and hair flowing, walked around the table with a book in one hand and a cane in the other. He was very poor – again in fine accord with tradition – and informal. His wife would often arrive in the middle of our lessons and discuss with him all kind of family and community affairs. She used to ask for money for the housekeeping. He would habitually answer that there was none, whereupon, after further argument he would reach into his pockets and 'find' some. Other people used to come to our *Heder* on various errands

Teaching was done in the old-time 'rote' fashion – first learning to read the Hebrew alphabet, then chanting parts of the 'weekly portion' of the Bible – in Hebrew with a Yiddish translation. I happened to be a very good pupil: by the age of 5 I was able to recite quite well a certain amount of the Torah. So our teacher, Hirsh Meyer, prepared me for the first traditional celebration, that of 'Bridegroom of the Torah'. One Sabbath after the prayers at the 'Hassidic *shtible*' (the makeshift small synagogue) which our family frequented, my father invited everyone to our small apartment in the centre of town for kiddush (drinks and tidbits, vodka and herring). When they, and invited members of our extended family, packed our small home and had some refreshments, I – in a new blue outfit – was put on a chair. I started to declaim in a ringing voice the portion of the week and a short commentary by Rashi, the great authoritative medieval scholar. My grandfather, his long, white beard flowing over his gabardine Hassidic black coat, was sitting opposite me, his eyes shining and head nodding in approval. When I finished, he blessed me and kissed me, as did most of those present. And so I became a 'bridegroom of the Bible' at the age of 5.

The next stage of my orthodox education was at a Talmud Torah. This was a serious establishment in a separate wooden house with several rooms fitted out with identical wooden tables and benches and manned by the same type of Hassid with flowing beards, long sidelocks, and *tsitsit* under the black kaftan. My teacher there happened to be a red-haired fellow who used to sweat profusely and clear his nose with a large dirty handkerchief to the accompaniment of loud noises. He carried the proscribed cane more like a symbol than an actual tool for promoting education. Here we learned not only some part of the 'portion of the week' but were introduced to various commentaries and to a few passages of the Mishna.

By the age of 7 I was enrolled in a Polish primary school, and then the problems started. At that time in Poland, state-run schools were very much a Catholic religious concern. An icon of Jesus on the cross and of the Madonna with a lamp beneath adorned the front wall of every class-room. Studies started and finished every day with prayers and the singing of religious hymns. A Catholic priest was vice-principal: he officiated at mass on festivals and delivered sermons in front of the entire school. Lessons on 'religion' were given by a priest five times per week. Jewish pupils had to stand during prayers though they were exempted from saying the prayers. During lessons on the Catholic religion we had to march out of class. Not to be left without religion, a rotund and kindly elderly Jewish teacher plied us with a sugared interpretation of Judaism at special periods for Jewish pupils. These lessons were often an hilarious and outrageous affair, since some of us knew more about Judaism than the teacher, while others were totally bored and disinterested and so engaged in all kinds of frolics.

For a Jewish child, school was a place of anti-Semitic hatred. Teaching was six days in a week, including on the Sabbath. Once enrolled one had to attend school every day. With a special permit issued by the principal, Jewish pupils could be allowed to be absent on Saturdays, provided that they learned the lessons and did the homework on Sundays. This meant actually finding another pupil who attended Saturday studies, copying his notes and learning from him what the assigned homework was.

This involved going to the home of another pupil and persuading or bribing him to give you his notes and explain the assignments. Often the price was doing his homework for him. Later, when I attended a 'gymnasium' (high school) – enrolment in which was especially difficult for a Jewish youngster – I was not allowed to be absent from lessons on Saturday. My father agreed to my going to school on the Sabbath provided that I did not engage in any activity that is forbidden, such as writing. So when there was some kind of written test on the Sabbath, I sat there with my arms folded and explained to the teacher that 'I do not write on the Sabbath day.' Some anti-Semitic teachers who knew about it used to amuse themselves and entertain the class by calling me out in front of the blackboard, asking me some question and then telling me to write the answer. When, as expected, I refused, laughter and merriment engulfed the entire class. The teacher acted naive: 'But why do you Jews do so? ... Tell me?'

As it happened, there were four Jewish students in our class and the three of us were the best. Our mathematics teacher, a fat, bald Pole often berated the class: 'You cursed dumbheads! Why is it that whenever we deal with some difficult problem only the *Zhidki* (Yids) know the answer and you (non-Jews) sit there like the fools you are?' He used to walk around in class, come from behind and give a pupil a hard smack over the head with his heavy fat hand. He specialised in inflicting such blows on Jewish students, for nothing at all.

The students were no better. Often they used to call us all kinds of abusive names, blackmail us to allow them to copy our homework, steal our sandwiches or mockingly offer us their food knowing that we would not eat non-kosher. On frequent marches, for example, at various national festivals and demonstrations, they would suddenly kick me in the ankles or punch me from behind, and then pretend total innocence. There was practically no contact between us, the Jewish students, and the non-Jews.

Anti-Semitism was rife outside school. On my way home from studies I had to pass a small, narrow side-street, next to a cemetery. This was a danger area. While passing there we were often beaten or attacked with stones. One youngster, Stashek, was a particular scourge to us: of dark complexion, often barefoot, with a cane in hand, he accosted us, demanding money, sweets or cigarettes. Even after I gave him some of these he did not forgo the opportunity to give me a smack with his cane or to throw a stone while I was departing. One day we decided to teach him a lesson: we invited several strong Jewish boys to follow us in this street. When he accosted us as usual the others joined us and we started beating him. He began shouting loudly: 'Yids are beating a Christian for blood! Help! Help!' Soon a few members his gang came running and we had to retreat rapidly in case a policeman came and put us in prison. As a matter of routine, Polish law enforcement was eager to act against Jews and utterly unwilling to defend a Jew against violence.

In the late 1930s, Hitler's German Nazism became more and more influential in Poland, and anti-Semitism increasingly virulent. We were very lucky at our school; at some schools and universities Jewish students were put into separate corner seats – a kind of ghetto; at others they were forcibly prevented from attending, thrown down from balconies and steps, beaten up to a pulp. Huge demonstrations were held in all cities with ultra-nationalist bellicose slogans, organised by the pro-Fascist Polish government-sponsored movement – the 'Endek'. These demonstrations gained intensity following the German ultimatum to Poland demanding that Poland cede to Germany its only outlet to the Baltic around Gdansk (Danzig). I made myself look as much as possible like a Pole and went to observe one such demonstration in the main square of our town in front of the Sokol cinema. It was packed with young, rowdy men carrying flags, singing ultra-patriotic songs and shouting at the top of their lungs: 'Fight to the last', 'Death to the enemies of Poland'; and then – like thunder over the sea of heads: 'Poland for the Poles', 'Christians – do not buy from Judases', 'Jews – out! Jews out! Jews out! Jews to Palestine!'

This attitude of the Polish authorities had serious consequences. My father had a major food shop in the centre of town. Among our clients were quite a number of non-Jews. We also supplied a Polish army canteen with fresh food, and this was an important item in our business. Gradually our Catholic customers withdrew, and one day the Polish officer explained most courteously to my mother: 'We are very pleased with your supplies which are always fresh and of good quality. However, we have received orders to buy only from pure Poles. Sorry.'

It was not surprising, therefore, that these circumstances made us feel our Jewishness more intensely. Meanwhile, a crisis boiled over between my father and my deeply orthodox grandfather. When I started to go to a Polish state school it angered my grandfather very much, but at least I continued to study at the Talmud Torah in the afternoon. This became, however, increasingly inadequate and inconvenient. It was far from our home and often in the winter by the time we finished at six o'clock it was dark outside. There was scant lighting in the streets and we lit our way with little lanterns which we carried with a candle inside, it was very picturesque to see a myriad snow flakes swirling in the light of the candle lantern. But one such evening we walked home in a snow storm and got lost, until a passing carriage showed us the way. Also, as we became more educated in the general school, through reading, cinema, radio and newspapers, the old-fashioned and primitive teaching which we received at the Talmud Torah came to seem ever more inadequate.

Under the influence of our mother, my father moved us – me and my two brothers – into a more modern religious school, 'Yavne'. This was too much for my grandfather: that the grandchildren of Samuel Katz, of high priestly lineage and a pillar of the Belz Hassidic sect, should leave a proper orthodox school and attend a so-called religious establishment which taught the Bible in modern Hebrew, God forbid! Worse, this school was sponsored by religious Zionists, and there was nothing more hateful to the Hassids than these. My grandfather cut off all relations with us and would not talk to my father for quite some time.

As usual in our small town we had almost all kinds of Jewish groups and factions – from underground (illegal) communist groups through the leftist–Yiddish 'Bund', Zionist radical–socialist 'Hashomer Hatzair', general Zionist 'Hanoar Hazioni' and 'Akiva', to the right-wing nationalist–revisionists and their 'Betar' youth movement. One of the popular, fine and youthful teachers at the Yavne school started there a group of religious Zionist scouts, 'Hashomer Hadati'. Its activities were mainly held on weekends and in the evenings. In the atmosphere of virulent anti-Semitism surrounding us, Zionism (Jewish nationalism) found a profound response. We spent time singing the new songs of Jewish pride, and held marches and celebrations. At meetings, we listened as we were told about the great progress in building the 'Jewish National Home' in Palestine (the Land of Israel to us) where Jews were tilling the land, building new towns, villages, schools, even a Hebrew University ... And, yes, where Jews were not helpless weakling victims but defended themselves with weapons! There was one more powerful reason why we were so 'devoted' to the youth group: this was a framework for our gender liberation, the only place for free informal contact with ... girls, girls, girls! And what girls we had at the group – golden-haired and green-eyed Regina, fine-looking Salka with brown eyes and a warm personality, diminutive Itka of a delicate complexion, robust Sara sporting long, black plaits. And this was the only place we could have something we did not have at the general or at the religious school – friendship with other boys: curly-haired, lively little Israel ('Srulik'), the tall, argumentative, long-faced David ('Duvciu') – and many others. Together we clandestinely smoked our first cigarette (I choked and coughed – and have been a non- smoker ever since), broke in without tickets to the local stadium to watch football games, sat at the only ice-cream parlour in town commenting critically about passersby ... It was within this group that we had our first romantic adventures, first kisses and embraces. For some time I became enamoured with Salka, but also had a 'do not touch' admiring relationship with Regina. These experiences were especially intense on excursions and even more so during summer camp where we often slept in the same hayloft

... Not that things 'went too far', as they say. Generally, these youth organizations were puritanical in spirit.

After one short school year, the teacher who organized our group had to leave. He earmarked a team of five of us to be a 'provisional leadership' team for our group 'until the central agencies of 'Hashomer Hadati' could send a replacement for him. As time went on the promised replacement did not materialize. Our team decided to continue with our activities and elected me as the 'leader'. And so, at the ripe old age of 12 I became responsible for this 'religious Zionist youth group' in the Jewish community of Yaroslav. We arranged group discussions and festivities, excursions and study weekends like any other group in town. Meanwhile, we became less religious, while not far from us another, much larger Zionist youth group developed, 'Akiba'. This group had a richer programme and a proper adult, instructor. While less religious than our group it was still very much traditional and somewhat 'mystical'. For example, it indulged in long singing sessions 'at the outgoing of the Sabbath'. A large crowd of youngsters would pack tightly the narrow, rented premises of the club, sitting on the floor, on the window sills, on the tables. They would gather at sunset, while it was still light, and sing along for hours until total darkness. From time to time someone would read some poetry, tell a story, speak briefly on some topical issue – all in the rosy light of sunset and then in the darkness. As we became less religious and more grown up, we felt that our group was becoming too narrow for us – so we joined 'Akiba'.

It was with this organization that I went for the first (as it later turned out, also the last) summer camp just a few weeks before the start of the Second World War, in July 1939. It was the greatest and most enlightening experience of my youth. We spent more than two weeks high in the East Carpathian mountains, housed in an isolated store-house, sleeping on hay mattresses and eating simple country food. For the first time in my life I was 'free' from close parental supervision, within a commune of close to 200 young people from many cities. How magical were the early mornings, when we sat out before sunrise on a promontory high in the mountains and watched in awe the red disc of sun rising somewhere below, painting in flaming red the slowly, majestically moving clouds there. We were above, yes above the sun and the clouds – in heaven! How beautiful were the evenings without electricity, sitting around a huge blazing fire, singing and jostling late into the night. How wonderful the excursions into woods and green valleys in the vicinity. How perfect also were our camp leaders, highly educated, good-looking, friendly young people, almost all in training at various places for going soon on *aliya* (emigration) to be pioneers in the Jewish Homeland in Palestine! Above all, here we were, young Jews among Jews, no anti-Semitism or estrangement, a minuscule Jewish 'state' . Little did we know what was going to happen only several weeks ahead ... Of all our close friends in our town and in the youth movement not one remained alive after the Holocaust.

3 • 'Jews Out!' – We are Exiled to the Soviets

It was a quiet sunny morning, about two weeks after the Germans occupied our small town of Yaroslav in southern Poland in September 1939. Quietly a civilian member of the Gestapo, in a fine jacket and green riding trousers entered my parents' shop. Calmly he told us that all Jews had to leave town that day, and go eastwards to the other side of the River San, which passed through our town. *'Wer von den Juden bleibt nach drei Uhr in der Stadt wird erschossen werden'* ('Any Jew found in town after three o'clock will be shot'). It was after ten in the morning. We had less than five hours to deal with our lifetime's possessions and make whatever arrangements possible. Quickly we closed the shop and went home. My father was in hiding at the other end of town; my younger brother, 'Moishe the Catholic' went to bring him home.

On our way home we could already see large black official posters in Polish and German, with the eagle and the swastika on top, signed by the German military commandant with the expulsion order for all Jews, under the penalty of death. The poster spelled out instructions: Jews were ordered to gather at the local football stadium, where they had to hand over their keys in an orderly fashion, with explanatory notes and addresses, as well as surrender all monies and valuables. At the stadium instructions would be given as to where to proceed.

What were we to do? Leave all we had accumulated in a lifetime – our shop full of goods, two houses, including an apartment full of personal belongings, furniture, fur coats, silver and porcelain? We decided to do as Jacob, our forefather had done, divide our camp: the men of the family would leave while our mother and little sister would remain to guard our home and possessions. Surely the Germans would not do anything to them? Time was short. Quickly we put some of our valuables in three strong containers; one we hid beneath the roof, one in the cellar and one in an iron pail at the bottom of our coal shed. We decided not to go to the stadium but in a round about way cross the San river on our own. Who knows what the Germans might do to us at the stadium? Also, we decided not to hand in keys and valuables. We were afraid to take any valuables with us openly, so we hid some precious stones and money in our shoes and clothing. Mother took little sacks and made arm handles from ropes for them, thus we had something like a backpack. In each she put a few pieces of clothing, especially warm things, a towel and some toiletries. Just before three o'clock we took a last look at our house which had been home to us for years. We gave a last kiss to our mother who was not crying, and to our little sister who had big tears in her eyes, and we started walking. Will we return soon or never? ... Were we right to leave mother and sister? Will the Germans catch us? But if they apprehended us before the stadium we would say that we were going there; and if they stopped us after the stadium we would say that we had been there already.

As it happened, we passed through the town without interference. We met some Jews coming from the stadium. As we suspected, it was hell. Germans and 'Polish' police were making a personal search, forcing men and women to undress, beating them mercilessly whether or not they found any hidden valuables on them, forcing them to run round the stadium until they were exhausted. At least we were spared that, and we had a few of our hidden valuables with us. In front of us we saw now the wide, swollen waters of the River San. The bridge over it was destroyed. Along it we could see a pontoon bridge which the Germans had built. At its entrance two German soldiers stood guard, and along its side there was an inscription: *'Juden nach Palästina'* (Jews to Palestine), with an arrow pointing to the other side of the San river. Should we cross the bridge? But what if the Germans there got hold of us? We knew that about a kilometre downriver there were usually some peasants with boats who would take people to the other side. One boat owner agreed to do so for an exorbitant price, little did he know that we would have paid even many times more. Close to the other side the boat got into a dangerous eddy; we, the youngsters, helped with spare oars to steady the boat. At last we stepped safely onto the shore.

When we walked back to the main road on the other side of the bridge we soon realized that our troubles were far from over: the road was packed with columns of German military trucks and at the roadside military police were moving swiftly on their motorcycles. By now we had met some other Jews expelled from our town. We continued walking on a sideroad to avoid the Germans, but soon it was dark. At the end of a small village we saw a peasant house. At first the peasant shouted at us, but when we promised him an impressive-looking ring, he agreed to let us and some other Jews (we were afraid to stay there alone) sleep overnight in his barn. We were utterly exhausted, yet we could not sleep much. We were afraid that he might think that 'Jews surely have some gold with them' and attack us at night.

At dawn we decided to move on to a village some 20 kilometres from Yaroslav to the east of the San where an old business acquaintance was living. He used to come regularly for years once a week to buy various supplies from our shop. Father knew him as an outstandingly honest, religious Jew. 'He will not refuse us', father said. An additional important point was that his village was deep in the country, well away from the main road and the Germans.

Late in the afternoon we stood at last at his rather large, thatched house. It was situated at the fork of some dirt roads, next to a stream with a small wooden bridge and some ducks swimming about on the water. Out came an old man with a long white beard and a prominent white *tsitsit* shawl. He was greatly surprised when he saw my father and his three sons on his doorstep in that remote village, in bedraggled clothes and with sacks on our backs. He knew my father as a well-to-do merchant in what was to him the major town in the area. When he heard our story, he embraced us heartily and invited us to his house. A sumptuous meal was served. My father asked him for temporary shelter and offered to pay for it. It turned out that his sons and their families lived with him in this large house – one huge, extended family, so there was no room in the house itself. Also, the large entrance room served as a kind of 'all purpose parlour' during the day and in the evening it became a sleeping area for one of the sons and his family. Therefore, sleeping arrangements were made for us under the thatched roof, in the attic. As for payment, he would not hear of it! 'You have been uprooted from your home by the Germans, may their name be accursed. So this is your temporary home, as long as you need it,' he said.

So there we were, in the attic of this peaceful house in the country, far from the Germans. For some time we lived as if inside a Tolstoyan country idyll of a patriarchal family. At dawn all the menfolk in the house gathered for prayers in their *tsitsit* prayer shawls and their phylacteries. At the main meals the entire large clan would gather, and nobody would touch any food until the old patriarch had made the appropriate blessing. On the Sabbath, the main front room was turned into house of prayer with Jews from the nearby villages attending.

Meanwhile, a dramatic and unexpected change occurred. On the third day of our stay in that village, I was sent by father to go to the nearest small town, Holeszyce, to buy some medicine for his asthma. I was also supposed to find out what was going on, since in the village we had no radio or newspapers. I walked on a dirt sideroad, from which I could see in the distance what was happening on the main west–east road leading in the direction of Lvov. From time to time I stopped to rest and surveyed the villages which I passed, so my walk took quite a few hours. As I marched I noticed a remarkable change. At first the road was packed with motorized German military columns. After some hours, the eastwards German flow stopped. And then – I could not believe my eyes – an even more rapid movement of German military columns started – westwards! After some time traffic on the main road disappeared altogether. Unbelievably, the main road was empty.

As I reached the main street of Holeszyce, which itself was spread along the main west–east road, I found a curious atmosphere of excitement there. This small town was an almost entirely Jewish marketing town. Under the Germans, hardly anyone could be seen in the streets. Now, however large crowds were milling around the town, then they formed into two lines, one on each side of the main road. I asked a woman nearby what was happening. 'Haven't you heard? The Germans are gone – the Russians are coming!', she replied.

It was a clear autumn day and the atmosphere in town was as if there was some kind of festival. The road was empty. Suddenly, at the far end of it, which was slightly uphill, a hazy brownish mass started moving and the sound of heavy motors was heard from that direction. Soon they were upon us: first a column of heavy trucks, then several tanks and armoured cars, then a few detachments of cavalry and of foot soldiers followed by some more trucks.

The entire scene was at the same time one of climax and of anticlimax, exhilarating and depressing. On the one hand, the atmosphere was friendly and cheerful. After the German 'experience', the Jewish population of the town received the Soviets warmly: here and there people cheered and threw flowers. The passing soldiers waved and made friendly noises, while the foot column sang lively Russian songs. At some point the flow stopped. Opposite the place where I stood within the line along the road, a mounted officer got off his horse and approached us. Suddenly he opened up in Yiddish: *'Ihr zayt Yidden? Ich bin fun Odess!'* '(Are you Jewish? I am from Odessa!'). A short, friendly exchange followed between the overwhelmed local Jews and this Yiddish-speaking Soviet cavalry officer. In other places groups of people stood around the newly arrived Soviets and a friendly exchange in fragments of Polish and Russian took place.

On the other hand the general appearance of the Russian troops was frankly depressing. Especially in comparison with the western European-looking, clean, well-dressed and highly disciplined Germans. The difference was so glaring, that despite the criminal attitude of the Germans to us Jews we could not close our eyes to it. The Russians did not look Russian, they looked Asian. Many had Mongol faces. They were shabbily dressed in brown, badly cut uniforms. Their trucks – and even more so their tanks and armoured cars – looked badly designed, heavy and belched a thick, stinking smoke. The foot soldiers had bad shoes and their singing sounded strangely eastern. Altogether, the German army had almost no foot soldiers or horses. The Soviets looked somewhat backward even by Polish standards. But the friendliness of the Soviets was beyond all this. For what was the worth of the outward European appearance of the Germans when beneath they were worse than barbarians.

4 • Crossing the German–Soviet Border

Several days after I returned from Holeszyce and after we found ourselves under the Soviets, it became known that Germany and the Soviet Union had signed an agreement about a new border between them. It left Yaroslav on the German side, since the San river became the dividing line. In addition, the agreement stipulated an 'open border' for an exchange of population within two weeks. It soon became known that the bridge on the San river would be open for this exchange. This meant that there might be an opportunity for some of us to cross the San into Yaroslav and fetch our mother and sister who had remained there. It was decided that I should dress up as much as possible as a village lad in order not to look Jewish. With me went my younger brother, 'Moishe the Catholic'. Next morning we hid some money and valuables in our clothes and headed off in the direction of the bridge and the Germans.

Late in the afternoon we arrived at last at the San river passage, utterly exhausted after the long march. There we found real pandemonium: masses of people were pushing towards the bridge with Soviet mounted army and police trying to push them back. Carriages with horses were coming over the bridge from the German side but could not get through because of the mass of people who blocked their way. Other carriages were trying to push through towards the bridge. Soon we found out that in order to cross the bridge one had to get a pass from the Soviet border outpost nearby. So we went there and found a huge queue. Furthermore we were told that they did not give permits to youngsters. By that time it was growing dark and the bridge was closed.

For a considerable payment we were allowed to stay overnight in a peasant hut nearby. It was not possible to lie down since it was packed with people, so we slept a bit in a sitting position. Dawn found us at the bridge again. At first it looked as if there was no way for us to make the crossing and we were thinking that we would have to return 'home' defeated. Then we noticed that some of the carriage drivers had youngsters with them on the driver's seat, apparently their sons. The border guards were not challenging this at all. This opened a way much quicker for us than even for those who had to wait in the very long queue clutching their permits. However, it was not easy to find a driver who would risk taking us on his cart through the German guards as if we were his sons. In the end we found one such driver who agreed to do so in exchange for a lovely ring with a red stone in the centre (he explained later with some relish that it would be greatly appreciated by his mistress in the neighbouring village). We put my 'Aryan' brother on the front seat beside the driver, and I sat backwards so I was barely seen behind the driver. For good measure, I pulled my cap down over my eyes and arranged my hair to stick out wildly from beneath it like a real peasant lad. When asked by the Polish policeman at the other side in front of Germans, the driver answered simply: 'These are my lads, they help me with the heavy luggage'. I sat there shaking – they only needed to search us or simply order us to pull down our trousers and they would soon discover the truth. The Germans dealt most severely with those who attempted to cheat them. But there was an immense crush of other carts behind us and in a moment we were waved through. We were on the German side.

Within an hour we stood in front of our house, knocking heavily on the main entrance door. How great was our shock when an alien voice asked angrily: 'Who is it?' Our mother and sister were no longer there. When we heard this my blood froze, fearing the worst. It turned out that when they had heard about the exchange of population arrangement they hired a cart, loaded onto it whatever they could of our things – bedding, some furniture – and left for a crossing on the San river at another point at Sieniawa, not where we had passed early in the morning. Mother and our sister had been in good health when they left.

Having said that, the occupants of the house tried to close the door on us, they would not allow us to go in. But we explained that we had also come on a special errand that even our mother did not know about: to dig out some valuables which we had hidden when we left. We promised that if they would allowed us to get them, we would give them a valuable part of it, otherwise they would never find it on their own. After some consultation behind the closed door, the elder lady, who was the senior there, said that they would give us an answer later in the afternoon when her son came home. But that was exactly what we had to avoid: we were afraid that a man might rob us of the valuables once we found them – or even kill us. So we made out that we had to leave soon in order to cross the border and there was no time to wait.

Eventually they agreed. We asked for a spade, a pick and a lantern. They opened the door to the coal pit for us and we started to dig. At several points it seemed that we hit a metallic object, but it turned out to be a stone. We shifted the coal and wood to the other side and started digging there. By then we were black all over, covered in sweat and struggling to breath because of the coal dust. But we would not give up; we realized that this might be our only chance. At last, after about an hour of work (which seemed to us a millennium) we 'hit the jackpot'. Slowly we uncovered a blackened pail inside which some metallic objects rattled. The moment of danger arrived: we were afraid that those ladies who had been standing by the door while we were digging might now wrench from us the 'treasure' or hand us over to the Germans. From one corner of the pail we quickly took out a necklace and some other valuables which we gave to them. Then we grabbed the pail and marched off as quickly as we could. We were lucky not to be killed or even robbed.

Only now did we face our next difficult problem: how do we get back over the river and how do we smuggle the valuables through the German border guards? In a secluded place on our way back to the river, we pried open the iron pail and peered inside: there were some rings, necklaces, armbands, silver wine cups, candle holders and so on – a treasure trove! Speedily we transferred the contents into two small and inconspicuous sacks which we had brought with us. We wrapped these in some of our clothing in case the Germans opened the sacks, draped them like a bundle over our shoulders and set off.

By the river we found a long line of carts waiting to cross the bridge, with German guards on both sides. Luckily, there was quite a commotion there with some of the carts which had come over from the other side pushing to get into the line. Having learned from our previous crossing, we searched for a lone elderly wagon driver who could 'adopt' us as his sons/helpers. After a prolonged search we negotiated successfully with a rather flamboyant elderly fellow with a pipe who, for a very high price, agreed not only to take us in his cart but also to hide our two sacks within his driver's straw seat. We explained that we had there all kinds of tools which were important to us and which the Germans might confiscate. The driver and my 'Aryan' brother sat on the seat with the sacks inside and I sat with my back leaning on it and slowly the cart moved forward to the border control post. As we came closer to it, it started to rain. We were afraid that the rain would loosen the straw of the seat and – oh horror – the sacks would be revealed. The wagon in front of us was being thoroughly searched, all things were taken off, some undeclared things were found there. The Germans were shouting and beating the people and the driver. By then we could not do anything but move on. Two rather tired-looking Germans approached, asked questions and circled the cart suspiciously. The driver explained: 'We, I and my sons who help me, came over this morning from the other side with some civilians who within the exchange of population got a permit to move westwards. Now we are returning home to the east side.' All of this in broken German while my brother and I sat there frozen with fear. One German looked beneath the cart, the other raised the worn blanket at one end of it and gave the drivers seat a slight shove. The rain grewstronger. The Germans decided to leave and shouted '*los*'(move on). After a few long minutes we were over the bridge. How glad were we for once to see the huge red hammer and sickle emblem on the Soviet border post.

We stayed at a village hut for the night, again without much sleep for fear of being robbed. Next morning, we marched home in heavy wind and rain. As we walked along a railway line, I was astonished to find in the mud a silver cup and then another … I called to my brother who was walking in front of me. We examined his sack; it turned out that as a result of the incessant rain his sack had developed a hole. We searched the area walking backwards and found in the mud a silver armband, a ring and a cup. We tied my brother's sack so that the hole would be covered and continued on our way. Soaked to the bone, shivering from cold and dead on our feet with exhaustion, we arrived at last at our 'home'. We were happy to tell the news that our mother and sister were alive and well and on their way (we had told our mother when we left that we would be heading for this place). We proudly presented the spoils of our 'expedition' and told them the story of our 'miraculous' crossing of the German border. Then we went to sleep for some 12 hours. Our mother and sister did not arrive.

What happened? Did the Germans get hold of them? Did she go somewhere else? After dark, while we sat and planned a search for our mother on the next day, a cart rolled up in front of the house. There, inside a warm cover were our mother and sister – dazed and crying but safe! The last days had been a terrible trauma for them. At first, the Poles who came to live in our apartment in Yaroslav would not let mother take some of the things and she had to fight it out with them. Then, close to the border crossing in Sieniawa they were suddenly surrounded by a crowd of peasants. They got hold of the wheels of the wagon, turned it violently over so that its contents and passengers spilled out on the road in the rain. The peasants started beating people and looting whatever was close to hand. In the cart was also a woman hunchback, an elderly neighbour of ours. She received a bad blow to the head when falling onto the road and started to scream with all her might. My mother joined in as loud as she could. Suddenly, at the end of the road some German soldiers arrived. The bandits took fright and ran away. (Robbing the Jews was reserved for the Germans themselves; they would not allow the Poles to do so.) The wagon owner would not agree to go with them any further, so they sat in the road in the rain for hours until one cart driver had pity on them and took them over the border. Then they had to find another wagon to bring them to this village. (The woman hunchback went into shock as a result of the blow. She never recovered and died several months later.) Despite the theft on the way, some of our belongings had survived, since our mother had stretched herself over them. We were especially pleased to see some of our winter clothing. With much elation we kissed and embraced our little sister Ruth. Despite all tribulations and crises she remained cheerful and full of beans. Here we were, a united family again, knowing little of how far the future was going to take us.

5 • Under Soviet Rule in 'Liberated' Western Ukraine

By October 1939, more than one month after the start of the Second World War, after the Germans occupied our town of Yaroslav in southern Poland and our family was forcibly driven from there eastwards, we found ourselves under the Soviets. Our mother and little sister remained at first in our town, but after some weeks we were reunited at the house of my father's friend in a village about 30 kilometres to the east of our Yaroslav. We could not stay on at this house, and we could not just sit and do nothing. Where would we go? What could we do?

After checking out the area we found that in the nearby main village, which was close to a railway station, a rich peasant was willing to rent a room to us. It was of medium size, with a separate entrance and windows looking out on a road-crossing. And, what was of major importance, it was situated in the centre of the village, called Nova Grobla. My parents immediately saw the possibility of turning the room into a shop of some kind. This matter has to be related to the general problem of commerce under the Soviets. During the first days after the arrival of the Soviet forces the shopkeepers opened their establishments as usual. Before the war, under Polish rule, the shops were full of goods of all kinds and shop windows presented a fine display of merchandise. One of the first measures of the new, Soviet administration was an announcement that the Russian ruble was equal in value to the Polish zloty. In Poland, the zloty was hard currency. One American dollar was equivalent to about five zloty. For ten zloty one could get a good pair of shoes or an inexpensive ladies' dress.

Within a week or two, the shops in the areas under the Soviets were empty of any goods and the windows were practically empty. Why did this happen? I witnessed one such incident which may serve as an explanation. On my second visit to the nearby small town of Holeszyce, I entered a shop in the centre. It displayed in its window some elegant colourful ladies' shoes. As I lingered in the shop, a high-ranking Soviet officer entered. He got a friendly reception. He pointed to a pair of shoes in the window and asked for the price. When he realised how cheap the shoes were compared to the price 'at home', he took out a wad of newly printed rubles and asked the shop owner for all the ladies' shoes in the window. After a long argument between the salesman and the officer it was agreed that five pairs would do. (We learned later that in Russia itself it was well-nigh impossible to get such elegant shoes.) The officer left, no doubt to scavenge in other shops. The shop owner frantically started to remove all the remaining shoes from his window and shelves. With great frustration he fingered the bundle of useless rubles in his hand. The point was that he had no way of renewing his stock. Indeed, the rubles were of little value. Shortly after their arrival the Soviets nationalized all banks, private industries and workshops. Their owners were proclaimed to be 'bourgeoisie' and systematically put in jail and sent to Siberia. Despite government decrees which demanded that all economic institutions must continue functioning, much of production and commerce came to a virtual standstill.

That of course did not mean that people stopped eating, dressing or living. It simply meant that parallel to the extremely contracted official economy, a grey and black market rapidly developed. The value of the ruble was quickly tumbling in this real economy and prices were climbing rapidly. And as one might have expected, Soviet officials and officers adapted quickly to this situation: as long as nobody supervised them they bought and sold on the 'unofficial' market. It appeared that they had plenty of expertise of that kind of thing in their perpetually hungry-for-goods economy.

Having come from generations of traders, my parents realised the possibilities created by this situation. Obviously, they were only able to utilise them on a small scale. This activity provided us with some income so that we did not have to live by selling our few valuables, and it gave my father and all of us something to do. Furthermore, strange as it may sound, it gave us a feeling of fulfilling an important, useful function. Once a week, my father and one or two of us sons, used to march to the nearby railway station. We carried with us some village produce (cheese, butter, vegetables, onions). We travelled by rail to the nearest large town, Lubachev. Country produce was scarce in town and we were able to sell it there at some profit. My father had some previous contacts there and soon we established trust with some 'unofficial' traders. As a result we got some merchandise which was generally not available – good cigarettes, sugar, coffee, matches, chocolate, sweets, combs, brushes, warm socks, elegant ladies' socks, salt, pepper, wicks and oil for lighting lamps. We carried our heavy bundles from the station to our room in the village a distance of several miles, in rain, snow or in the scorching sun. There was no proper road to the station and no cart driver at it. We laid out our goods on the beds, on the table and even in the small entrance hall. Word about our 'shop' spread rapidly through the village and soon we were inundated with 'customers'. While the prices naturally bore no relationship to those officially fixed, the villagers were often very thankful that the particular merchandise was available at all, since many of these items were not to be found elsewhere. One day, a woman farmer came in: 'For two nights we have sat in the dark because we can't find a wick for our oil lamp.' We sold her two wicks, matches (these had also run out), tobacco for her husband ('He will be very glad to have it') and some salt and soap. She added a pair of warm socks for her daughter and a pair of stockings for herself, paid and went home a very happy person. She became a steady customer coming in at least once a week.

Our small business flourished, keeping us quite busy, especially with Christmas and the New Year. During the dayour room became a shop; for the night we collected all the merchandise in cartons and suitcases and arranged our beds to sleep. As it became ever more difficult to get supplies, we had to travel to Lubachev more than once a week.

One autumn day I surprised my parents: 'I want to go to study! Here in the village I shall come to nothing.' Mother was immediately for it. Father was persuaded at last when I explained that while studying in Lubachev where the nearest high school was situated, I would be able to buy in advance some of the scarce goods. Then I would be able to bring some of it 'home' when I returned each weekend. Also, we found out that a neighbour of ours from Yaroslav, of the same family as the hunchback woman who came through the German border with my mother, lived in Lubachev, not far from the high school. So, on our next trip to that town we visited them and they gladly agreed that I could stay at their place for a reasonable monthly rent. I was very happy about it, also because their pretty daughter, Salka, was my girlfriend. We lived in the same house in our town, belonged to the same youth club, and from time to time spent an evening together.

For me, the transfer from the village to town, from tending the shop to studying, from being alone to living in the same apartment with Salka, was nothing but a miracle. I had brought a bundle of my things with me, so father went back to Nova Grobla on his own. A folding bed was put up for me in the corridor; the family slept in the main room which served during the day as a tailor's shop (Salka's mother was a seamstress of some renown). Next morning, in my best outfit and with a little case with some notebooks, pens and pencils, I proudly but somewhat shyly presented myself before the school secretary. She took me to the principal's office. Here my first surprise awaited me: he looked completely opposite to the Polish principal that I had been used to at 'home' in Yaroslav. He was in black boots, a shabby jacket, a black shirt without a tie; his hair was combed back and curly. From the first glance I realised that he was Jewish; which was immediately confirmed when the secretary addressed him as 'Comrade Aron Moiseyevich'. Moreover, he knew no Polish; he spoke Ukrainian and Russian. 'You understand that you will have to study in Ukrainian and that you will have to catch up with the material that has been learned so far,' he said. Somehow, with the help of the secretary I understood. When I promised to do my best, I was marched off to the appropriate class. And so my studies started.

How different this school was from the Polish one I had known. Religion was non-existent; there was even teaching on Christmas Day (but not on New Year's Day, since this was a recognised Soviet holiday). Instead of religion we got a lot of Soviet communist ideology – red flags, hammer and sickle, revolutionary and Red Army songs – and endless adulation of Lenin and, even more so, of Stalin. However, things did not work out entirely to the Soviets' liking. Many of the teachers did not know Ukrainian or Russian, and of course, many of the pupils did not know these languages either. There were no textbooks in these languages, so a large part of our studies were in Polish and from textbooks in that language – especially in exact sciences. As time went on, some teachers arrived from Russia, especially for teaching Russian language and literature, history (in the Soviet communist interpretation – with a lot of quotes from Lenin and Stalin) and geography (mainly of the Soviet Union). The trouble was that these teachers seemed to us rather inferior and uncultured. They, and especially the women teachers, were badly dressed, with badly fitting peasant dresses and boots instead of high-heeled shoes. They usually wore funny berets or hats. Their hair and fingernails were done in peasant style. They wore no lipstick or cosmetics. Their teaching methods were backward, mechanical and parrot-like. Nevertheless, studies were quite intensive, with a lot of homework and in three languages. At first, it was difficult for me to even understand the lectures. But after two or three months I was catching up. By the end of the school year I passed the exams (under the Soviet system there were exams at the end of each year) as one of the best in the class.

The small town of Lubachev where I lived and studied was something of a microcosm of that former part of Poland which under Soviet rule was called Western Ukraine. While there I did get my intensive and many-sided 'Soviet communist education'. To me it was both fascinating and appealing. With its immense enchantments and nightmares, it was as if a new world suddenly opened up before me. I was then a youngster, only 15 years old, but quite developed for that age. I had lived all my life in Yaroslav, and travelled beyond it only for brief visits to some nearby cities. The largest of these was Lvov where I was overwhelmed by seeing the opera house and the trams. In Poland everything to do with communism was strictly forbidden and almost nothing was taught at school about the vast neighbouring country, the Soviet Union.

At Lubachev I was suddenly hit by an immense onslaught of the Russian–communist 'civilization' and the 'unofficial' reality. These two were so obviously contradictory, so glaringly opposed to each other, that sometimes it made my head spin and took my breath away. Soon I came to realise that had I seen the communist literature 'at home', in Poland, without observing the realities under Soviet rule, I could have fallen for it, despite my Zionist background. Paradoxically, it was the 'real communism' under Soviet rule which I was able to observe at close range, first in Lubachev and then inside Russia, that cured me of accepting communism as a personal creed.

Since communist literature was unknown to me and forbidden in Poland, I was curious about it. Now it became available, I read it avidly and soon became quite knowledgable in it. At school we were fed it in many ways. In history lessons we were taught about the glorious Great October Socialist Revolution, about the victories of the heroic Red Army during the Civil War, about the unprecedented achievements in 'building socialism' in the USSR, in the 'Fatherland of All Toilers' in the entire world under the glorious leadership of the 'Father of All Nations', Comrade Stalin. Such was the case with almost all other lessons. The literature teacher read to us passages from Soviet writers and poets on Lenin, on 'socialist construction'. In geography we learned about the greatness of the Land of the Soviets, about great new industries built as a result of implementing the Five Year Plan, and so forth.

No more old-time holidays and celebrations. In their place came an entire range of new festivities and memorial days. In October we celebrated the anniversary of the 1917 Bolshevik Revolution. At New Year we marked the great successes of the Soviet Union over the past year and the great plans for the next. Major festivities were held in February around Red Army Day. At the beginning of May, parades, public dancing and festive meetings were arranged for May Day, 'the international solidarity holiday of workers of all countries', and so on and on. There was teachers' day and medical workers' day, farmers' day and postmens' day – there was hardly a week without some celebration. We marched in parades, we sang 'revolutionary' songs, we waved red flags with the hammer and sickle emblem, we danced to the blaring of military brass bands. Major rooms in town were turned into Public Halls where Soviet films were shown free of charge and various performances were held. Needless to say, the films were full of glorification of 'Revolution', Lenin, Socialism and Stalin.

Above all, the theme of 'Soviet democracy' was impressed upon us. Capitalist democracy is a sham and sheer falsehood. It is a chimera to hoodwink the masses and make them submit to the exploitation and rule of capitalist oligarchy. Only in the Soviet Union is there a true People's Democracy. 'Bourgeois' leaders speak about equality, liberty and brotherhood; but what equality is there between a very rich and influential capitalist and a poor unemployed worker who has no money for his daily bread? To cap it all we were given intensive lessons on the 'Stalin Constitution' of the USSR. It was presented as the most democratic and progressive constitution in the history of mankind. And so it was, at least on reading through it. It featured extensive paragraphs about rights and freedoms 'of all citizens' – freedom of assembly, religion and conscience, of speech and the press, the right of all to work, free education, state-run health care, inviolability of person and of personal correspondence, and so on. All this could be very persuasive and impressive if it were not for another part of the picture – stark reality. And this presented a total contradiction of Soviet official assertions. Immediately after the Red Army entered our area, we were told that it came to 'liberate' us from the yoke of the 'Polish bourgeoise rulers' – not from the Germans with whom the Soviets concluded an additional treaty of friendship. All official spokesmen and media were telling us that the Second World War had been unleashed by the capitalist rulers of the West. Not a critical word was allowed about Hitler's Germany, which only a few weeks previously had been branded an 'enemy of mankind' by Soviet leaders. Any mention about persecution of the Jews by the Hitlerites in Germany or in occupied Poland also disappeared. These flaming manifestations of 'eternal friendship' between the two recent sworn enemies – communist Russia and Nazi Germany – were in our perception blatantly false and utterly wrong. The entire official establishment was revealed as full of lies. Being Jewish, we were torn by a severe dilemma; on the one hand the entrance of Soviet forces into our area saved us from the Nazis; on the other hand we could not accept the alliance of the USSR with Hitler.

Immediately after the arrival of the Red Army, Soviet secret police followed and a wide-flung but very discreet reign of terror was unleashed. Entire categories of citizens were its object. Systematically, the secret services were sweeping the country. First, all top officials, estate owners, capitalists and high-ranking officers of the Polish army were arrested and condemned to long prison sentences. Every month or so another group was taken: all former policemen; activists of political parties; many church leaders; editors and media people. Among the Jews many were victims of this terror – Zionists, *Bundists*, rabbis, bankers, merchants, intellectuals, 'speculators' (as all those engaged in the 'unofficial market' were branded). All this was done in an 'invisible' way. People were taken in the middle of night or were invited to come to some office and arrested there. Often people would simply disappear; sometimes some information about them was given, which in turn was often false (for example, 'they have been resettled in big cities inside Russia' when they were actually sent to the Gulag camps in Siberia, the Arctic north or the deserts of Central Asia). In many cases no information was forthcoming. Sometimes the entire family would be arrested and sent away without a trial, even without ever knowing what they were charged with. Such were the lucky ones – at least the family remained together (as was the case with my own family). But more often, the head of the family was taken first, usually to a harsh prison camp in a faraway, inhospitable area, and after some time – inevitably – the jailers would come for the wife and children. She was often a 'living widow' and the children virtual orphans, since in most cases they never saw their husband/father again.

While this was going on, the area which had formerly been Galicia or the southeast part of Poland was proclaimed to be Western Ukraine. An assembly of 'representatives' was convened by the Soviet authorities in Lvov, the capital of the area. Not surprisingly, the assembly unanimously and enthusiastically petitioned the Supreme Soviets both of the Soviet Union and of the Ukrainian Republic (part of the Union) to incorporate the 'liberated' area into their respective bodies. Both Supreme Soviets approved this request promptly, unanimously and no less enthusiastically. As proper democratic procedure would demand, 'free elections' of members of the various Soviet bodies – regional, republican and federal were announced. A shrill, intensive and thorough 'election campaign' was launched, which, not surprisingly turned out to be a huge propaganda and brain-washing onslaught. The fly in the ointment was that the residents of the area had a considerable experience of elections in former Poland. Though far from ideal, these elections were held within a multi-party system, with wideranging freedom of the press, assembly and opposition to the government. Immediately after taking control of the area, the Soviets suppressed all political parties and activities, closed all newspapers and publications, took full control of the radio and disbanded all social, cultural and entertainment bodies. The 'free and truly democratic elections' were run while the reign of terror was in full swing. The Soviet-controlled media published acre after acre of ecstatic articles, letters to 'Great Comrade Stalin', reports about mass meetings of 'the elated liberated populace'. Not one word about arrests or suppression; the exile of entire categories of the population, not even about rampant inflation; mass unemployment, total breakdown of the entire trade and supply system; or the painful shortages of goods.

In the midst of the 'election campaign' the pupils of the top classes in our school were given a short training course and then sent as 'volunteer instructors' teaching groups of 'voters' about the supreme democratic merits of the 'Constitution of the USSR'. Amongst others I was also selected for this noble mission. Late in the afternoon we were collected from school and driven to a nearby village. There a local organiser dispersed us to various peasant houses where groups of villagers were assembled. Just picture me, a boy of 15, obviously urban, Jewish and 'intellectual' sitting there at a table with an oil lamp in front of a circle of peasants. Many of them were illiterate. They wore heavy rough winter clothing (it was often quite cold in the hut). Some were smoking pipes or rolling simple tobacco cigarettes. There I was reading to them in broken Ukrainian the various articles of the constitution and mouthing the relevant commentary exactly as I had been told. My 'listeners' pretended to be listening; those in front nodded approvingly with their heads. Most of them indulged in the ancient peasant art of sleeping while sitting erect – at which they were especially good due to the darkness outside the circle of light of the lamp.

From time to time one of the 'supervisors' came in. In a second, the entire scene changed radically: the peasants were immediately awake, nodding their heads, issuing exclamations of wonderment and profound satisfaction, even asking 'appreciative' questions. The moment the 'supervisors' left, everything returned to the previous routine.

So here I was, preaching the joys of the 'most democratic constitution in world history'. About freedom of expression where nobody could express anything that he really felt and thought – not the farmers, not me, not even the 'supervisors'. I pretended to believe in what I was reading, the peasants pretended that they were listening and agreeing; the supervisors pretended that they were supervising. Actually, they spent most of their time drinking beer in one of the huts. If it were not so sad, it could certainly be quite a comedy of the absurd. For many years afterwards, this particular experience impressed itself on my mind as the quintessence of the Soviet system.

6 • My Father: Prison and Release

The spring of 1940 was fine. The situation in Soviet-ruled 'Western Ukraine' stabilised somewhat: no official market developed but the unofficial one filled the vacuum; the arrests and forcible exile of various categories of 'anti-Soviet' innocent citizens continued regularly; the newspapers went on telling us how enormously thankful we were to the Soviet Union and to 'comrade Stalin personally' to be liberated from the 'capitalist yoke of the Polish rulers'; they also wrote persuasively that it was the 'Imperialist West' – that is, France and Britain – that unleashed the war against Nazi Germany, with which the Soviet Union had friendly relations.

My parents, two brothers and little sister went on living in a room in the centre of the village Nova Grobla where they slept at night and ran a little shop during the day. I continued to study at school in the nearby town of Lubachev. On Friday afternoon I used to go on foot the ten or so kilometres 'home' to spend the Sabbath with my family. Early on the Monday I used to walk back to school in Lubachev. I lived there with a Jewish family who had been lodgers in our house in Yaroslav. The daughter of the family, Salka, had in some ways been my 'girl' in Yaroslav; the friendship carried on in Lubachev, so I was not lonely there.

Then disaster struck, like a bolt from heaven. On one occasion, on returning home to the village, I noticed immediately that no goods were displayed in our room and no customers were around. It turned out that two days earlier a couple of Soviet 'economic inspectors' and a policeman had come to our room in the middle of the day. They carefully inspected the 'goods', asked in detail about prices, wrote an extensive protocol and made my father sign it. Then they officially accused my father of 'speculation and infringement of Soviet law'. My parents tried to explain that even the officers from the Soviet Army base nearby would not be able to smoke if we did not sell them matches, or that many peasant families would have to sit in the dark in their homes if we did not make some lamp oil available. True, we did not sell at official prices, since these were unrealistically low and no goods could be obtained at these prices at all. It was quite obvious that 'objectively' my parents were fulfilling a vital function – like the entire 'informal' economic network – without which life would become impossible. But all their explanations were to no avail. The 'police' took statements from some of the neighbours, took some goods with them as 'evidence' (or for their own use), ordered my father to 'desist from any further commercialism'and left. They said that they would hand over the case to the investigation authorities in Lubachev and my father was forewarned to wait for a call from there.

My family remained without any livelihood, with nothing to do. But this was nothing, compared with what was to follow. Three weeks passed, nothing happened; we thought and hoped that this trouble would pass. I returned to my studies in Lubachev. Then one day my father arrived unexpectedly at my lodgings. He had received an order to come to the investigations office in Lubachev. Since he did not speak Russian or Ukrainian, and in order to assist him in case of need, it was agreed that I should go with him. I skipped school and we went together to the office in the main square of town. After a wait of almost two hours we were called into the office of a small, black-shirted 'comrade' who smoked incessantly some acrid, low-grade cigarettes (I could not stop wondering what he would do if he lived in our village after we closed and cigarettes were not available). He did not take much time to deal with us; he showed my father the protocol made during the search at our home in the village and asked whether it was true. My father tried to argue and explain. He cut him (me, I was translating) short: 'Explain to the district procura- tor, not to me.' He filled out a form, and gave it to an attendant policeman, who told us to go with him. When we left the build- ing, the policeman told my father to walk straight in front of him and took out his revolver from its holster. It was at that moment that I realised that my father was in great trouble. We marched to the district procurator's office where a thin, red-haired man simply looked at the form written by the chief investigator and endorsed it with his signature. No time was allowed for 'explanations' as had been promised. The same policeman then took the paper and marched us without a word of explanation to the other end of the square. I realised soon enough that this policeman was Jewish – a thing utterly impossible in Poland before the war. I remember thinking how paradoxical the situation was: a Jew, a Soviet policeman with a revolver in hand, escorting another Jew, hitherto a well-to-do merchant, whom the Germans had expelled from his home, as if he was some kind of criminal. And all because of some small commercial activity which actually fulfilled an acute need.

We went on walking through the square and I prayed that no one who knew us would see us in this situation. At the other end of the square we were faced with a massive gate. Our escort produced the papers, the gate opened and my father was told to go inside. When I tried to follow him I was pushed back by a burly guard. The gate closed and I remained outside. Only then did I read the inscription at the side of the gate which in one word said everything: 'Prison'. I was utterly shaken and had to muster all my strength to prevent myself from crying there publicly in the square. Looking around I realised that the prison was on my way to school yet I had never noticed it before.

One can imagine my bleak mood as I returned home, this time by train; how was I going to tell my mother that father was in prison? As it turned out, there was no need to explain; my mother understood immediately when she saw that I returned alone with tears in my eyes.

Before leaving the prison gate, I found out that it was permitted to bring 'parcels' for prisoners and to apply to the procurator for information about each case. Soviet regulations did not allow the intervention of a lawyer. At the procurator's office they were only prepared to say that when a date for the trial was fixed they would let us know. The parcels were received over several weeks, but no permission was granted to visit our father in prison. Then, after some time, a parcel was returned with a note: 'This person is no longer here.' Further inquiries yielded the information: 'He was transferred to the central prison in Lvov.' Oh horror! Our father was incarcerated in the 'Brygidki' prison, infamous for its cruel treatment and conditions.

What should we do to save our father? In a roundabout way we heard that Brygidki was so overcrowded that 40–60 inmates were kept in cells designated for only a few; food and water were scarce and there was hardly any air to breath. It was a living hell and my father suffered from an acute asthma. We were in despair: how long could our father survive under such conditions?

My mother became as if possessed: she could not sleep or eat, she grew thin and highly distraught. At last our constant trips to Lubachev started to produce results, albeit in an unforeseen way. Our frequent visits to the procurator's office, our depositions and inquiries yielded nothing. But informally we learned through the Jewish family I was lodging with, who were tailors, that another woman tailor in town had access to the Russian wife of the procurator. This wife had already 'helped' somebody. My mother dressed in her best and went to see this woman tailor. She offered her money and all kinds of goods, she cried and begged for pity – to no avail. The procurator was afraid of the consequences of the previous case and would not hear about another. My mother, however would not give up. She went to see the woman tailor again and supported her plea with some weighty assets: a pair of beautiful diamond earrings, a fine gold bracelet and a medical document stating that father suffered from acute asthma. She added an elegant, long, black evening dress, an embroidered blouse, a pair of coloured ladies' shoes and a considerable sum of money. It was not clear which of these treasures would remain with the woman intermediary – but it looked a serious chance.

A week later we were called to the procurator in Lubachev. He received us personally: 'Information has reached me that prisoner Katz is suffering from asthma and tuberculosis. Under Soviet law he can be released from prison on parole until his trial, provided that two persons become guarantors for him. I suggest that you sign a petition for his temporary release under these conditions.'

On the same afternoon my mother and I did not return home but went straight to the family in the next village with whom we had found refuge when we had been expelled from our home in Yaroslav. They were friends of my father who had known him for many years. We hoped and prayed that they would agree to sign as guarantors, and actually, when my mother tearfully explained the situation, stressing that it was a matter of life and death, they agreed unhesitatingly. They were old-time religious Jews, and 'saving a Jew from prison' is regarded as a primary obligation and a great *mitzva* (religious good deed).

Early the next morning a cart was travelling to Lubachev. In it sat the two elderly members of this family, in their Sabbath gaberdine, their long, white beards flowing. I was also in the cart, in high spirits, hoping that soon father would be free. How great was our disappointment when we were told that guarantors must be less than 55 years of age. The two who arrived with me at the procurator's office were over that age (actually they came forward because it was believed that as senior citizens they would seem to be more solid guarantors).

Back went the cart to their village. I was tormented by the thought: 'What if the sons, who were not personal friends of my father like their elders, would not agree to be guarantors?' When we arrived at their home it turned out that the wife of the second son had objections: 'What if something happens (my father would run away?) – then my husband might be arrested?!' But after some persuasion both sons agreed. They had some urgent matter to attend to during the next day, so we travelled by cart again the day after. This time they were accepted and signed. A few days passed and then my mother was called to the procurator. 'Here is a letter of release to the prison authorities in Lvov', he instructed her. 'You hand it to the prison warden himself, not to anybody else. Then he will release your husband into my custody. But I allow him to stay at your home.' My mother held the writ in her hand as if it were some holy script. She went straight to the railway station and took the first train to Lvov. Late the same afternoon the door of our room in Nova Grobla opened – and there was father!

At first it was difficult to recognise him: he had a thick beard, he was emaciated, his eyes were bulging and his face was very pale. My mother told us that she had waited for hours at the prison gate; but when she saw a thin, bearded man coming out surreptitiously she did not recognise him; it was father who recognised her. It was difficult to perceive what those weeks in prison did to him. His tale corroborated the horror stories we had heard previously about the Brygidki prison in Lvov. He was locked in a small cell together with some 50 other prisoners. Pails with some *kasha* (corn porridge) and water were shoved through the door several times a day. But the violent criminals established themselves close to the door and got hold of the food. They ate and drank as much as they wanted and then what remained was handed over to the other inmates. Worst of all, there was not enough space to lie down, so sleep was only possible in a sitting position; and there was no air to breath. My father was a very meek, passive man, but in the cell he fought his way to the door, since he felt that otherwise it would be the end of him. This might well have been the case had he been incarcerated for any longer:

he demanded to be taken to a hospital when he became ill and was hardly able to breath, but there was nobody to speak to. The wardens opened the door only to shove in food, to fetch someone for trial and to carry out the dead, which occurred quite frequently.

It was several weeks before my father started to become himself again. Meantime Passover came and went. I returned to my studies in Lubachev and passed the end of year exams. We lived on borrowed time: my father was released officially 'until trial'. We had no work and no income. Luckily, the Soviets started to build a railink near our village. A call for workers was issued and we decided that the three of us were going to work there. It would give us some income and other bonuses. Early at dawn one day in May, we climbed on a rough truck which drove the workers from our village to the railway building site. There a striking picture revealed itself to our eyes: as far as the eye could see a human beehive with carts, horses, tractors and trucks was building an earthen track for the railway. When we came closer we realised that the railway had brought thousands of workers from inside Russia for this construction. They made an appalling impression: rough peasants, in rags, dark-faced from working in the sun, in shabby shoes, smoking cheap tobacco.

During the first days, it appeared to us that we would not be able to work there. The foreman put us to the heavy work of carrying 'stretchers' filled with wet, heavy earth uphill to dump it at the top of the new railway track. This, while the sun was beating mercilessly down. We could not believe our eyes when we saw some of the imported Soviet workers almost running uphill with the stretchers. An overseer stood at the top of the hill and wrote down how many stretchers each team brought up. Pay was according to output, and there were bonuses for surpassing the required amount. At the end of day, we had barely made half of this, whereas the Soviet teams made a half as much again. The Soviet authorities were greatly concerned that the railink be built as quickly as possible, since it was close to the German–Soviet border and was thought to be of strategic importance. It was because of this that they brought over thousands of workers from inside Russia.

After the first few days we learned to adapt to the work. We came to work with a wide-brimmed hat and in appropriate dress and shoes; more important was the change in our work. The Soviet workers were not interested in working at the top of the track, levelling and hardening the earth which was brought up by various means. This work was not quantified and it was not possible to earn as much as by carting earth where the pay was higher. We did not meet the target in any case, and were only too pleased to be paid the flat daily rate. Work at the top of the track was much easier: it also allowed periodical rest, when no new earth was brought up the hill. So the three of us brothers – aged 17, 15 and 14 – worked on the railroad. This gave us two important things: an income, small but steady, and a standing as 'proletarians'. We hoped that this would be taken into account when father's trial came about – if ever.

However, late in June that year (1940),----------------- on a Friday evening, something happened that changed our lives completely – we were exiled to Siberia.

7 • Deportation: A Long Journey into Russia

'Vast is my country
with many forests, fields and rivers.
No other country do I know
where Man breathes so freely...'*

On Friday, 20 June 1940 (almost exactly one year before Nazi Germany started its war against the Soviet Union) our family gathered at our room in the village of Nova Grobla. In the evening, mother lit the Sabbath candles, father said the prayers and made Kiddush (blessing on the wine). We sat down at the table covered with a white cloth to a traditional Sabbath meal, singing Hassidic Sabbath songs.

It was very hot night. Since our house owner allowed us, we, the three boys, decided to sleep in the barn which was cooler than the room in which our parents and little sister slept.

Suddenly, in the middle of the night we heard some heavy-hammering on the door of the barn. Mother's shrill voice was heard: 'Get up immediately and come to the room ... The police are here.'

At first we thought that they had come again for our father. When we reached our room we realised that it was something entirely different. Two men with revolvers, obviously Soviet judging by their dress and general appearance, addressed us in Russian: 'You have two hours to pack one bundle per person – and you must leave with us.' No other explanation was given. We immediately recognised one of them as being Jewish. Later he even said a few words in Yiddish. 'Where are you taking us? And why?' we asked. As the packing went on, they, and especially the Jewish fellow, slowly opened up: 'All refugees who came from the other side of the border and did not become Soviet citizens are

---

* A popular Soviet song at the height of Stalin's purges.

being evacuated to deep inside Russia. You should not worry, you will live there in big cities and there is proper work for you there .'

We were reminded of the two registration drives for all non-local residents who had originally lived on the other side of the then Soviet–German border. All local residents received Soviet citizenship automatically, whereas refugees had been asked in the two consecutive registration drives: 'Do you want to stay and become a Soviet citizen, or do you chose to return to your previous place of residence?' For various reasons we registered at first to stay and then, the second time, to return to our previous residence. Rumour had it that unless one registed for return, one would not be able to do so even at the end of the war. So now we were being evacuated because of this.

Packing took longer than the two hours they allowed us. After some time, they allowed me to go to the neighbouring village, to the Jewish family with whom we had first taken refuge when we were expelled by the Germans. I woke them up, told them what was happening to us and gave them a quickly scribbled authorization to deal with the things which we left behind (by that time we had a Singer sewing machine which was regarded as being of considerable value). We also notified the owner of the house that we were leaving the things to that family (otherwise he could easily just help himself). By that time, close to dawn, a horse and cart requisitioned by the authorities arrived; we were told to get onto it with our two 'guardians', and off we went to the nearest railway station, in Lubachev.

The KGB had obviously planned that the entire operation should be conducted at night, unwitnessed by the local population. But either because June nights are so short, or because of some delay at its start, it continued well into the early hours after dawn. Also, it was a large-scale operation and the streets of Lubachev became clogged with the many carts carrying 'evacuees' and their 'guardians'. The entire population of this town lined the street leading to the railway station. We passed by the house where I had been lodging when studying in Lubachev. The entire family stood there. They recognised us but could not get to us. The women cried openly and blessed us from afar. I tried to jump off the cart and run over and talk with them, but was firmly held back by one of the KGB men.

When we arrived at the railway station we saw at its end a long goods train surrounded by soldiers with rifles fitted with bayonets. Beyond the circle of soldiers there was a circle of family and friends of the deported. The entire scene was like something from a horror film. The soldiers were not able to control the situation: from time to time a mother, sister or close friend on one side of the circle of soldiers recognised their closest family or friend on the other side. They would run through the soldiers to each other, embrace, kiss, exchange papers, money, valuables … The soldiers ran around shouting, attempting to separate the people, to push the deportees back to the train. To enforce their orders they started beating people with the butts of their rifles and threatening them with the bayonets. Not far from us an elderly man got badly hit by a rifle butt on the side of his head; he fell to the ground screaming and covered in blood. Two soldiers were carrying away a screaming and kicking girl; twice she succeeded in freeing herself, she ran to a nearby carriage shouting 'Mother!' The soldiers pushed her roughly to the ground, bound her legs with a belt and carried her away.

In the meantime embarkation took place. There were no steps at the entrances to the goods carriages. The young and fit were able to climb in, but the elderly, and especially the women, could not make it. They had to be pulled and pushed by those around. This was especially difficult when some of them would not part with their bags and belongings. Embarkation was therefore very slow. The officers were running and shouting, the soldiers started pushing and beating. Some carriages were full, but more and more carts were arriving and more people were pushed into the carriages. The heat was rising, it was almost noon. Finally, the heavy sliding door of the carriage was closed and locked with a huge bolt. Then the locomotive whistled and the long prison train started moving.

'We are prisoners!' The full horror of the situation sank in. All previous talk about 'evacuating' us evaporated. When taken to the railway station the KGB officers had given us the impression that we would travel on a normal passenger train, which were quite comfortable. Instead, we were packed like cattle, some 40 persons, 12 families, into a goods carriage, which was fitted only with a wooden shelf on both sides of the wide, locked door. A fight immediately broke out for the better places in the corner of the upper shelf, by the small barred windows and as far away as possible from the makeshift 'toilet', a term which was much too flattering for the contraption in the middle of the carriage, opposite the door. It was a hole in the floor surrounded with a low sheet of tin. We managed to make a place on the upper shelf for our parents and sister, and we lay down on the floor beneath the shelf, together with our bundles. The carriage was very crowded, the heat was stifling, several of the 'passengers' in our prison on wheels broke down, crying and screaming. One elderly woman lost consciousness. We had no water, the stink from the 'toilet' became overwhelming. We banged on the door, screamed 'Help!', shouted 'Water! Water!' through the small windows – all to no avail.

After several hours the train stopped. We resumed our banging and shouting with great vehemence. At last the door opened partly; three KGB blue-capped, soldiers and an officer stood there with their rifles poised. Two pails of water and two with yellow *kasha* (corn porridge) were pushed onto the floor of the carriage. Immediately a scramble for water and food started, but the officer shouted: 'There must be order and quiet, otherwise you will be severely punished! We have here a carriage which is a punishment cell, and I would not suggest that anyone try it!' With these words, he picked a burly fellow near the entrance: 'You will be the orderly here, responsible for this carriage. Any disruption, and you will pay for it.' The heavy door was closed with a bang.

There were ladles on each of the buckets. Jacob, the burly fellow, appointed three other men to stand at each bucket and apportion one ladle of water and *kasha* per person. Meanwhile, the heat subsided. Slowly the various families sorted themselves out and prepared for sleep. After some time the train started moving again. In the darkness, when most were asleep from exhaustion and the terrors of the day, the train stopped again. Several loaves of bread and buckets with some kind of soup were shoved in. In the meagre light of the carriage, close to midnight, food was again distributed and consumed.

And so our long journey inside Russia started. On the second and third days of our travel we noticed similar trains to ours. On several occasions our train stopped alongside such a train. Through the small windows we were able to shout to them, despite the guards'warnings. In this way we learned that the refugee evacuation operation had been conducted on a large scale throughout Western Ukraine on the same Friday night. The refugee prisoners in all trains we encountered were all Jewish, as in our train.

When I woke up, on the morning of the third day, the door of the carriage was slightly open. I looked at the station building, at the countryside; everything looked different. The realization hit me: we were already within Soviet territory. The place looked somehow more coarse, people were poorly dressed, the buildings showed signs of neglect. We asked the guard: 'Where are we?' 'Somewhere around Zhitomir', was the answer.

As the train moved deeper into Soviet territory, our guards became more relaxed. They soon realized that our kind of people would not run away. We would not leave our families, and we had nowhere to run without papers, in a country foreign to us. Besides, our fate was not yet clear to us; the KGB guards kept on assuring us that we were going to be 'resettled' in big cities inside the huge Soviet Union where we would be able to live 'quite comfortably'. Actually, there were campaigns for enlisting skilled people (tailors, builders, dentists, electricians) from former Polish territories for work inside Russia. While some of these people returned deeply disappointed, others wrote that they settled there quite well (especially tailors, shoemakers, and so forth who could produce goods in the 'Western style' which were not known in Soviet lands). So we hoped that what the guards said was true. Especially since we were with children, old and ill people. Many of us were skilled and could contribute well in some city environment. Who could have, in his wildest imagination, guessed that we would be forced to live in camps deep in the Siberian forest?

Anyway, as we travelled deeper into the Soviet Union, the regime grew more relaxed. The guards allowed us to keep the door partly open while the train was in motion, and as time went on we were able to talk with them and give them some presents and cigarettes. They then began to allow us an open door at stations, which completely changed our travel conditions. Often, our train was put on hold because of heavy priority traffic and kept at a station for many hours. At almost all stations there was a little bazaar. We, especially the youngsters, used to jump off our carriages, run to the bazaar and exchange a 'Polish' pair of socks, a blouse or money for some fruit, vegetables, milk, cheese, tea ... Also, at each station there was a tap for *kipiatok* (hot boiled water). These 'riches' made it possible for us to make tea or soup of our own and to supplement the food apportioned to us.

These shopping excursions were, however, far from innocent. They were actually fraught with considerable danger. It was only possible to leave the carriage if no soldier could see us, especially not an officer. Often our train would be shunted onto a siding; to get to the bazaar or to the *kipiatok* tap meant sprinting underneath a number of trains and hiding underneath when railway guards appeared. There were special red-capped railway police and we had to hide from them. Also, the expedition had to be excuted with utmost speed since we never knew how long our train would remain at the station. Sprinting over trains was dangerous in case the train started moving quickly and one had to jump from it while it was moving. It was even more dangerous to slip beneath trains; if it started moving it could maim or even kill you. We youngsters were agile and escaped quickly in such cases. But some others were severely injured. On one occasion, we heard an elderly man screaming madly; we saw him quite close to our carriage being pulled underneath a train opposite us. When he raised his arms we saw that they were practically severed and oozing blood. Later we heard that he died of his wounds.

On one expedition we were very lucky with our transaction: a peasant at one of the stalls was selling *bulochky* (traditional Russian breadrolls) and another sold us fine apples and strawberries. We quickly gathered our treasures and started our trek back. However, two trains were moving and we were delayed. By the time we arrived at the place where our train had been, we could not believe our eyes – it was gone. We asked a nearby railwayman: 'It left about 10 minutes ago', was his answer. I was there with one of my brothers. We despaired: 'What shall we do? Who knows whether we shall ever see our parents again? And surely we shall be punished.' Having no other recourse we went to the station-master's office and he took us immediately to the railway police. We presented an innocent story. 'We went behind the next train to attend to our needs, the train must have left so quietly that we did not hear it.' (It was forbidden to use our carriage 'toilet' while the train was at a station; and of course we had thrown away our shopping goods before returning to the station.)

The railway police officer was utterly perplexed. We did not know the identity of our train or its destination. Furthermore, we had no papers whatsoever. He made some frantic telephone calls. Our problem seemed insurmountable even after he established contact with the nearest station at which our train would be arriving. We had to get there, but we had no ticket; we were prisoners, so we were not allowed to travel unescorted, but he had nobody to send with us. At last he made up his mind; he wrote some official paper, stamped it with his stamp, then took us personally to the next train which was going to the next major station where our train was due to stop. He handed us over to a carriage attendant and gave him the paper on which he had written. Within several hours we arrived at that station. The attendant handed us over to a railway policeman there and gave him the paper. It turned out that our train, which was slow, had not yet arrived. We were treated to tea and some sandwiches (a royal feast!) and fell asleep on the floor of the railway police room. After midnight we were woken up: our train had arrived. How great was the joy of our family when we were reunited in our prison train! Our parents had feared that they might never see us again. Nor were we surprised to see that the guards were also very happy to welcome us back.

Day followed day and our train moved ever deeper into Russia. We passed bridges across mighty rivers. The first was the Dnieper, close to Kiev; but we passed it at night and did not see it properly. Then we travelled south of Moscow and crossed the Volga; it was so wide that we could barely see from one side to the other. Inevitably, we remembered the River San in our town of Yaroslav in former Poland; in midsummer it was so shallow that we used to cross it on foot. As we journeyed on, it became apparent that the train was travelling steadily east, and it became almost certain that we were being 'evacuated' to Siberia. We came to the foothills of the Ural mountains, and then travelled across them, until one morning we realised that we were actually in Siberia. Our guards kept on asserting that there were great, highly developed cities even in Siberia, but we finally lost all confidence in their comforting words. By then we had come to realise that they themselves did not know our final destination. Naturally, as we travelled into Siberia our mood became increasingly gloomy. There were some cities and fertile areas, but vast areas were covered by endless woods and wasteland.

Yet, despite all this, the atmosphere on our train became almost friendly. By then we knew each of our guards quite well and on occasion engaged with them in long talks. Some of them were very curious to hear about life in Poland and Europe before the war. Some of our 'passengers' had travelled widely, even to America. As Soviet people isolated from the outside world, the guards were fascinated to hear from people who had seen it with their own eyes. The weather was summery, not too hot, and as we travelled through the huge stretches of Russia, the Ural mountains with their breathtaking views and then through the vast lands of Siberia, we could not help being deeply impressed. It was like a holiday in the middle of a nightmare journey.

As usually happens with youngsters, we became friendly with

others on our train, and soon we formed a kind of 'gang'. During the long waits at stations we engaged in games and excursions along our train. There was an empty carriage at the end, the door of which was open. Often we skipped to this carriage and travelled sitting at its entrance with our feet dangling outside. We sang, told stories and sometimes even danced (away from the entrance door so that the guards would not see us). The train journey was to most of us something of an adventure, since we had not previously travelled beyond our immediate surroundings. Also, travelling on this train was like being in an eerie, suspended-time capsule: we could do nothing but live from day to day and wait to see what would happen.

Soon enough the 'picnic' was over and the horror of our situation gained the upper hand. Our train passed Novosibirsk, the capital of Siberia, and then it started moving deep into the foothills of the Altai mountains, not far from the Mongolian and Chinese border. At a small station several of our carriages were uncoupled from the train on which we had been travelling for more than three weeks.

'This is it, you have arrived at your destination!' our guards announced. We looked around in horror: apart from some houses next to the station we could see nothing but endless woods climbing higher and higher up immense mountains. 'How are we going to live here?' we thought in despair. Little did we know that we were not even to be allowed to live in this village, but were to be incarcerated in small barrack camps in the depths of the endless Siberian forests. We also did not know that, ironically, by removing us from the German border many thousands of miles away, the KGB actually saved our lives. Exile in harsh conditions to Siberia turned out to be an inadvertent rescue operation. Almost all of our family and Jewish friends who were not exiled, who cried over us during our deportation from Lubachev, perished in the Holocaust. We never saw them again.

8 • In a Jewish Prison Camp in Siberia

'Siberia, Siberia – I am not afraid of Siberia.
Siberia is a Russian land as well...'*

For more than three weeks we travelled under armed KGB guard – some 50 people in each goods wagon – through the Ukraine, central Russia, over the Ural mountains and the endless plains of Siberia. Finally, we arrived at a small God-forsaken railway station. It was – as we later found out – at the foothills of the Altai mountains not far from Siberia's borders with Mongolia and China. With our meagre possessions, we were unloaded onto the platform under the open sky – still under guard. From time to time small trucks and horse-drawn carriages loaded with barrels and other goods came by and collected a group of the newly arrived exiles. Soon our family of six were precariously located on top of empty barrels and crates, and on we went. That we actually arrived at our destination seemed to us nothing short of a miracle: the small truck wove along a very narrow forest lane through hilly terrain, climbing higher and higher. Some parts were muddy or sandy and the truck slipped and stalled. In some places thick branches practically covered the trail. These hit against the barrels producing a frightening noise, and worse: the branches often hit us, knocking us off the little truck. With all our strength we clung to each other and to the barrels. At one point our little sister Ruthie began to fall, had she done so it might have resulted in her being maimed for life, or even dead. She got hold of the sideboard and with an incredible effort, and luck, we pulled her back on board. All our appeals to the driver to slow down and drive with more care fell on deaf ears – he just laughed. On and on we went through a mountainous ancient forest – with trees as thick as

---

* Popular Russian folksong.

entire houses – higher and higher. On the long trek, which lasted several hours, we passed several tiny settlements, each consisting of several wooden barracks. We were neither allowed to stop there nor to exchange a few words with anyone.

After a few hours of this ordeal we finally arrived at what was to become our home and prison. In a small clearing in the ancient wood, at the edge of a small lake we saw several wooden structures. The biggest was a long, low, black barrack with a tarred roof and small windows. Further on were three houses of light wood. One turned out to be a supervisors' 'office', another with big windows was for their families' lodgings. The third was some kind of warehouse-cum-shop.

We were told to get off the trucks and gather in front of the long barrack. A tall, thin fellow stepped forward from the group of several local 'supervisors' and addressed us in a harsh voice:

'You have arrived at Barrack 9. You are absolutely forbidden to step outside the perimeter of this enclosed area. You must work, all of you, including women and youngsters. Those who work will receive the ration of a pound of bread and other food when available. Those who will not work will receive nothing.

I am sure many of you think that this is only your temporary place. Get that idea out of your heads! You will not leave this place until you die. This is where you will live, and here on the nearby hill you will be buried. So you had better make the most of it. Today you will have some rest and settle into your barrack. Tomorrow at dawn you will go out into the woods for work and you will return at sunset. That will be your schedule every day … The slightest insubordination will be severely punished?'

We were too shocked and frightened to react immediately to this 'life sentence'. Deep in our hearts we simply did not accept it, and with the benefit of hindsight, we were right. It took us only a little more than a year to get out of there, but of course, we could not know this at that time. We looked around: was this God-forsaken clearing in the endless forest and this long, black barrack to be our world from now on? What also frightened us immensely was the contrast between us, the exiles, and our local 'bosses-to-be'. Most of us came from cities in former Poland, and many were from well-to-do families. Many were dressed in their best finery, which they had put on when they were taken into exile for fear that if they put it into a bundle it might be lost (or stolen) on the way. Many of the men were in suits and good shoes, while the women wore fashionable dresses and elegant shoes. In the middle of the Siberian forest we looked like a displaced island from some remote, fashionable, European world. Our bosses were dark and shabbily dressed in forest fashion, coarse boots and felt hats. They looked to us like woodland creatures which bore a certain resemblance to humans. 'And these are to be our masters here?' we thought. Little did we know that in only a few days we would look very much like them – only worse.

We were given a piece of black bread and some *kasha* and then marched off to our 'lodgings' in the black barrack. It was obviously not designed to accommodate such a large number of people – some 40 families. From one end to the other of a long, poorly lit corridor there were small doors covered with sacking material leading into tiny cubicles. Our family of six – parents, three brothers and our little sister – were packed into a room barely the size of a small bathroom. It was separated from other such cubicles by makeshift wooden partitions and one could easily hear what was going on on the other side. There was, mercifully, a small window at the end with a small table and two rickety, wooden chairs. On the right, there were three narrow bunks fixed on the partition one above the other. When we were all together, there was only room to stand, and, as it was summer, it was unbearably hot and stifling; but we were not permitted to leave the 'apartment.'

Naturally, we were deeply depressed. Throughout the long journey we had been told: 'Do not worry! You are being evacuated from the border areas in former Poland to cities inside the huge Soviet Union where the conditions are comfortable and people with your skills will find good employment.' We sometimes suspected that we were being lied to, but often we wanted to believe in it. Even when we had passed the Ural mountains on the Trans-Siberian railway deep into Siberia, the officers of the security guard went on reassuring us: 'There are large modern cities there and you are going to live there.' And now we were here and heard 'the life sentence' pronounced by our local jailer and boss. This was not the first time we had been lied to by the Soviet authorities, nor was it to be the last.

Somehow we managed to sit on the two chairs and bunks, unpack our few things, cover the bunks with whatever we had and prepare for what we hoped would be a forgetful sleep. Soon it turned into a night of unbelievable torture. The narrow bunks could not accommodate two people each; they were hard and uneven. Loud noises were heard constantly through the thin partitions. Mosquitoes started buzzing around. But all this was as nothing compared with the main plague: within minutes of lying down we were covered with a blanket of all kinds of hungry vermin. We were bitten all over by a hungry host and there was no way of protecting oneself from it. Where did this army of vermin come from and how could one escape it?

At last the hour of salvation arrived – at dawn we risked leaving our infested, stifling 'dwelling'. To jump ahead: in the nights that followed we learned to sleep leaving the oil lamp burning, which diminished the activity of the vermin. Also, despite the smothering heat, we learned to wrap ourselves hermetically with covers so as to deny the vermin access to our bodies. By the third or fourth night we were exhausted through lack of sleep and hard work during the day, and we became so used to the biting, so that we slept solidly, despite everything. It is in the nature of Man to be infinitely capable of suffering and adjusting.

OUR FIRST DAY AT WORK

At dawn our door was torn open. One of the 'supervisors' stood there yelling: 'Get up! To work!' We dressed as quickly as possible and rushed outside. There we had to wait a good hour until the bosses got ready. We were provided with a lump of black bread, a little of the eternal *kasha*, some work tools and were marched off in small groups into the endless surrounding forest. For mile after mile we walked on a barely visible trail passing by small ponds or bogs where from time to time rather large snakes moved around. To our great pain we quickly realized how little our 'superior' clothing agreed with the Siberian mountain forests into which we marched deeper and deeper. Our feet were soon covered with blisters; our elegant shoes slipped on the boggy parts of the trail; branches of the trees and the rich undergrowth tore our trousers. The women among us suffered even more, some of them in frilly dresses and high heels. How we envied our masters in their harsh boots and tight, dark, working clothes!

With the first snow and frosts which started early in September this problem became more acute. We were forced to go into the frozen snowy forest in light European attire and shoes. We suffered from cold and frostbite despite the fires which we were allowed to kindle. Slowly some special winter equipment arrived, albeit in an odd sequence: small winter boots, very large padded trousers without a front opening, tall flapped hats ... Still as the winter progressed, the main body of workers were gradually equipped with appropriate clothing. It had to be so: when the cold reached -40° Celsius anyone without it would quickly freeze to death.

After more than an hour of trekking through the forest we were told to halt at a clearing which was flanked with an artificial cave – a dugout inside a hill with a door. We discovered later that such hill dugouts were quite frequent in the forest. They served as storage and rest areas. On occasion they actually saved our lives, when caught in the forest during a storm, or when we suddenly had to attend to our needs when working in a 'mosquito cloud', or simply when we were in danger of freezing to death in the winter.

One of the bosses now gave us our first instructions about our future work, which was for us a totally unexpected and unknown quantity. It was not logging or clearing the woods as we had thought, but producing sap from the ancient trees. This was regarded as a precious chemical which was collected in the barrels of which we knew from our trip to the barrack. With the help of a huge, two-handled, semi-circular sickle, the boss cut the thick bark off a tree, creating a clear patch the size of a shield. Then, with another knife fixed on a long handle, he made a small vertical incision which created a central channel under which he fixed a small cup. He then made two horizontal cuts with an outlet into the central channel. Immediately thick yellow-green sap started to flow into the cup. A number of other 'shields' were made. After a while a woman with a bucket and a spoon went around and collected the sap from cups, then emptied the bucket into the nearest barrel. At intervals small horse-drawn carts went through the woods collecting the barrels and transporting them to the nearest road. From there they were moved to the nearest railway or waterway, and then to a huge chemical factory near Barnaul, the capital of the Altai mountain region. According to our informers the sap was raw material for a number of chemical products including some for military uses.

We were then ordered to do the same as our boss demonstrated. Before long we were in agony. We were not used to hard physical labour. The bark turned out to be as hard as steel. The dust poured on our faces and made it difficult to breath. The sap was like glue, the buckets grew heavier and heavier as we filled them and as the hours dragged on. In the forest it was hot and humid, and as the work continued our arms and backs became stiff and aching with each cut we made in the trees. Exhausted and aching all over, dirty and with sap in our hair and covering our clothes and hands we marched back home, where there was nothing to clean oneself with except sand and dry tree branches. We were given some soup with a few vegetables and off we went to bed. At first I couldn't sleep – my entire body was in pain. But soon enough, after such a day I was sound asleep, vermin and all.

Next day we were allotted our 'estate' in the woods. Every able- bodied exile was given a portion of the wood which he was to work. I was then aged 15 and my younger brother, who teamed up with me, was 13. We were both obliged to work if we wanted to earn a working man's food ration. We were allocated a portion of the forest some five kilometres from our barrack – bounded by a small lake at one end and a clearing at the other. It contained 2,000 trees, and was properly marked as belonging to us. Some of the trees were so thick that several men with outstretched arms were not able to span its girth.

We were overwhelmed: 2,000 trees! Wow! We never imagined that we should strike that rich – and in Siberia of all places! We were less impressed when told that there would be periodic inspections to ascertain that we serviced all the trees in our 'estate' properly. Luckily, in time we found out that 'our' wood had some blessings to compensate for its negative side: several fields of blueberries, rather a lot of edible mushrooms and some wild fruit at the edge of the lake. Once in a while free-ranging cows would saunter into our neighbourhood, and soon we learned to milk them. So occasionally we would return 'home' laden with fruits of the forest. These added immensely to our meagre food rations. We would scoop a handful of blueberries or chew some edible mushrooms and put into our mouth a crumb of bread to enjoy the taste. Mushrooms played a particularly important role. We collected as many as possible during the abundant autumn and dried them. Our little cubicle was full of rings of dried mushrooms. During the following winter months of virtual starvation we were often saved by a pot of mushroom soup. I had so much of it during that winter that for years after the smell of mushrooms would make me heave.

9 • Yom Kippur in the Forest

So we found ourselves at 'Barrack 9' in an all-Jewish prison camp in the Altai mountains of Siberia. The second night after our arrival was Friday night. Both my parents were from deeply religious families. As the holy Shabbat approached, my mother pulled out from our bundles one candle, broke it in two, and covered her head with a scarf. She then covered her eyes with her hands and as she pronounced the traditional prayer and lit the candles two small tears flowed slowly down her cheeks. In our cubicle room we started quietly to say our prayers and sing the well-known Sabbath songs. Through the thin partitions we heard others singing in their 'rooms'.

Suddenly the door to our 'room' was torn open violently. In the open frame stood one of our bosses, a huge threatening man. 'I am warning you – none of this nonsense! Next time you will be punished severely', he shouted. 'What do you think this is, a synagogue?' he sneered. He stepped forward into our room, blew out the candles, turned around and left, closing the door violently behind him. We remained in the dark. We, the young in the family, were non-religious, but this struck us as a reprehensible case of anti-religious coercion. Therefore, on no account did we stop lighting some lights (though we did not always have candles) in honour of the Sabbath because of this incident. Nor did we refrain from singing our Sabbath songs. We posted sentries of our own at the entrance to the barrack to warn us if any of the bosses were coming, and we conducted our singing and prayers quietly – in case of informers in our midst. More difficult was the problem of going out to work on the Sabbath. We had to work on that day and could do nothing about it. Several of the deeply religious among us found ways to avoid it by working harder on Friday, to cover up for not working on Saturday. But this was only possible as long as they were working alone in the woods. When supervisors were present they had to work.

The showdown came soon enough. Towards the end of September, the most solemn day in the Jewish religious year arrived – Yom Kippur. This Judgement Day Jews always spent fasting and praying; any manner of work was most strictly forbidden. Any infringement of the strict rules of Yom Kippur was regarded a most serious religious transgression deserving inevitable and severe punishment from Heaven. We made up our minds: no matter the risks we would find a way to mark this ancient Jewish Judgement Day. Not that I myself was religious, nor were many of us, especially among the young, but Yom Kippur was deeply embedded in our tradition. We found a way to mark it even during our brief time under the Germans. Besides, in the barrack conditions, this was a matter of 'national–ethnic' self-assertion, of being Jews.

On the day of Yom Kippur we went as if to work in the most distant part of 'our' wood. On the previous day we had done more work than usual to cover for not working next day, as long as we were not supervised. We agreed with all the others who were not under guard to meet at ten o'clock in the morning at a remote dugout in the woods. Opposite its door there was a huge trunk of a cut- down tree on a small hill. In the absence of a Torah scroll we placed on it a small Bible which one of us had somehow managed to keep; we wrapped an old prayer shawl around the trunk. Then we proclaimed it to be the Holy Torah Ark in front of which prayers are customarily said in a synagogue. Our small group gathered around the makeshift Ark, with heads covered according to religious law, and started our Yom Kippur service. We posted some young members of our group as sentries at strategic places so they could warn us in case any of our bosses approached. I looked around; all the participants were quite aware that if we were discovered, it might end in severe accusations: forming an illegal assembly, refusal to work, conspiracy, and so forth. Such matters were punishable by years of harsh imprisonment and separation from the family with little hope of seeing them again. The people around me were just as frightened as I was at that moment and yet we did not falter. The prayers started.

But how could we pray when only two of us had prayer books, and even these were tattered. One elderly person with a small beard who had such a book stepped forward and started intoning the ancient prayer of *Kol Nidrei* (it is generally said with great solemnity at the opening of prayers at sunset on the previous day, but as we could not do it in the barrack, we said it now).

'By permission of the assembly above, in Heaven, and with the permission of the assembly here below, on earth, we allow to pray with sinners ...

All our vows, limitations, oaths from today and to the next Yom Kippur day ...' The old man must have been some kind of cantor since he sang and intoned the prayers in the traditional and well-known manner. My two brothers and I used to sing in the little choir in our small synagogue back at home. So we joined in and together it sounded much as a proper service. Some of the participants couldn't hold back and cried openly while beating their breasts:

'Our Father, our King we have sinned before thee, be merciful, forgive us, have mercy upon us ...' Since we were without prayer books we simply repeated the words after the leader. And though we were trying to be quiet for fear of being heard by the supervisors, it seemed that the ancient forest was reverberating with the prayers rising straight to heaven. I looked around again. Could one ever envisage a more bizarre picture: a mixed bunch of people in bedraggled dress, with work-blackened faces, standing around a huge tree-trunk in a remote, hidden corner of a primordial wood and intoning melodies as strange to this place as could be: 'O God of Israel, save thy People Israel! Return us to Zion, to Your Holy City – Jerusalem!'

'What could be further from us in a corner of the endless Siberian forests than Jerusalem?' I thought at that moment. Then we intoned the customary prayer in memory of the dead with grave solemnity:

O Lord, let there come before thee
the shining memory of those
who departed this world.

Suddenly we froze. From afar the barking of dogs could be heard. This meant only one thing: our bosses were searching for us. Disaster was near. Our sentries came running back: 'Run! Disperse!' Within seconds the prayer shawl was off, the books hidden and we were sneaking off rapidly in all directions. Either we were lucky or the bosses were not that keen to find us out – we were all able to return to the barrack as if nothing had happened.

Once at the barrack we learned about what had happened there. Some of the people at our settlement, especially the old, were deeply religious. One of them, Abraham Kaufman, was from our town in Poland. I remembered how he used proudly to stand, with his long white beard, in front of his dry goods emporium, a highly respected citizen. 'You can do to me whatever you like – beat me, arrest me – I shall absolutely not work on Yom Kippur', he told the bosses. They tried all kinds of ways to break him but he stood his ground. Then one of them – an especially evil type – went over to him and whispered something into his ear. Kaufman's face became as white as chalk. Then with a considerable effort (he had been fasting since the previous sundown) he stood up, got hold of a saw and together with another bearded ancient they started sawing wood in the courtyard of the barrack. While working both intoned the holy prayers of the Day of Judgement, with tears flowing from their eyes.

What did the evil boss whisper into Kaufman's ear? At first we did not know since he would not reveal it. Within several days of this incident he was dead. His heart could not withstand the strain of the humiliation and coercion. This was the first death since we had been incarcerated in 'Barrack 9' and we were afraid that the bosses would not allow a burial with traditional religious rites. However, they apparently had a bad conscience about the way they had treated him. All the exiles came early before sunset from work in the woods. The bosses were nowhere to be seen. We gave Kaufman a traditional Jewish burial. His body was washed, wrapped in a white sheet. It was put in a coffin of wooden planks covered with a prayer shawl and carried in procession to the nearest hill where a grave was dug. He was eulogised by one of the elders and then the two sons said Kaddish. Another old, bearded man intoned 'El Malei Rahamim', the prayer for the dead. We dispersed quietly, unhindered.

One of the sons of the deceased eventually disclosed what the evil boss whispered into Kaufman's ear on that Yom Kippur day: 'If you do not start work immediately we shall take away not only your food ration card but also those of your entire family, including your grandchildren's. Then you will be responsible for their painful death from hunger. And don't delude yourself – we shall certainly do so.' Kaufman worked on Yom Kippur to save the life of his grandchildren. According to Jewish religious tradition *Pikuach Nefesh* – saving human life – overrides even the laws of Yom Kippur.

A small marker remained fixed on the fresh grave on the hill: 'Here interned for his final rest lies ABRAHAM KAUFMAN the TZADDIK'. Abraham Kaufman, a deeply religious orthodox Jew was a humane person. Also, it is indeed an obligation of a non-religious Jew to defend the right of a believer to uphold his religion without hindrance. Anti-religious coercion, much like religious coercion, brings about a reaction -- the opposite of the one intended.

10 • Winter and Spring: Hunger, Frostbite and Mosquitoes

'Even though I walk through the valley of death
I fear no evil ...'

(Psalms, 23:4)

Winter came. The situation in our Barrack 9, lost in the Siberian Altai mountains, became desperate. Heavy snowstorms covered the small mountain roads to our settlement. For several days – sometimes for a week or more – we were cut off from the outside world. We had no electricity, no radio, no newspapers and of course no telephones. The frost often reached more than –40° Celsius. For months we could not see the sun: it did not rise above the tall, ancient trees around us. Night fell soon after 3 o'clock in the afternoon and day arrived close to 9 in the morning. It was possible to move outside our barrack except on makeshift skis supplied to the workers among us by our bosses. The skis were actually narrow planks of wood with some nails in the middle around which some thick strings were bound. We were supposed to put our foot in the middle of the plank and bind the strings as tight as possible, and off we went. Only we had to pray all the time: 'God in heaven! Grant that the strings will hold', because if they broke or slipped off the plank into the deep snow it could be a matter of life and death, especially if you were alone. It happened to me once when I went through the woods to find some food under the snows for our cow. The strings on the 'skis' broke, I fell into the snow which was between two and three metres deep. No matter how I tried I was unable to get out. I started yelling for help. For almost an hour I was stuck there thinking: 'This is the end. I am going to freeze to death here.' Especially since snow had started falling heavily and night was coming. Luckily I was not far from a trail that led to our barrack and two of my fellow prisoners were just returning there after work. They pulled me out and so I was saved.

Of course the most serious matter was hunger. It was not possible during the harsh winter to gather any wild fruit or mushrooms. When the roads were blocked no bread or porridge was distributed. Many families were faint with hunger, and when food was brought in they could not control themselves; they consumed it all at once. As a result they were permanently hungry, at the end of their strength.

The situation for our family was amongst the best in our barrack. We had our cow, Murka. Every day my mother supplied a cup of milk to several 'customers' in exchange for some flour, rice, potatoes and any other edibles. When bread was not available she cooked mushrooms soup or some milk and a little rice. When bread was delivered we had some of it with milk or home-made cheese. Her potato soup was also very popular with some bread crumbs or sweetcorn. Early in the winter we were transferred from the common barrack to a small room of our own with a large window in a newly built small house. We did not suffer from cold except when outside for work or for our personal needs. (Naturally the toilet was outside – and try attending to your needs during a major snowstorm and a severe frost!). A large iron stove was placed in the middle of our room. There was no shortage of wood: we found a dry tree not far from our room. During periods of clear weather we used to go out with a sledge and a sharpened axe; we chopped as much wood as possible and then transferred it to a lean-to by the wall of our room. We had to guard this precious resource by day and night.

Another very precious resource was fodder for our cow. We searched the forests around for some clearing where some straw or dried vegetation remained under a thin layer of snow. We walked miles and miles to the nearest settlements where we received a little fodder in exchange for all kinds of goods which we carried with us. Then we pulled the precious cargo on sleighs through the mountains – always hiding from the KGB.

ALMOST IN PRISON – BECAUSE OF OIL FOR OUR LAMP

In the middle of winter a new trouble befell us – no oil for our lamps. Darkness enfolded us from late afternoon till late in the morning. The endlessly long nights were unbearable. Especially so since the windows at the officers' dwellings were brightly lit. All our efforts to find a supply of oil failed.

At the end of our settlement, along the small road, there was a huge tank with oil for tractors. During the day a guard was usually there, but at night none was to be seen in the darkness. In desperation we decided to try and 'lift' some oil from this tank, despite the obvious risk involved. One dark night after midnight my mother and I put on warm, dark clothing, took a large pail and a long rubber pipe with us and walked surreptitiously towards the tank. No guard was to be seen anywhere. We came to the foot of the huge tank and I climbed its ladder. With enormous effort I lifted its heavy cover, lowered the pipe into it and started to suck oil from the tank into the pail. How heavenly was the sound of that precious fluid pouring into our pail: no more darkness, we were going to have light!

Suddenly we froze. 'Hey, who is there? Get down from there immediately with your arms up! You are under arrest for stealing government property and for sabotage!' The strong voice came from the darkness behind the tank. Soon the tall figure of the guard, wrapped in a huge, long winter coat appeared. He carried a rifle which was aimed towards us. We were stunned: if he really were to hand us over to the police we might easily end up serving a sentence of several years in a harsh prison away from our family, with a strong chance that we would never see them again. Theft of government property was punished most severely, especially when committed by exiles like ourselves.

I instantly pulled out the rubber pipe, poured back the oil from the pail into the tank, and threw away the pail and pipe as far as I could into the nearby trees, so that no material evidence would be available. How surprised was the guard when he saw in front of him a boy and an elderly woman with their arms raised – true 'state criminals'. He himself turned out to be an elderly bearded man. My mother started to cry loudly: 'I have an ill daughter and we must have some light to care for her,' she sobbed. 'Have mercy! Would you hand over to prison a woman with four children and a chronically ill husband?' At first we tried to promise him all kinds of things, but he would not hear of it. This was very dangerous since we could be accused of attempting to bribe a government guard.

Guessing that being an elderly peasant he would be religious my mother entreated: 'Please let us go and God will surely repay you!' Suddenly he embraced me tightly: 'I have a son your age ... We are all prisoners here.' Here we stood, embracing in the darkness of a forest after midnight – two victims of Soviet rule in a rare moment of solidarity. 'Go with God ', he said to us, and he did not have to repeat his words. We beat a hasty retreat since if someone else were to see us we could still end up in prison. How happy we were sitting in darkness, but together with our family and not in jail. Some time later we got some oil for our lamp from one of the drivers in exchange for a shirt.

On the clear winter days we were obliged to go to work, though only the younger men and those with proper winter clothing. We were dressed in padded jackets and padded trousers. We had also special pressed felt boots called *valenki* and heavy flapped hats. Inside the *valenki* we put several pairs of winter socks and wrapped our feet with additional warm rags, and around our faces we wrapped scarfs so that only our noses and eyes remained uncovered. Despite all that we often suffered from frostbite, especially when moving on skis on an open lake with the wind against us. We constantly checked each other's cheeks and noses; if any part started to become white we stopped immediately, turned away from the wind and rubbed the white area with snow until it was red again. In the wood we searched at first for any dry wood which we chopped, and started a fire. We worked by rotation: one team worked while another warmed itself around the fire, and though the fire was usually huge – an entire tree or entire heap of wood – we were often hot in front but frozen from behind. We worked at various winter work, felling some of the trees, or cutting off the bark on standing trees in preparation for sap extraction, and so on. When we went out to work at 8 o'clock it was still dark outside with the moon shining. Usually we moved on our skis in one long line on the lake. Sometimes we had to return hastily to the barrack just before a heavy snowstorm. Once the storm caught us on the lake several miles from 'home'; the wind was so strong that it pushed us sideways on our skis, and the snow fell so heavily that we could not see a yard in front of us. Half dead from exhaustion we made it into the safety of our settlement, but some of us were suffering with severe frostbite as a result of it.

A NEW PLAGUE: MOSQUITOES

By early May the long, terrible winter was drawing to an end. In the warmer weather the mounds of snow started to thaw. Instead of snow we had heavy rain. The entire countryside turned into one impassable bog. We were once again cut off from the world, and consequently had no bread or other supplies. But the greatest, and hitherto unknown, torment came in the form of tiny creatures: mosquitoes. They started as a few here and there; but soon they came in cloud-like swarms. They settled on our clothes like a cover; if another person was even one yard away it was difficult to see him because of a virtual cloud of mosquitoes in between. They were whirling, buzzing loudly and biting any piece of exposed flesh. One could die from the multitude of bites if not properly protected. We had to put on netted headcovers which protected our faces. We dressed in such a fashion as not to leave any part of our body uncovered. Our hands and nets we smeared with a repellent black tar. We all looked like devils in hell. It was a disaster if the netting covering your face got torn on some tree branch – an army of mosquitoes immediately buzzed through the opening and the terrible biting started.

The worst of all was if you suddenly had to attend to your needs. To crouch and expose any part of your body was painful and dangerous. One had to run to the nearest dugout, light a fire at the entrance so that the smoke from it would keep the little vermin away. Then it was possible to proceed – provided the wind did not blow the smoke inside, in which case you almost choked. The same routine applied to having a meal or a rest. To keep the mosquitoes out of our room we kept the windows and door permanently closed, and yet somehow they succeeded in buzzing in. Before going to sleep we spent quite some time swatting them, down to the last one if possible.

By early summer the mosquito plague diminished and became bearable. We worked hard in the forest. Week followed week, month followed month, and we started to wonder whether perhaps the KGB officer had been right after all when, on our arrival, he had told us that there was no way we would ever get out of this place. Little did we know that in only a few days, the world situation was going to change radically – as would our own lives.

11 • A Cow Called Murka

We were a family of six. My elder brother, Lemmel, was 17 and he worked a portion of wood not far away from me and my younger brother, Moshe. My father, Leib, was then aged about 40. Back in Poland he had suffered badly from asthma. Miraculously, in the mountain air of the Siberian Altai he felt better. Needless to say, he lost a lot of weight, which was also good for him. Nevertheless he was not regarded as fit for heavy work in the wood and was assigned to light work around the barrack itself. At first he was employed in all kind of cleaning activities, but soon enough he was a construction worker when two new wooden buildings were erected at our settlement. He switched to this work of his own volition: a construction worker was entitled to a larger food ration and pay. My mother, Batia, was somewhat younger than our father; yet she had problems with her circulation and some varicose veins in her legs. She also had to look after our little sister, Ruthie, who was 6, and to attend to the needs of the four workers in her family. Consequently, she was not pressed into the heavy work of collecting sap with a bucket in the woods. She soon found a way to work on our own little 'farm' – a vegetable patch which she established behind our barrack. Even Ruthie contributed to our food supply: together with some other children she walked the surrounding woods and collected wild fruit and mushrooms. Once, while trying to reach some fruit at the edge of a bog, she started to sink into it and had to be saved by other children. Another time, when walking barefoot in the forest, she stepped into what turned out to be a snake's nest. Luckily she escaped unharmed, but the picture of the hissing and curling snakes attacking her remained with her for a long time.

All in all, our family was regarded as being in a relatively good situation. Next to us in the barrack was a family of seven – two adults, one youngster of 14, and four little children. The father was a weakling and the mother could not work at all. Their food ration was very small, they had no other resources and they were rather passive. This family was permanently on the brink of starvation. They used to steal each other's bread rations, and in consequence, as well as because of their chronic hunger, they consumed their bread ration the moment they received it. Then they had to wait until the next bread ration was handed out, some 24 or 48 hours later, without food, for there often was nothing else to have (they were not into collecting wild fruit and if they did have any they gobbled it up at once). From their quarters we often heard screaming, beating, fighting and noisy accusations being hurled. In the next terrible winter when food supplies could not get through the snowy mountains, and we remained without bread for several days in a row, this family locked itself up in their room ready to die and put an end to their constant suffering At first we did not suspect anything. It was during a major snowstorm so nobody was moving about much outside. Then the snowstorm was over but their door remained locked, and what was particularly strange was that their room remained very quiet. When not one of them answered our urgent calls we broke the door and found them lying half dead on their bunks. Ironically, just about then a huge food supply arrived in two trucks. We received their bread ration and made a collection from almost everyone of some food and vegetables. I shall never forget their faces when they were faced with this abundance of food ... From then on arrangements were made to collect food for several 'weak' families in our settlement – and not one person died of hunger. At a neighbouring Polish barrack quite a number of people died of hunger and cold during that winter.

As it happens we found out soon that even inside an exile barrack there remained and developed further major differences between rich and poor, resourceful and passive, strong and weak. We were amongst the rich – both in terms of workforce and of resources. Though we arrived with only a few bundles we somehow succeeded to hide a few pieces of gold and other valuables as well some good clothing and other articles. At the station bazaars during the long railway journey we had managed to exchange a lovely towel or elegant set of underwear for some white flour, buckwheat or potatoes, so we did not arrive at our barrack without any precious supplies. Though we were almost totally isolated, we were occasionally able to exchange some goods or valuables for some food given to us by the drivers or the wives of our bosses.

Also, when we were arrested back in former Poland to be sent to exile, the security officers had allowed me to go to a friendly family in the next village to inform them of what was happening to us. I had asked them to get whatever we left behind, sell it and transfer to us the monies recovered. Remember: we were told that we were being resettled in big cities inside Russia! At first we were allowed to write to them from our barrack and send them our address – so from time to time we received a parcel packed according to our instructions. These parcels were a virtual lifeline for us: they included valuable items which were good for exchanging for food. For one elegant skirt that arrived in one of the parcels we received over a period during the winter half a quart of milk each day from the mother of one of our supervisors who kept a Siberian cow. It was from her that we learned that a small, half-blind cow was for sale at a settlement not too far away.

In our family, it was always our mother who had the gift for ideas, innovations and solutions. In our home town of Yaroslav in the south of Poland, after the First World War, she had had the initiative to open a small grocery shop at the market entrance. In time it grew to become one of the main businesses in town which allowed us a comfortable living. It was her business acumen that made it possible for us to buy two houses. One of these was a rather prestigious villa formerly occupied by a minor member of the Polish landed aristocracy. It was in this villa that we lived until – at the beginning of the Second World War – the Germans occupied our town and expelled us to eastern Poland where we found ourselves under Soviet rule. Then in turn, the Soviet secret police exiled us to Siberia, to 'Barrack 9'.

So once again, it was our mother who took the unprecedented initiative in buying a cow. We heard that the cow was with an old couple, both ill and no longer able to find food for the cow during the harsh winter. They would be prepared to sell her for a reasonable price – part money and part things to keep them warm. My mother packed a warm blanket which we had somehow held on to till then, a good shawl and sweater and some other things. We sold some of our valuables to the wife of one of our supervisors and got some money. We informed the prospective sellers about our offer and received the answer that they were prepared to bargain with us if we would come to their hut, which was more than ten miles away across the snow-covered mountain. We then paid a truck driver to inform the old couple that we were coming. My mother decided to go there and, as was usual in such ventures, to take me with her.

Only then, when we were ready to go, did we realize how difficult and dangerous a venture we were about to undertake. We
were strictly forbidden to leave the confines of our 'barrack-
prison'. If caught outside we could both be jailed for several years.
I could only go during a weekend when my absence from work
would not be noticed; and if anything were to happen and we
couldn't return by Monday, my absence from our place would be
noticed and I might be declared an escapee – with dire consequences. And how were we to march more than ten miles through
the mountains when the snow was piled as high as a tall man?
Especially on the way back – if successful – with a cow? And what
if a major snowstorm were suddenly to develop – we would
freeze to death in the mountains.

However, nothing could weaken my mother's resolve. We
dressed in the warmest clothes and best boots of the entire family,
took with us a small sleigh with additional blankets and food in
case of emergency, and off we went. We prepared our excuse in
case of being caught: my mother was ill and I was taking her to see
a doctor.

At first we moved on quite well along a narrow trail without
anyone challenging us. But then the trail led through a neighbouring large prison settlement at which – we had been warned –
KGB officers were stationed. Moreover, they had dogs who could
smell fugitive prisoners from afar. Cosequently, well before we
reached that settlement we had to leave the security of the beaten
trail and go around it through the deep snow. This turned out to
be extremely slow, exhausting and dangerous: not only was the
snow very deep but under the snow there was often bog into
which one could sink forever. We trod cautiously, but despite this
my mother slipped several times into such a quagmire. Luckily it
was not me for I was strong enough to pull her out, it would not
have been the case the other way round. The sleigh also helped
because we could push it in front of us to check the ground.

Suddenly we heard the dogs barking. We hid behind a clump
of bushes, sunk deeply in the snow and froze. The next half an
hour seemed to us an eternity, but eventually the barking stopped
and we moved on. How relieved we were when, after marching
again for a mile or so along the trail, we reached the blessed major
'Ice Road'. Here we could proceed more openly. The ice road was
many miles long, stretching from a high mountain to the nearest
waterway. Along it moved a lively traffic of huge sleighs loaded
with logs. They were pulled by tractors towards the river bank

where they were unloaded. In spring the logs were bound into rafts and floated down river to their destination. The ice road was constantly watered and cleared of snow by huge teams of prisoners under guard. But here and there were some bundled-up civilians, so nobody paid much attention to a woman and a youngster walking along.

What luck! A horse-drawn cart passed by and we persuaded the driver to give us a lift for a suitable remuneration. Following the instructions we had been given, we left the ice road and covered the last mile on a side trail. The sun settled behind the huge trees, it turned dark, twice we took a false turn and lost the trail. Finally, half dead from the cold and exhaustion, we knocked at the door of the old couple we were seeking. 'Who are you? What do you want? We don't know you!' they shouted. They would not open the door. We were stunned. We gave them our name and the name of our supervisor's mother who was supposed to make the arrangement – nothing helped. Obviously, the truck driver had taken the money but had not delivered our message. Finally we explained that we would freeze to death if left outside in the cold through the night, and promised to give them a fine gift if they let us sleep over.

Once inside, after several cups of hot tea with sugar which we unpacked from our bundle, and especially after we spread in front of them the various goods we had brought with us, the atmosphere changed. The old couple did not even haggle much. The old woman explained that she felt sorry for the cow because lately they had not been able to find fodder for her. 'She was looking at me with her hungry eyes', she said. And we did not even examine the cow properly: we saw her behind a partition, small, reddish, half-blind but alive. After all we were not in a marketplace where we could choose and bargain, and in any case we would not have the means to buy a better one.

Utterly exhausted, but happy, we fell asleep in a corner of the warm hut. The next morning was clear again. After completing the deal the old woman parted lovingly from the cow – their only possession – and we were off. My mother was leading the cow in front and I was pulling the small sleigh with fodder for the next few days which the old couple had still had at the hut. Where we would find food for the cow after this meagre supply was finished, we had not the faintest idea. The journey back proved even more difficult than the way there. On the narrow path it was imperative to lead the cow along the narrow trail. Once in a while she would slip into the deep snow and we had to pull her out. On the ice road she often slipped and fell. By the time we arrived at the settlement with the KGB post, which we had skirted round in the morning, it was dark and we decided to go through it along the main trail. We hoped that the dogs would not bark since they were used to cows and prayed that no prison guards would see us. We were stopped twice, but the cow saved us. We explained that we were bringing her for one of our bosses, and they let us pass. The idea that we, as prisoners, might be taking the cow for ourselves did not occur to them.

By the time we arrived at the entrance to our barrack it was dark. Now we faced the final but very dangerous part of 'operation cow': we had to slip her in unobserved and settle her within a makeshift lean-to behind the barrack wall. Hidden from sight we waited, frozen to the bone, until after midnight when all activity had ceased. Then very quietly we led our cow behind the wall of the barrack. You can imagine the faces of our family when they saw us emerging from the darkness leading the reddish beast ... they had been expecting us early in the evening and here we were arriving towards the morning. They thought some disaster had befallen us. Excruciatingly tired and aching all over we went to sleep. But how happy we were: from now on we had a nourisher, a cow. Next morning we woke to a blessed sound – my mother was milking our cow – and we were all presented with a royal treat: half a mug of warm, foaming, fresh milk.

12 • A Letter to Stalin and an Answer

'Citzens of the USSR have the right to
education ... ensured by free provision
of all forms of education... universal
and compulsory.'

(The Constitution of the USSR, 1936, Art.21)

Since August 1940 our family – parents, three brothers and a little
sister – had been incarcerated in 'Barrack 9', a small settlement in
the endless forests of the Siberian Altai mountains, close to the
Soviet Union's borders with China and Mongolia. At the barrack we
were all obliged to work. I was then 15, having just completed the
4th grade in high school. There was of course no school for many
miles around our tiny settlement in the woods. Instead of being
educated at school, I was forced to engage in work in the forest
which was too hard even for a strong adult. Working conditions
were extremely harsh: from sunrise to sunset, trekking through
mountainous forests for many miles every day with very little rest
or food. Everyone had a daily quota of labour to fulfill, and if he
failed to do so he was punished severely, primarily by cutting his
and his family's already meagre food ration but also by restricting
even further his already heavily restricted movements. The climate
was very harsh: hot and humid in the forest in summer, temperatures down to $-40°$ Celsius and heavy snowfalls in the winter.
There were snakes, bogs, clouds of mosquitoes and vermin in the
rooms in the barrack.

Before we were taken in the middle of the night and exiled to
Siberia I had been studying for one year in a school which was set
up by Soviet authorities in a nearby town. While large-scale
arrests and purges were going on, and any possible opposition to
Soviet rule was harshly suppressed, 'free' elections were
proclaimed. The population of former eastern Poland – liberated

by the Red Army – was about to 'elect' its representatives to the various local and central Soviets (formal legislative councils). All elder students in my school were given an intensive and speedy course of instruction in teaching the Soviet constitution, 'the most democratic constitution in the world', and, like many others, I was sent as a propagandist to teach this constitution to a group of uneducated residents in one of the suburbs of Lubachev.

Made wiser through their knowledge of the KGB mass arrests for the slightest dissent, the residents punctiliously attended the evening sessions taught by me and other instructors. Both parties to this exercise knew full well that the entire constitution was one immense fraud, but the terror forcefully unleashed in the land achieved its goal. The Kafkaesque or Orwellian spectacle repeated itself regularly: I, along with other propagandists, extolled the great freedoms included in the Stalin constitution, the like of which there is not to be found in 'bourgeois England' nor anywhere in the whole world. The attentive listeners nodded their heads approvingly and had no questions except when a Soviet supervisor was present. This was very lucky for us, for we were obliged to report any dissenting 'anti-Soviet propaganda'. If we failed to report it, but an informer passed on information about it, we could be severely punished. In this matter there was of course a major difference between us, the population of former Poland, and that of the Soviet Union. The latter was totally isolated from the outer world, whereas the former was well informed about the situation in the democratic countries of the West; and before the war Poland too had been a country with a democratic system, albeit with limitations. So both the instructors and the listeners, as former Polish citizens, knew very well how untrue the perorations about Soviet democracy were.

I am recounting this here because of one of the paragraphs (article 121) of the Stalin constitution that impressed itself strongly in my mind stated that: 'All citizens of the USSR have the right to education.' We also taught something that was not included in Stalin's constitution of 1936 but was later incorporated in Brezhnev's 1977 constitution (article 58): 'Citizens of the USSR have the right to lodge a complaint against the actions of officials and state bodies ... which contravene the law or exceed their powers, and infringe the rights of citizens.' I had always wanted to study and here I was denied my right to education at school though I was of school age.

I decided to demand my rights by the the only means with any chance of success in those days: appealing to Stalin himself. Turning for justice to the supreme ruler – the Tzar or the top Commissar – was an old, established tradition and a large number of citizens' appeals were continuously addressed to Stalin.

Doing it turned out to be very difficult. It had to be done in total secrecy: the KGB officials could inflict harsh punishment for it and my family would think me crazy and do everything to prevent me from implementing my plan. By then, we were not allowed paper, envelopes or stamps as we had been before. So I had to do with whatever I could get. Somehow I scrounged a sheet of paper and wrote in Russian (I learned it during that single year at school before exile to Siberia) as follows:

To: Secretary General of the Central Committee of the CPSU (Communist Party of the Soviet Union) Comrade JOSEPH STALIN the Kremlin, MOSCOW.

Dear Comrade Stalin,

The Constitution of the Soviet Union, which in the eyes of the people is connected with your name, states in article 121: 'All citizens of the USSR have the right to education.' In my previous place of residence I attended school. In fact I was a foremost student in my class. But here at our barrack I am not given the opportunity to study, though I am of school age. My constitutional right to education is therefore not implemented. I very much want to study.

I appeal to you to direct the local officials to make it possible for me to go to school for which I shall be very grateful to you.

Yours with the greatest respect,
Wolf* Lvovich Katz

Here I gave my full address and additional details about myself. My hands were actually shaking while I wrote. From time to time I broke out in a cold sweat and my knees felt weak: here was I, a mere boy and a prisoner/exile to boot, illegally writing a letter to a ruler who seemed to me then the mightiest on earth … And what if the bosses found out?

---

* 'Zev' means 'wolf', which was my name before coming to Israel.

Despite my fear and hesitation I decided to go ahead. Not having an envelope I folded the sheet of paper into a double closed triangle in a fashion then common in Russia when envelopes were scarce. I wrote on the outside the Kremlin address (but not mine as sender, for fear it might hinder delivery). Now I was ready to send it off. But how? The only way was to bribe a driver of the small trucks which came through the mountain trails. They delivered food and other goods and took out wood and barrels of sap which we extracted from the trees to the chemical factory at the nearest railway station, many miles away. I had no stamp, there was of course no post office or even a postbox within many miles of the forest, and even had there been one we were not allowed to post letters on our own. So I took the risk, gave a driver who looked decent a pair of fine socks and some money for a stamp. He swore to deliver the letter as necessary.

There followed now long weeks of waiting. Nothing, no reaction whatsoever. Desperate about the amount of time passing while I was not at school I decided to repeat the exercise. This time I gave the letter to a driver of a horse and carriage who looked poor and sympathetic. I gave him a more alluring 'present' – a set of fine underwear the like of which he had apparently never seen. But weeks passed, autumn was drawing to an end, and I was now realizing that: even if the authorities were to direct them to allow me to go to school, the officials here would have the excuse that the roads were impassible or that they could not accept a pupil in the middle of the school year. As I continued to work hard in the forest I gradually gave up any hope of a reaction to my appeal. Could it all have been in vain?

Then one snowy day a runner came to the forest where I was working. Suddenly he called out: 'Prisoner Wolf Katz! You will immediately go with me by order of the (KGB) officer!' All through the several long miles of the walk I was turning over in my head what might be the sin for which I was being marched urgently from work to see the officer – and what might be the punishment for it. Had I said something 'anti-Soviet' and someone reported on me? Had I not fulfilled the work quota? Or perhaps they had found out about my letter to Stalin, and who knows what punishment they would inflict on me for that?

As I entered the bosses' house I was directed to a side room. To my amazement I found in it all the supervisors including the top officer of the KGB who had addressed us on the day of our arrival at this barrack-prison. I was covered with dirt from working in the woods and in tattered working dress. As I came into the room they looked at me as if I were some kind of rare animal.

'So this is the fellow who keeps up correspondence with Comrade Stalin!' the officer said in a sneer. I just stood there dumbfounded, paralyzed. 'Do you admit it?' he asked me.

I had no choice: 'Yes,' I whispered.

'So there is an answer', he said and put before me on the table a paper with Kremlin insignia. I was even more shocked than before: Stalin had answered me – a mere mortal!

'Read it loud' – the officer ordered. I read:

> To: Wolf Lvovich Katz, Respected comrade,
> Your letter reached us and we examined your request. We cannot determine from here what the schools' situation is in the area of your residence. We are therefore transmitting a copy of your letter to the responsible officials in your area – with an injunction that if a school can be found you should be able to exercise your right to education.
> Signed (name which I could not decipher)
> Assistant to the Secretary General
> The Kremlin, MOSCOW

'And now read the following paper', the officer commanded. I noticed that another paper was attached. It was from an assistant to the head of the regional Education Authority (OBLONO). In it I was informed that the matter has been looked into. 'Upon advisement of the appropriate authorities [the KGB, I assumed] no suitable school was located. Regretfully yours ...'

'Now the punishment will come', I was inwardly sure. All this time I stood before them with my head down while they were enjoying all kind of fine foods and drinks on the table. I raised my head and looked at them. I suddenly realised that they found the entire episode rather amusing: a boy prisoner at a Siberian barrack writing to Stalin – and receiving an answer! Who knows, maybe the secretary would follow up the case? Better to be careful ...

Now the commandant of our barrack spoke: 'This time we are just giving you a warning – no more illegal letter writing! You may return to work. I shall keep an eye on you – remember!' I turned round on my weak legs and walked out of the room. When outside I started shaking, I could not stand on my feet. I sat down on a log nearby. Soon one of the junior bosses came out.

Surprisingly he spoke to me: 'You are a lucky devil. The local commandant wanted to send you to jail. But the superior officer said one should go easy with this case and that was also the opinion of the regional secretary'. I could not believe my ears: the regional secretary knew about my case!

I did not return to work. It was sunset soon anyway. I walked to the edge of the wood and returned to the barrack with the others. I did not disclose what happened at the bosses' house as commanded. But somehow the people at the barrack learned about the whole thing. It sounded to them like a fable from Krylov or Ali Baba, and some of them came to gaze at me as if I was some strange creature: 'Look at this little fellow: he had the audacity to write to Stalin himself, and received an answer from the Kremlin. Even the bosses here deal cautiously with him.'

For me nothing changed. I had to go on working in the woods, fearing that I should never go to school, even a letter from the Kremlin had not helped.' In fact I did, within less than one year, at another place, and as a free person, I went to school.

13 • 'Our Dear Polish Allies' – Strike in Siberia

Summer came. The mosquito plague diminished as the heat increased. June 1941 – one year since had been exiled to Siberia from the territory of former Poland. We worked in harsh conditions in the forests of the Altai mountains. In our little barrack in the woods we were entirely isolated from the world outside: no radio, newspapers, telephone.

Several days after 21 June we started hearing rumours that Nazi Germany had attacked the Soviet Union and that the Red Army was retreating rapidly. We were told nothing. We went on working in the woods as if nothing had happened, so we did not know what to believe.

Soon enough, it became clear that the rumours about the war were indeed true. The younger ones among the truck drivers and some of the better trucks started disappearing; they were mobilized for the army. We succeeded in getting hold of the occasional newspaper and could not believe what was printed there: German forces were on a full offensive deep inside Soviet territory. They had completely occupied the Soviet-held former Polish lands where many of us had close family and friends. We were very frightened and worried – for their fate and for ours. What would happen to us? Supplies were becoming increasingly erratic as more trucks and drivers were called up.

Then one day towards the end of summer several of our supervisors arrived suddenly in the forest at our place of work: 'Stop working!' they ordered. 'You are all to return forthwith to the barrack!' Once we arrived there we were herded into the main hall of the administration building. At a long table confronting us and covered with a green cloth were gathered our bosses including the commandant himself. There were long benches in front of the table, and for the first time since our imprisonment in the barrack we were invited to sit down. We were stunned: the entire situation was unprecedented – stoppage of work on a working day, the politeness of our supervisors, sitting down in front of our jailers as if we were free citizens.

Suddenly the door at the back of the room opened and in came two people: one military and one well-groomed civilian. Immediately our bosses stood up, and seeing this we also stood. The important guests sat down and so did we. Then the civilian stood up and addressed us: 'OUR DEAR POLISH ALLIES'. Immediately a hubbub rose in the hall. Hitherto we had been addressed as 'exiles' or 'prisoners'. This new title given to us was like a revelation: we were now citizens, and what was even more important to us – POLISH citizens and ALLIES!

Stunned and surprised we listened to the speaker: 'As you know [certainly not officially] the hordes of Nazi German forces have treacherously broken their treaty with us and opened a murderous attack on our holy land. We are now involved in a Great Patriotic War to liberate our Fatherland and to save all mankind from Fascist tyranny …' In this worldwide struggle the anti-Fascist forces alliance was already forged: mighty Great Britain, the Free French, a number of other governments in exile have already declared their alliance with the Soviet Union in it's war against Germany. The United States of America and other countries, though not in the war, have also expressed their support.

One of the governments that entered an alliance with us is yours, which is presently resident in London. It has the full support of Great Britain, it is recognised by the USA and other countries. We have good relations with your Prime Minister, General Sikorsky. As a result of an agreement between our countries an amnesty for all former Polish citizens is being imple-mented.' Here he appealed to us that the work we were doing was important and therefore we should continue with it until it became possible to transport us away from here. Conditions of work would now change and we were to be paid like workers.

For several weeks after that memorable day we continued to work in the woods, but things were rapidly changing. A repre-sentative of the Polish Sikorsky Government was appointed for our area. He sent information and newspapers into our, as well as surrounding, barrack-prisons. We designated some elders from among ourselves and they presented our demand to be evacuated from Siberia as soon as possible. But the days passed and nothing happened. The first snows fell and we were becoming very anxious that soon it would not be physically possible to leave.

Also, rumours reached us that we were soon to be moved from Siberia to Soviet Central Asia.

Desperate needs demand desperate measures – a strike. In the end it was more than that: we declared that we were going to return the tools and refused to work any more at all. Now our bosses were stunned: the thing was unprecedented – a strike and total refusal to work in a Siberian camp, and in wartime! They threatened us with all kinds of countermeasures, but it appeared that they no longer had any power over us. On the morning of the appointed day we refused to go to work in the forest. Instead we formed a long line in front of the tool warehouse. With tools in our hands we demanded that the tool-keeper receive them and provide us with official receipts. The tools were government property and if we were to leave without such a receipt we could be arrested for stealing. The keeper and the supervisors threatened us, ordered us to leave for work forthwith, declared that in any case the warehouse would not be opened and the tool-keeper would in no way provide us with the desired receipts. The line however did not budge for hours. We elected some elders to go and talk to the commandant himself. They returned having made no obvious progress, and yet, about lunch-time the disgruntled tool-keeper suddenly appeared. He started to accept our tools and provide us with the precious piece of paper. We understood that this was done following consultation with officials 'above' and saw in this an important victory. The KGB's power over us was totally broken! But still no official means of transportation was put at our disposal to leave the barrack for the nearest railway station some 40 miles away through the mountains. In the meantime we heard to our surprise that at that station, which was flanked by a village, a large number of Polish exiles were gathering. The Polish representative informed us that a special train would come to that station to take us to warm lands in Central Asia. There we would be able to live and work until the end of the war when it would be possible to repatriate us to Poland. We were elated: we are going to get out of Siberia before the terrible winter and go to the warm lands about which we had heard were rich in food and opportunities to make a living. Moreover, the hope of getting out of Soviet Russia and returning home to Poland – hitherto a distant dream – now seemed a reality. We did not have even the slightest doubt about an allied victory over the Nazis, though Russian forces were retreating across the entire front and the United States had not yet joined the war.

But how were we to get to that great haven of salvation and hope – the railway station. By now we were desperate: the train might arrive any day and who knew whether there would be another one. We would be stuck in Siberia for the winter! The solution was there before our very eyes: the drivers. By then the fear of KGB intervention no longer existed. Therefore we simply proposed to a passing truck driver that we would pay him handsomely if he took us to the station. He could not take all of us; so my father, my younger brother and myself climbed with part of our belongings onto the barrels and off we went. We were supposed to find a place to stay and then the rest of our family would follow.

It is difficult to describe my feelings as we drove away from the barrack; it was only a little more than a year since we had first been imprisoned there, but it felt like an entire century. On leaving I caught a glimpse of the commandant who had promised us on arrival: 'You shall never leave this place – for sure! This is where you will work, and this is where you will die.' I wanted to shout: 'Look at me ! I am leaving – for ever!' But I did not utter a sound.

Next to the railway station was a sprawling village, in the roads and open spaces of which we could see Poles and their families camping with their belongings or walking about on their business. After several hours of searching we found a peasant who agreed to lodge us in his warehouse for quite a high price. Despite that we were very pleased since some hours later it began to rain. All those camping outside rushed to find shelter and the price for any accommodation rose steeply.

Next day the rest of our family joined us, after a nerve-wrackingly long search for us walking in the rain with the rest of our bundles on their backs. Several days of uncertain waiting followed. Every time a train came into the station hundreds of the Poles ran to it hoping that it would take them away. At last, on the fifth day, a representative of the Polish embassy in Moscow arrived. He gathered us together and promised that he would not leave until a train came several days later. In the meantime we had to be officialy registered since in Soviet Russia nobody was allowed to travel, work, reside anywhere, or get a food ration card, without official papers. An official registration group from the regional soviet started work the next day and immediately a long line formed. Among others we also received the precious document. It was just a sheet of paper which stated:

USSR MINISTRY OF INTERNAL AFFAIRS CERTIFICATE

Person [Lev Samoilovich KATZ (my father for example)]
a former citizen of the REPUBLIC OF POLAND
born in 1900 in Yaroslav, Poland
and his family consisting of
[here came the names and personal data]
are under the auspices of the
Embassy of Poland in the USSR in Moscow.
The above persons have the right
to travel, reside, work, rations etc.
much like any other citizen.
All respective authorities are herewith instructed
to act accordingly.
signed [name]
Director
[place, date, official stamp]

Four days later a long goods train finally arrived. We did not know whether to laugh or cry. We expected a passenger train in which we would leave our prison life with some dignity; whereas here was a dirty goods train. There was a rush of people with their bundles, pandemonium! People were afraid that there would not be sufficient space for everybody; also everyone wanted to get for themselves the best places (by a window, on the upper shelf, not by the door or by the makeshift toilet ...). At the same time we were elated – at last we are going to leave Siberia! Warm lands of Central Asia – here we come!

14 • A Home in Northern Kazakhstan–Semipalatinsk

After two days of waiting, a locomotive was coupled to our train, the siren blew and slowly we started leaving the station of Tikhonkoe in the foothills of the Altai mountains of southern Siberia. We were elated. Here we were: free people leaving Siberia, travelling ever further south. From Novosibirsk, the capital of Siberia, and a major centre on the Trans-Siberian railway, another major railway line starts. It is several thousand miles long and loops across the lands of Central Asia before rejoining the main Trans-Siberian line. It was on this Central Asian railway that we were moving on and on southwards.

But we were also deeply anxious. Where were we heading? How would we live there? Would we be able to find housing and work – for we had almost nothing left. For three days and nights our train moved slowly south. At each station we talked to people, to railway attendants, anyone, in an attempt to find out more about the unknown lands we were travelling to. The picture we received was as follows: there are great, prosperous cities in Central Asia, like Tashkent or Alma Ata. But they are capitals of Soviet Republics and we were not allowed to live there. There are also other cities like Dzhambul where many of the freed Polish exiles had settled; but rumour had it that no more were allowed to settle there and that presently many were being settled in *kolkhoz* farms (collective farms) even against their will. Conditions in these farms were harsh and the work was back-breaking. Also the climate there was very hot, like in a desert, and some epidemics were raging. My father suffered from a acute asthma and, ironically, the air in the Siberian mountain prison camp had been good for him, we feared that it might not agree with him in hot Central Asia.

We heard that the first major city out of Siberia and into Kazakhstan was the town of Semipalatinsk. We had never heard this name before; but the closer we got to it the more good things we were told about it. Though it was nominally within the Kazakh Soviet Republic and therefore also part of Central Asia, it was said to be predominantly a Russian city. The climate was 'continental' and dry – not with a very hot summer. Moreover, there was a major meat-packing factory there as well as textile factories; and above all – food was relatively abundant! Also, while some Polish refugees and exiles had settled there recently, they were not too numerous.

As the train neared Semipalatinsk we wondered: should we get off on our own into an unknown place? It was a momentous decision: if it turned out to be a disaster, we might be trapped there since further travel on our own might not be allowed. We had our belongings ready for disembarkation. When the train stopped there we were told that it would stay there for several hours. One of us remained to guard our bundles and the rest of us went into the station and some distance into town to reconnoitre. Soon we met some Jews who had been evacuated from western Russian territories occupied by the German army. Then some local Jews approached us and even one Polish former prisoner. Their report was quite positive, and what is more they confirmed the rumours about epidemics in the hot areas of Central Asia. What finally decided us was that father felt that the air there was dry and good for him. We returned to the train, asked for permission to stay in Semipalatinsk, took off our belongings and moved into the main hall of the railway station. We never regretted our decision.

There was pandemonium at the railway station: it was packed with people and their belongings. Entire families were sitting and lying everywhere on the floor. Some men were sleeping and snoring loudly; women were unashamedly breastfeeding their small children. At first we had no place but to stand holding our belongings. More people entered and the congestion became unbearable. However, some time later another train arrived. We fought our way to a corner just before an additional crowd from the train engulfed the station. It was late afternoon and we could not face the idea of a night at the station. But where could we go?

It was decided that my mother and myself would go into town to see whether some accommodation could be found. The prospect of speedy success was minimal; the rest of the family remained in the station hall to guard our bundles and the corner we had secured there so that we would have an emergency place for the night.

My mother took some 'goods' – a shirt, a pair of Polish elegant ladies' shoes, a fine table cover, as well as some money–and off we went into the unknown city. We soon found out that the centre of town was 'Russian', good wooden or concrete houses; prices there were astronomical and there was hardly any room available. We learnt that we might stand a better chance if we went into the 'Kazakh town' stretching around the city core. We plodded off in that direction and soon found ourselves in a world which looked as it must have centuries ago: unmade roads full of sand, low clay houses with flat roofs, outside toilets, no telephone or bus service. Here and there we noticed donkeys or camels (for the first time in my life). There were no shops or public buildings. In a word, a total contrast to the modern 'Russian' centre. Yet here we thought that we might find something.

We walked from house to house for several hours, but everywhere we encountered the same negative answer: 'No room! We do not take in strangers.' In despair we decided to go back to the station, but along a different route. In front of one of the clay houses an elderly Kazakh woman was resting. To our great surprise she was willing to rent us a large room at the back entrance of the building. It had an alcove with a stove which could serve as a kitchen. Actually, her eyes lit up when she saw the Polish ladies' shoes: 'My son has been called up to the army, but I have a daughter and these shoes will be a lovely present for her. Her friends will die of envy.' As an afterthought she remarked: 'Good that you are Polish (we had shown her our documents showing that we were Polish citizens) and not Jews ... I have never met any, but I have heard that they are from the devil.' We had already given her the shoes and money for rent and it was already late. We said nothing but walked quickly back to the station where we announced to our surprised family: 'We have found a room.' To transfer our heavy belongings several miles to our room we hired a kind of rickshaw – a man who pulled a cart on two wheels. There was of course nothing else – no taxi or horse and cart. It was also important to hire the man since he knew the way which we were not certain of in the rapidly descending darkness. Little did we know that this was to be our first lesson in what was soon to become our own profession.

The first winter in Semipalatinsk was very difficult for us. While formally part of Kazakhstan which is (again formally) included in Central Asia – it is actually similar to southern Siberia. It has a hot summer but also a very long, cold winter, down to

–40–50° Celsius. It soon turned out that our room, which was comfortable enough as long as it was warm outside, was nowhere close to being properly sealed for a harsh winter. One could actually feel the cold wind blowing through it and the northern wall was practically covered with ice. There was no proper way to heat the place; the cooking stove had to be heated with wood which was non-existent. During the first weeks of winter we bought a few bundles of dried wood branches at the bazaar. As the cold and snow grew the supply dwindled and the price rocketed to the equivalent of a week's salary. Our experience in the woods of Siberia came in handy for once: we dressed in our warmest clothing and marched off, my two brothers and myself, into the deep snow of the nearest wood to bring bundles of dried branches.

The wood was some miles from our room. Then we had to go several miles into the deeper wood since the nearer trees had been picked clean of any dry branches. At first we walked briskly along a main road; then we found a narrow track into the wood; then even that disappeared. We moved on in the deep snow often sinking in it so that the two of us had to pull the other out of the snow. At last we arrived at an area where there were some dry branches on the lower part of the trees. Luckily we picked up en route some long sticks with which we were able to reach the dry branches high on the trees and knock them off. Then we collected them, bound them into bundles, put these on our backs and started our trek back. We were extremely lucky: a snow storm started when we were already at the edge of the forest. Had it started blowing when we were still deep in the forest we might have lost our way and not been able to get out. Even so, moving through the deep snow in the forest with heavy bundles on our backs and then marching several more miles during a snowstorm on the road exhausted us completely. When we reached home, we took off our bundles with a triumphant expression and then practically collapsed. The cold room felt very warm indeed; the mattress on which we were able to lie down and stretch our legs felt like paradise itself!

To our great shame, when our mother put some of the branches which we brought with us into the oven and tried to kindle a fire it turned out that many were not dry enough; they did not give off much warmth but they did produce great quantities of smoke which smothered our room. So this was the first and last time we went to the forest for wood. We had to find other ways to earn enough in order to buy wood at the bazaar whatever the price.

Our other affair to do with wood was also a total failure. Looking for some gainful employment in town we saw a notice about the need for a stoker to keep the fire going in the central medical clinic. We – my brother and myself – presented ourselves for the job. All males were mobilized for the war so there were no other candidates. We argued that though we were both teenagers we had experience from our stay in Siberia and the two of us would do the work of one. So we were signed on for a trial period.

For the first two weeks it looked as if we would manage; it was still warm outside and the wood was dry. But soon enough trouble set in. It became very cold; there was not sufficient dry wood, so we had to use some wet logs, and often the fire would die out amid plumes of smoke. We had to get up at 4 o'clock in the morning, to begin to stoke the stoves at five, and as it became cold er and the wood became wetter we had to work harder – more logs had to be carried from the cellar several floors up to the many stoves and it was heavier. Soon we were so exhausted that after a few hours of work we were not able to carry on. Then we overslept several times, so that we started to stoke the stoves late. When the doctors arrived for work the clinic was cold and full of smoke – chaos! In short, after several weeks both the manager of the clinic and we ourselves came to the obvious conclusion that this was no job for two teenagers.

We were looking for some other way to work and survive, and it was our father who found a solution. To go to work in a factory was tantamount to entering forced labour: work was often 12 hours a day, including Sundays, the slightest work infringement was harshly punished; wages remained at pre-war levels, while prices were rocketing – a monthly wage was barely enough to buy a loaf of bread and a bundle of wood at the bazaar. My father was a merchant before the war in Poland; but he had already been imprisoned once in a Soviet prison for such activity before we were exiled to Siberia, since in the eyes of the Soviet authorities all private commerce was speculation. 'I am not going to indulge here in commerce at the bazaar – I do not want to find myself in prison again', he said.

One day he went out to the bazaar, sold some of our remaining possessions and bought a two-wheeled cart and a long, thick rope. Next day he dressed in warm working clothes and went to the railway station. Since there were no taxis or carts with horses the Soviet authorities gave licences to 'recognised porters' – so it was legal activity. There were by that time only three long-distance passenger trains per day arriving at Semipalatinsk station – one late at night. They were often hours late.

By late autumn/early winter of 1941 ever-growing numbers of refugees and evacuees from Soviet areas occupied by the Germans were arriving in Semipalatinsk – almost all of them by train. Many of them were Jewish. After many days and often weeks of travelling in packed carriages, they arrived often in the middle of night in rain or snow, in a strange city. They frequently had nowhere to go or had a slip of paper with a name and address. They were terrified that they might loose the few possessions which they brought with them or that these would be taken from them by robbers, who were quite common. In many cases these were women with children or old people without men to protect them. Some of them were Polish like ourselves.

It was on such occasions that we stepped into the action. We rotated waiting for the trains: usually our father met the trains during daytime, together with one of us brothers. I preferred to meet the train at night together with my younger brother; it gave us the opportunity to attend school (which in war-time was in the afternoon). Also, it soon turned out to provide a good wage and often – which was more important – food. I remember one of many cases: long after midnight during a rather strong snowstorm and a severe frost a woman with three children arrived. She yelled for a porter but there was none. The train was soon to leave with her suitcases since she was unable to unload them because of the children, one of whom had a fever. The station area was dark, the other passengers were sleeping, and I was there with my younger brother. We approached her and realised soon that she was Jewish. We said to her a few words in Yiddish and offered her our help. Quickly we climbed on the train, got her belongings out through the window and carried them to our sleigh. We had some blankets so we arranged a kind of cushion for her sick child; the other two were able to walk. The woman explained that she had come from Kiev – two weeks on the train. Her husband was a colonel somewhere on the front. Kiev had been taken by the Germans and she escaped at the last moment. Here, in Semipalatinsk she had a sister; she had a slip of paper with her name and a rather unclear address. We recognised the place – it was at the other end of town, many kilometres away. In the meantime the storm abated somewhat, so we started our long trudge to the given address. How great was our grief when we arrived there totally exhausted at 4 o'clock in the morning to be told by the people in the house, through the closed door, that the sister was no longer there. The woman started crying again and the two children collapsed on our sleigh.

Fortunately, the people had the new address of the sister – several kilometres further. With the remainder of our strength we pulled the sleigh with the three children the extra distance. By the time we found the new address it was dawn, and we were completelywhite and frozen. Yet, how great was the joy, the screams, the embraces and crying when the two sisters met! We were taken in, given hot tea, bread and sausage. We were well paid and given some of the sausages, a small sack of white meal and – unbelievably – a huge bar of chocolate. 'This evening you have saved our lives!' the Kiev woman kissed us. 'May God himself reward you' she exclaimed and collapsed on her sister's bed.

15 • At a Communist College at Kazakhstan University

After a few weeks we realized that it was possible for us to survive in the harsh conditions of north Kazakhstan by working at the railway station as described above. We started looking beyond our narrow surroundings. I was of school age and eager to study after the enforced break during our imprisonment in Siberia. My elder brother dreamed of becoming a driver and here was an opportunity to do so. Going to school did not interfere with my working at the railway station; school was in the morning (class space was overcrowded and scarce) and our work at the station was when the night train arrived after 10 o'clock in the evening.

I arrived at school quite a few weeks after the start of the year but it was wartime and evacuated children were also arriving late. The principal looked at me and at my certificate stating that I had been released from Siberia with some scepticism. 'You have not studied in Russian so far so how will you manage?' – he asked. I assured him that I had taught myself Russian on my own and that I would do my utmost to catch up with the others. I was put in the grade before the top and found it heavy going, especially after night work at the station. Yet, by the end of the school year I was among the best pupils in the class, with top marks all round, including in Russian language and literature. The principal recommended therefore that after some intensive special summer preparatory courses I should be allowed to take entrance exams to the local Pedagogical Institute (teacher training college) linked to the University of Kazakhstan. Having passed these exams successfully, I found myself by the start of the next school year at a Soviet Institution of Higher Learning. It was one year only since I had been a prisoner in the endless woods of Siberia.

From then onwards, September 1942 until early summer 1946 when we were repatriated to Poland, I led a kind of a double life. On the one hand, I was a successful student at a Soviet university. At the same time I worked, first at the railway station and then at the Altai warehouse. Studies at the college were arranged very much like at a high school – from 8 o'clock through until 2 or 3 o'clock in the afternoon. There was no choice of lectures or lecturers; a rigid timetable was fixed by the college authorities. Attendance at all lectures was obligatory. Soviet law dictated that all working-age citizens had to work. This was most rigorously implemented in wartime. Studies at the college were officially recognised in lieu of work, and as a student, I received a small scholarship, a food ration of a working person and hot lunches at the student refectory.

So each morning I dressed in my best clothes and walked some two kilometres to the college (there was no public transport there during the war). There I sat at the lectures, some of which were rather boring, but some of them of a high standard and fascinating. Often in the winter, we sat in class fully dressed in our warmest winter attire, since there was no fuel for heating and the temperature outside often reached –30° celcius and lower. After the lectures we walked to the student refectory about a kilometre away where we waited in line for a meagre but hot lunch. Reinforced by food and some tea I walked home, a distance of about one kilometre. After some rest and an early evening meal, I changed into working clothes and walked to the railway station often pulling our cart or sleigh. Work there went on till late at night depending on the time of the arrival of the train and the distance of the place to which we had to bring the client on that particular night. We arrived home late in the night, often frozen and deadly tired.

Luckily, I did not have to go to the station every night, only several nights each week. And soon during our second winter in Semipalatinsk we found a new and far more rewarding employment. It related – who would have believed it, in far away Central Asia under Soviet rule – to gold. It turned out that in the nearby areas of the Altai mountains and northern Kazakhstan some gold mining was done by a rich state trust named 'Altai Zoloto' (Gold of Altai). The Soviet authorities were so hungry for gold that they endowed this company with extraordinary powers and supplies. The company opened shops in the major cities in the area which bought all kinds of gold wares from the population. Before the war payment was in money at rather high prices. In wartime when the Soviet ruble was practically worthless, pay was in coupons in exchange for which all kinds of rare and fabulously expensive goods could be obtained. In the harsh conditions of the war, virtually nothing was available in the state-run shops – all enterprises produced exclusively for the war effort. The Altai shop was therefore very much like an Aladdin's cave. A man or (mostly) a woman, could walk in with a little bundle of some old gold things – a bracelet, earrings, a gold chain, grandfather's gold watch – and leave with a sack of white wheat flour, a winter coat, a fine fur hat, boots or galoshes, good sausages and cheese ... In war conditions these were treasures beyond value. A sack of flour and several pounds of butter and meat meant actually an end to perpetual hunger for a family. A winter coat and good pair of boots with galoshes meant being saved from freezing in the terrible cold. Alternatively, these could easily be sold at the local bazaar for a fabulous price and then bread, vegetables, wood or coal and almost anything else could be bought. In time the coupons themselves became something like a hard currency; they were sold and bought at a price which fluctuated depending on the benefits which one could get by exchanging them for goods at the Altai shop. The greatest benefit was possible when the shop had galoshes, tea or fat of any kind; the shop took relatively few coupons for these goods, and the price for them at the bazaar was very high, since they appeared very rarely at the shop and it was impossible to get them anywhere else.

At first, we exchanged some gold items for some food at the Altai shop, during the first and hungry winter of 1941–42. Apart from our bread ration, we had little else to eat. Often there were breaks in the supply of bread; huge queues formed in front of the bread shops, despite rain, snow and frost. One of us used to go out at night or before dawn and take our place in the very long queue. This person would go out dressed in double layers of our warmest winter clothes. Closer to the opening time of the shops some of us would join the queue at the place held by whichever one of us had gone first. In such a way, if they gave a certain portion of bread per head, we were able to get several portions. Often, the amount of bread was not enough for the entire queue; suddenly the doors were shut and the remainder of the people in the queue had to trudge home empty-handed and hungry. Much of the shortage was due to widespread stealing. A loaf of bread was sold at the bazaar for a price equal to an average monthly wage. Rationed bread was sold at the state shops at the official price of less than a ruble per kilogramme – a pittance. Not surprisingly, everyone who had something to do with the distribution of the bread often indulged in acquiring some bread which was later sold at the market. Also, apart from selling bread by the front door, there was also selling by the back door to officials, police, friends, family and so forth.

In time, I started working at the Altai shop. Adjoining it there was a huge basement warehouse. It contained goods and supplies not only for the local shop, but also for the nearby gold-mining bases. It happened that a young new manager was appointed to run it, and he needed trustworthy and efficient helpers, and it happened that I knew him quite well since his sister was studying in same class at the same college as me. I used to come to her home to do our homework together. In time we became friends and often went out together. When he proposed that I come to work with him, I naturally accepted his proposal eagerly. Officially, I was a porter there, and I used to load and unload trucks with heavy bales and barrels. We did this sometimes during a severe frost of –40° Celsius. At first we carried the loads down the steps into the basement fully dressed in our winter attire. But after a few gulps of vodka to warm us up and after running with the loads several times sweat covered us. We took off our clothes and worked naked to the waist despite the frost. It was on one such occasion that a wager was made, whether I would be able to drink an entire bottle of vodka all at once and then walk straight, without falling or faltering, to the other end of the courtyard. I was young and strong, with my Siberia training behind me, and I won the wager. Mind you, after arriving at the end of the court-yard my legs could not carry me. I sat down there in the snow with my back leaning at the wall. And, I have to admit I cheated. Before drinking the bottle of vodka I went down to the basement and ate some butter from a barrel there. When the stomach is lined with fat, alcohol is not as potent as otherwise.

There were many advantages to working at the Altai warehouse. First, one could eat there food that was but a dream outside: good sausages, cheeses, canned meat, with cucumbers and vegetables. It was possible to drink there real coffee and tea with lemon! From time to time it was possible to take home a sandwich full of sausage or cheese – enough for a meal for the entire family. But more than that was the knowledge of what kind of goods were being supplied to the Altai shop. When high-profit goods were unloaded, I was among the first to know about it. We usually bought some gold coupons and kept them in reserve for an opportunity to exchange them for fur coats and hats, sugar and tea, galoshes and flour, and so on. These goods fetched a high price. We were able then to buy new coupons and wait for the next opportunity. After I had worked there for some time, trust was established so that I was getting the information about the arrival of profitable goods without having to work there. After all, it was often back-breaking and the official pay was negligible.

Not working made it possible for me to devote my efforts to studying at the college. Actually, like many Soviet citizens, I lived in two diametrically opposed worlds. At the college I had to sit at lectures on Marxism–Leninism, the history of the Communist Party, the history of the USSR, Soviet literature, and so forth. At these lectures an idealistic world was presented about the 'dictatorship of the proletariat', 'glorious socialism' and the 'only true democracy' which exists in the USSR. In real life, we saw the immense poverty, slavery conditions and hunger of the workers and even more so – of the peasants. The years of my studies (1942–45) were years of the great Soviet war against the Nazi invasion. At first there was the disastrous retreat of Soviet forces to Moscow, Leningrad and Stalingrad. The catastrophic military defeats of the Soviet forces during the first period of the war were totally incomprehensible in the context of official Soviet imagery. Official Soviet media endlessly asserted that the 'mighty Red Army' was so strong that it would immediately inflict a crushing defeat on anyone who dared to attack the Soviet Union. This was engraved in the mind of every Soviet person through newspapers, speeches, film and radio. One popular song asserted that 'if anyone dared to cross our holy border in aggression – we shall crush him and carry the fire of war into his beast's lair'. Instead of this the Germans initially achieved victory after victory. Of course, the Soviet population did not know about the disastrous mistakes of Stalin and his leadership in the first year of the war. Only after the Russian victory at Stalingrad and the great Soviet victories starting in the third year of the war did the situation justify the former official Soviet conception.

At college, much like outside, the atmosphere was super-patriotic, the slightest critical remark was punished most severely. One of our best teachers was Professor Viktor Nefedov, an evacuee from Leningrad University, where he was known as a leading psychologist. Thin as a rake, old-fashioned in manner and speech, with simple round glasses on his nose and a glittering smile, he was in our eyes a unique specimen of that unique stratum, the traditional Russian intelligentsia. Rumour had it that he was in trouble with the authorities because of his acceptance of some

Freudian ideas which were anathema to 'Stalinist psychology'. He read his lectures from a carefully written text with plenty of proper (and sometimes utterly improper) quotes from Marx, Lenin and of course Stalin. One day he did not come to his lectures–he disappeared. Nobody mentioned his name; no explanation was ever given. Nobody asked (we knew better than that). Several months later one of our students, who was especially close to him, received through a released prisoner a little note written on a scrap of cigarette paper: 'For God's sake, please, please send me some soap, also please some tobacco and food if you can. If I shall not be eaten here by the vermin I shall surely perish here from hunger and slave labour ... I shall not see you again, farewell, Nefedov.' The note carried the post mark of 'Camp 8', a notorious prison on the Irtysh river, which had a reputation that no prisoner could survive there for more than a few years. Later we learned that he had been denounced by another lecturer at our college for remarking: 'If the Soviet forces continue to retreat as they have done so far, what will happen to our country?' He was accused of 'spreading defeatism' and condemned to seven years of hard labour. We never saw Nefedov again.

It transpired that it was another member of faculty who turned Nefedov in. It was the lecturer on Marxism–Leninism and Party History', Friedrich Futler. He was a rather strange creature: a cripple who always walked with the help of crutches, a German evacuated forcibly to Semipalatinsk from the former German Autonomous Republic on the Volga. This Republic was totally disbanded immediately after Nazi Germany attacked the Soviet Union and its German residents were exiled into far away areas. Futler had been one of the top leaders of the German Republic and apparently had to earn the trust of the authorities in Semipalatinsk. He regularly reported on professors and students at our college.

Another victim of his was our lecturer in Russian Literature, Vassily Sovsun. He was the complete opposite of Futler: round-faced, rotund, with frizzy flying hair, his lectures were a delight. Much like an actor, he used to declaim in his huge booming voice entire portions of poetry, dramas, novels – without a single note, all from his voracious memory. Attending his lectures was much like going to the theatre, to a one-man show by a superb actor. Whereas Futler was well-dressed, especially in winter, in a fine leather coat, boots, warm gloves and thick fur hat, Sovsun would run around in a thin worn coat, a pair of light shoes, hatless and without gloves. In the unheated lecture hall, he used to try to warm himself by jumping around on his feet and constantly rubbing his red, swollen hands. For his birthday we, the students, collected some money from our meager stipends and bought for him a pair of warm fur gloves. (He was so grateful when we presented them to him!). Though he always filled his lectures with the official point of view and quotations, he got in trouble with the authorities, apparently as result of a report by Futler. His lectures were cancelled, but somehow he got over it and returned after several weeks. He had been evacuated from Kiev where he had been known as a major literary authority and it seems that that helped him to get off the hook.

THE IRON LAW OF THE IMPOVERISHMENT OF THE PROLETARIAT

Soon I myself was in trouble with Futler and the authorities. As mentioned above, he used to lecture us on Marxism. Always at the end of his lectures, he used to call upon a student or two and ask whether the material had been understood. One day he enlarged upon the so-called 'iron law of the impoverishment of the prole-tariat'. This 'law' was regarded as a major principle of communist theory. It asserted that the more developed a capitalist country the more impoverished its working class becomes. Futler asked if I understood this 'law'. Here my previous knowledge betrayed me. After all, as distinct from my classmates, whose knowledge about the West was from Soviet sources which, for example, presented New York only through pictures of the unemployed searching through the rubbish bins in the streets, I knew about the situation there from my years in pre-war Poland. I knew from books, films, accounts and journals about the situation in the 'capitalist' West, and that the material standards of the 'proletariat' there were incomparably higher than in Soviet Russia. So I ventured to ask: 'But isn't the material situation of the workers in the West, in England for example, much higher than in backward countries?'

Futler did not answer immediately, but at the next lecture he indulged in a long explanation. The imperialist countries are plundering the colonies and handing out part of the spoils to 'their' proletariat. Also, Marx did not mean an absolute impover-ishment, but in relative terms: as imperialist capitalism develops the bourgeoisie becomes richer and though the proletariat gets some crumbs from the table it becomes poorer by the standards of society. He asked me specifically whether I understood the 'law' now; obviously, I said 'yes'.

I thought and hoped that this was an end to the matter. However, about two weeks later I was suddenly called to the office of the rector 'to clarify a point about my studies'. When I arrived there, I was directed to a side door. 'A certain comrade wants to talk to you', the secretary said. She closed the door behind me, and for two hours I found myself in a tête-à-tête with an elderly 'comrade', whose identity could not be mistaken. He consulted with some papers on his table and knew a lot about me: my family, my studies, what I said to my friends at a recent get-together of our class, and so on. Suddenly, he asked 'So you have some doubts about the validity of the "iron law of the impoverishment of the proletariat"?' I went cold inside, realizing how great was the danger: if I failed to explain this matter properly, I might be accused of 'anti-soviet ideological propaganda' since I expressed publicly criticism of a Marxist–Leninist dogma. For such a serious 'crime' one could easily receive quite a few years of imprisonment in a 'camp of correction'; I realised immediately that it must have been Futler who had 'reported' on me. Carefully, I indulged in an ideological explanation in line with the official doctrine about the 'relative impoverishment' and stressed that I had asked because I wished to understand it better.

'So who else in your class has doubts about our ideology?', the 'comrade' shot me a question. He questioned me about the lecturers and about a number of students, and what do the 'Poles I knew' think about the 'situation' and so on. Again, I had to be very careful: the slightest irregularity might have been used against those people mentioned as well as against me. If for example, I were to indicate that some others had 'ideological doubts' this could be built into a 'cell of Trotskyite opposition'. Worst of all, I could not know what others had told him about me and what I might have said on various occasions. So I kept as close as possible to the truth, carefully avoiding saying anything that might incriminate others as well as myself. 'So how come that you never heard any anti-Soviet talk?' he insisted. 'I am a very good student, I study Marxist theory diligently and nobody talks with me in an anti-Soviet manner', I answered.

The 'comrade' was an experienced interviewer in the best Soviet tradition; he asked suddenly the same questions again and again, sometimes repeating them rapidly several times. Part of the time he acted very friendly; then he would become threatening and shouting and sharp. When he allowed me to go, I was utterly exhausted and shaking inwardly, though I made a supreme effort not to show it. Also, it seemed to me that many hours had passed; I could not believe my watch which indicated that the whole thing took less than two hours.

This experience gave me some insight into the way the Soviet interrogators made people 'confess' to some fiendish crimes which they never committed. I realized that such questioning went on all the time. On the quiet, some of the other students admitted that they were 'invited to the comrade' from time to time. This was not the only occasion when I was called for a talk with a 'comrade'. As time went on, and they did not get any depositions from me, the threatening tone became more dominant. In the end they 'invited' me less and less frequently, I was lucky.

16 • Harsh Winters, Fine Summers and an American Vice President

So we lived in the city of Semipalatinsk, in northern Kazakhstan. Our condition improved in a cardinal way as time went on. During the first winter after being liberated from the prison-camp, we lived there in a kind of lean-to adjoining a Kazakh house. Its walls on three sides were of clay and sticks – apart from the side that connected it to the house, which was of wood. It was quite comfortable in September when we moved there. But soon we realized that it was a dangerous trap. Northern Kazakhstan, it turned out, was a very hot place in the summer; but in the winter the flat steppe country was open to the winds from Siberia. Temperatures reached more than −40° celsius, strong winds and storms were frequent. We had no wood even to cook a meal, and certainly not to heat the place. Even if had been possible to heat the large room, it did not warm the place since the strong, cold winds penetrated the thin walls. Though we kept on our winter clothing while at home and covered ourselves with everything we had for sleeping at night, we suffered constantly from the cold, actually more so than at the camp in Siberia. Often when we woke up in the morning we found the water in the barrel (there was obviously no running water there) frozen to ice, there was also white ice on the walls.

Despite all that, we would have somehow passed the winter with no harm – if it had not been for our mother's illness. In the middle of winter mother became very weak; she developed a chronic fever and could not take any solid foods. We succeeded in bringing a doctor to see her, but he was not able to diagnose the disease. Mother became increasingly weak until it was difficult for her to speak. There were no ambulances in that town, nor any taxis, all had been taken away to the front. It looked that unless some radical measure was undertaken, mother might simply fade away. When she was lying there in the icy room, white-faced, silent and immobile we often woke up at night and approached her bed to check that she was still breathing.

One mild, clear winter's day we decided to take her to the major clinic in the centre of town where she could be examined by specialists. We dressed her in all the warm clothes we had, bundled her around with a heavy blanket and, since she was not able to walk, we simply carried her on our back. This was not too difficult as she had lost a lot of weight during her illness ... The verdict of the specialist was shattering: 'Tuberculosis of the glands'. He gave her certain medicines which he explained could not cure but might 'strengthen her constitution'. The only cure possible was through 'treatment with rays' which hopefully would arrest the tuberculosis and restore the glands. Luckily, there was such a 'ray machine' at the central hospital in town. There was however no place anywhere at any hospital since they were packed way beyond capacity with wounded soldiers from the front. So the only way was for us to bring her in twice weekly to the hospital for treatment. Meantime he recommended – oh irony! – keeping her in a warm place and feeding her nourishing food. From then on began a period of our regularly transporting our mother to the hospital twice a week – a distance of several kilometres – sometimes on our back and sometimes on a sleigh adapted for this purpose. As warm spring air arrived and as the treatment progressed, my mother became stronger; she was able to get out of bed and slowly to return to normal. There is no doubt that the ray treatment saved her life, and it was all covered by the national health service, it cost us nothing at all.

After this terrible winter our material situation improved considerably. Father and my younger brother or myself worked as porters at the railway station which gave us a considerable income. We started dealing with 'Altai' gold, even if only on a small scale to start with. In the spring, our elder brother, Lemmel, successfully finished his training at a school for truck drivers. This made a major difference to us. There was indeed a great shortage of both trucks and drivers, since they had all been mobilized for the war. He was gladly taken on to work as driver of the single remaining truck of the regional pharmaceutical administration. It was not possible at that time to get any spare parts or arrange the necessary repairs officially. It was possible to do it only unofficially, at black market prices. The manager of the administration proposed therefore the following arrangement: each week for one day the truck would remain at the disposal of the driver, in this case, Lemmel, and as his responsibility; in exchange for this he would take care of all necessary repairs and make sure that the truck would worked for the administration all the other days of the week. This arrangement was fraught with many difficulties and dangers, and yet it worked for several years. In a way it gave each side what it needed: the administration had a truck that otherwise would have been immobilized – and this was the only truck at its disposal. Without it, it would not have been possible to bring medical supplies or fuel and coal to the hospitals and clinics in the entire area. Our brother on the other hand was responsible for repairs – which was nearly a 'mission impossible'. But he had at his disposal a truck for a day each week, which was a great asset. One of the crucial benefits became clear at the beginning of the next winter: one afternoon we went with our brother to the nearby woods and brought to our house a truck of dry logs. Next winter our home was wonderfully warm.

Slowly, we started some kind of 'good life' in those harsh war conditions in Semipalatinsk. Among the various institutions which had been evacuated to this town was also the Ukrainian National Theatre from Kiev. This was one of the foremost theatres in what was then the USSR. It settled in town with its leading actors, directors and orchestra. It put on a regular programme of classical Russian, Soviet and Western plays as well as some Ukrainian operettas. Some of these shows were of a very high standard indeed. It was not difficult to get tickets and they were not at all expensive. From time to time concerts were given by the theatre orchestra, visiting musicians and singers. There were also several cinemas in town, rather rough and technically inadequate (projection was often interrupted and the sound used to disappear frequently). Most of the films were propaganda yarns about the heroic fighting of the Soviet army at the front. But they also showed pre-war Soviet films such as *Circus* (somewhat similar to a Hollywood great) and historical classics such as *Potemkin, Ivan the Terrible* and *Alexander Nevsky*. These were not of much interest to the Soviet public, since they had seen them many times due to the rather limited number of films shown (only those that received the personal approval of Stalin could be presented; he found faults in many and nobody would then dare to show them). To us, however, many of these were new and interesting.

The greatest cinema sensation were the few American films which were allowed to be screened. The greatest success was that of *The Great Waltz* with Jannette McDonald, about the life of the Austrian composer Johann Strauss. I never understood why Stalin approved showing this film. It revealed to the eyes of the Soviet public, which lived in extremely drab conditions of chronic short-ages and sometimes acute hunger, a lavish and prettified picture of life in pre-First World War imperial Vienna. Moreover, instead of presenting an extremely negative picture of the Hapsburg 'feudal imperialist' court and ruler, it projected a glamorous court and benevolent Emperor Franz Joseph II. It was suggested that Stalin simply liked the leading lady and was influenced by his youthful memories when he had spent some time within the Austro-Hungarian state. Another great hit was *One Hundred Men and a Girl* with Deanna Durbin. Again, it presented a joyous, rich picture of life in 'capitalist America', totally different from the negative image usually presented of unemployed people search-ing in rubbish bins in the shadow of looming skyscrapers.

Summer was pleasant despite the great heat which sometimes reached 40° degrees Celsius. One summer pleasure was bathing and swimming in the huge Irtysh river which flowed through our town. Not far from our house the river created an inlet and a small island with a sandy beach. Since there were no lectures in summer, we were able to gather a small group of boys and girls and go to the river. There were very few people there, all were at work or otherwise occupied in those harsh war times. For us, these hours of splashing in the water, swimming to the island and playing around on the beach there, were like a private paradise.

Another matter that made summer pleasant was the dance in the city park. Overlooking the river, there was an enclosure with a dance floor surrounded by a bandstand and wooden benches among the trees. On most summer evenings a military brass band was there, giving a popular concert and playing dance music. It was open to the public for a reasonable entrance fee. It was like a bright island of joy amidst the sadness and drabness of life. Among the dancers there were very few men; girls danced with girls or with wounded and convalescing soldiers. From the second summer we, the three brothers, were able to dress in suits, put on fine boots or shoes and go to the dancing enclosure in the park. By that time we had come to know some girls and so took them with us. I did not know how to dance; but the girls did not let me off – they forcibly dragged me to the dance floor and taught me to dance that way. After dancing we went often for long walks in the park and along the river. Nights were very short there, so often by the time we arrived home to sleep, it was already dawn. Our parents got fed up with our coming home late at night, sometimes together, but often separately at different times after midnight, so it was arranged that we slept on mattresses under the roof, and did not have to enter the house and waken our parents.

The Soviet calendar was quite similar to the Catholic one – it was full of saints' days and holidays. There were the major holidays: May Day, anniversary of the 'October Revolution' and New Year. But there were also the anniversary of the death of Lenin in January, Red Army Day in February, Women's Day in March and so on until the 'Day of the Stalin Constitution' in early December. Every profession, group and cause in the USSR had a special day: railway workers' day, textile employees' day, teachers' day, miners' day and so on. Each of these was marked by festivities, marches, dancing and singing – especially after the situation at the front improved for the Soviet side.

Sometime in summer, we witnessed in our town of Semipalatinsk an 'historical' event: a visit by Henry Wallace, vice-president of the United States. To us it really appeared like something from another planet. Not that anything about it was published in the local media; but the entire town knew about it. Preparations for the one-day visit went on feverishly for a month in advance. For example, the lecturer in English at our college was mobilized to be a hostess for the visit. She was a rather pretty lady, evacuated from Leningrad, quite elegant and well-groomed, unusual in Soviet conditions. A lovely house, not far from our college, which had once belonged to a rich Russian merchant, was requisitioned and completely refurbished. The kindergarten that was located there was moved elsewhere. A search was going on all over town for fine furnishings, carpets, lamps and especially ancient silver cutlery. The place was turned into a small palace (there was no elegant hotel at all in town), and it was easier to keep an eye on the entire American delegation if it was located in one place away from the local townspeople. The visiting vice-president went to see some factories in the area. We had a friend at the huge local meat-packing plant. He related that the entire place was cleaned and painted anew; all employees who were usually dressed in old and soiled working outfits were provided with new shining clothes. The visitors were invited to taste some of the meat products – especially prepared and far superior to the usual fare.

The vice-president was also invited to see for himself the happy life of the Soviet people in the evening at the park. Of course, he did not come himself, but some of his party did show up. We went there ourselves on this evening. We could not recognize the place; the entire park was ringed with coloured lights, flags and decorations. A huge orchestra in fine military attire was blaring Soviet–Russian music liberally interspersed with American jazz (usually taboo!). Even more striking were the dancers: we had never seen so many young, well-dressed men and elegant, young dancing women on this dance floor in the park. We soon realized that the entire dance troupe from the theatre, as well as some of the security men, had been mobilized for the occasion. They donned fine suits and the 'ladies' were equipped with long evening dresses, (wonder of wonders!) fine stockings and long, white gloves. Under the trees with coloured lights elegantly dressed groups sat at tables enjoying delicious food served by white-jacketed 'waiters'.

We were dumbfounded and wondered whether the visitors realized that the entire thing was a show, as far from reality as the infamous Potemkin Villages (Potemkin was one of the 'favourites' of Catherine the Great; when she decided to travel in the country to see how the people lived, he had built entire fine-looking villages filled with dancing and singing happy peasants for her benefit). In any case, it was reported that the 'American delegation' were very pleased with their visit to Semipalatinsk 'where they saw that, far from the front, the Soviet people work devotedly and happily for the victory of the Democratic camp over Fascism'.

17 • We Volunteer for the Polish Army

The wages of the Second World War had definitely changed radically. After the great victory at Stalingrad in the winter of 1942–43, the Soviet army went over to the offensive. The Western allies also started an offensive of their own: the British defeated Rommel in North Africa and the Americans landed in West Africa driving the German forces from the continent. Meanwhile some political developments further threatened our situation in the Soviet Union.

As described earlier, we were released from the camp in Siberia on the basis of an agreement between the Soviet government and the Polish government in exile, which was located in London and headed by General Sikorsky. As a result of the agreement, which was concluded by the Soviets very much under British–American pressure, tens of thousands of former Polish citizens, including many former Polish officers, were liberated from Soviet concentration camps. They were allowed to form Polish army units under the command of General Anders, appointed by the London Polish government. Needless to say, after their taste of Soviet camps and persecution, the Poles did not demonstrate much love for Russia and were not keen on spilling their blood on the Soviet–German front, defending the Soviet regime. It was therefore agreed between the Western allies and the Soviets that the Polish army under Anders – together with their families, who were mostly exiled into Central Asia and Siberia – would be evacuated through Iran, then under British rule, to the Middle East. There they joined the British forces fighting the Germans, first in Africa and then in Italy. Quite a number of those who enlisted in Anders' Polish army were Jews of Polish origin; one of them was Menachem Begin, the future commander of the Irgun Jewish underground and future Prime Minister of Israel.

As the course of war turned in favour of Russia, and the Soviet offensive indicated a possibility that the Soviet forces would liberate

Poland in the near future, Stalin abruptly cancelled the previous agreement with the Sikorsky Polish government. Diplomatic recognition of the representatives was annulled which in turn caused a crisis in our citizenship status in the USSR. One fine day in the summer of 1943, we received notification that our previous documents, which had been given to us when we were released from the camp in Siberia and which recognized us as 'former Polish citizens', were no longer valid. Shortly we would be summoned to the local office of the Ministry for Internal Affairs to be given Soviet citizenship.

To us this seemed disastrous. Hitherto we had had special status, under the protection of the representatives of the Polish government. From time to time we even received parcels with food and clothing (in Western style which was highly appreciated in Russia) from the Polish consulate. We felt somehow protected and hoped that after a victorious end to the war we would be repatriated to Poland. Now it seemed that not only had we lost our 'special status', but also the hope of ever being able to get out of Russia, which was our most cherished wish. Moreover, this sudden change meant that we would soon be called up for service in the Soviet army and be sent to the front. The rate of casualties in the Soviet army was very high; and in any case, if we had to serve we wanted to do so in a Polish army, where conditions were less harsh than in the Russian one.

We lived in constant anxiety for months on end, but nothing happened. Then it became known that in Moscow a 'Council for a Free Poland' had been created consisting of pro-Soviet Polish persons. It was clear that Moscow intended to establish a pro-communist regime in Warsaw. Soon another Polish Army was being formed in Russia from the rest of the Polish citizens who had not enrolled in the Anders units. To beef up this new Polish army with pro-Soviet personnel, Moscow also transferred to it old-time Soviet citizens of Polish origin (some years later, the Soviet marshal of Polish ancestry, Konstantin Rokossovsky, was made supreme commander of the army of Poland under the Warsaw Pact). We expected any day a summons for service in this new Polish army, but to our surprise nothing happened. As time went on we became more and more uneasy, especially since it was rumoured that only those who served in this army would be able to be 'repatriated to Poland'. Also, many of our friends went to the front where many of them were killed or wounded. Also, more and more became known about the

German atrocities against Soviet citizens (it was not usually mentioned that they were Jews). We felt increasingly that we could not remain as passive onlookers. We succeeded in convincing our parents (especially our mother who would not hear of it at first) and one day in summer 1944 the two of us – my elder brother and myself – marched off to the recruitment office in the centre of town.

'We have come of our own free will to volunteer for the Polish army', we announced proudly. At first this unprecedented statement was met with astonishment and confusion. After considerable waiting we were called in to see the deputy head of the Military Recruitment Office of the area. He explained that since we were not Soviet but former Polish citizens he would have to refer our case to higher authorities. In the meantime, we were ordered to go through the usual recruitment procedures. We passed the prescribed health examination and wrote and signed a letter stating our request to be inducted as volunteers into the Polish army units. Another officer examined our readiness for military service; as it happened, I had had some military training since it has been an obligatory part of studies at the Soviet college which I attended. In the end, after completing the examination and paperwork, they sent us home: 'We shall refer your case to the proper office and let you know. You should be ready for recruitment any day now.'

We waited and waited. From time to time, we inquired at the induction office – nothing happened: 'We still have no response in your case. Wait patiently', they assured us. After several months we got to know one of the secretaries there. In great secrecy she revealed to us the mystery: 'If your name had not been Katz (obviously Jewish), you would have been called up for military service immediately. We are now recruiting men up to 50 years of age, married and no matter with how many children (Muslim men had many). But the Polish army let us know that they had too many Abramoviches already, they do not need any more. Having heard that, we decided not to exert ourselves in this matter; after all, why fight and face death in an anti-Semitic army? The matter hurt us deeply: even the privilege of fighting the Nazis as volunteers and possibly dying was denied to us, because we were Jewish.

By that time it became increasingly clear to us that while fighting the Nazis the Soviets themselves were becoming affected by the despicable bug of anti-Semitism. 'Jokes' such as these were popular: 'A Jew needs a crooked gun, so that he can shoot while hiding behind the corner'; 'Jews are fighting at the front ... of the bazaars'. A brother of our Jewish friends, an artillery colonel, came to our town for one month's home leave. He was highly decorated for heroic fighting exploits and was recuperating from his third wounding at the front. After two weeks of his stay, we became great friends. Before returning to the front he confided to us in secret: 'I think that I shall never see you again. Chances of death at the front are extremely high ... Only, unlike other soldiers, I shall never know whether I am killed by a German bullet from in front of me, or by a Soviet bullet from the back, shot by an anti-Semite in our own army.' Other Jewish servicemen, especially among the wounded who were recuperating in our town, reported in private about many incidents of anti-Semitism within the Soviet army. Those evacuated from the territories occupied by the Germans told of many cases when the local 'Soviet' citizens – Ukrainians, Lithuanians, Russians, Latvians – received the Germans with great enthusiasm and assisted them in murdering their Jewish neighbours: not just assisting them, but taking the initiative, not waiting for the Germans to come. When the German-occupied provinces were liberated, some Jews returned to their previous places, some after having been wounded at the front, some after years of fighting and hiding in the woods, others after evacuation in far away lands. They were confronted by intense anti-Semitic hatred; some of them were killed by anti-Semites after having survived in the camps or at the front. The ruler of the newly liberated Ukraine, Secretary General Nikita Khrushchev, even issued a covert order that Jews should not be allowed to return to their previous homes.

The Holocaust did not end entirely when the Germans were driven out, or even with the end of the Second World War. Jews, who somehow survived and returned to their previous homes often found Nazi collaborators there. These were living in their former dwellings, sleeping in their beds, using their furniture and kitchenware. Often it turned out that these were the same people who had betrayed members of their family to the Nazis or even served in the Nazi police or concentration camps. Some of the returnee Jews, who had fought in the Soviet army, took revenge upon the local Nazi collaborators. The Ukrainian nationalist underground, which was an ally of the Nazis and went on fighting the Soviets for some years even after the end of the Second

World War, also continued with anti-Jewish activities. We often heard about these matters, though the Soviet media did not mention a thing about them. It made us even more determined in our wish to leave the Soviet Union as early as possible. We believed that this would happen immediately after the end of the war, but we had to wait much longer until we were able to do so.

18 • The End of the War and My 'Miraculous' Graduation

The war was drawing to an end. On many evenings, usually at 8 o'clock, just before the main evening news, Soviet radio announced a new victory. At the start of the German–Soviet war, all radio receivers had been confiscated by the authorities. Using a radio on which it was possible to listen to foreign broadcasts was absolutely forbidden. Instead, in every household, public place and work place there were wired radio loudspeakers, which broadcast official programmes. These supplied only such information as the rulers wished to give the population. It was on this radio, especially during the last two years of the war, that the announcements about victories were made. They were usually given in the deep sonorous voice of Yuri Levitan (a Jew). They were accompanied by martial music played by a military brass band; a number of artillery salvos in honour of the victory from the Moscow Kremlin was usually heard at the end. The information on victories always came in the form of an 'order of the Supreme Commander' – Stalin.

The success of Soviet and allied forces against Hitler's Germany created an optimistic atmosphere; but in real life the situation remained very grim indeed, without any visible improvement. The bread and fuel shortages, the fantastically high prices for anything at the 'grey market' bazaar, pervasive corruption and the constantly felt pressure of the secret police – all these continued as before. As it happened, I became even better acquainted with these towards the end of our stay in the Soviet Union.

Having lived for several years in Semipalatinsk, and having become relatively well-to-do, we came to know some of the people in the 'social circles'. From time to time they would invite us to private parties and sometimes we gained entry to 'official' celebrations. While the majority of the population was extremely hard working and barely survived on insufficient supplies of black bread and potatoes, people at these parties would gorge themselves on meats, cheeses, fine sausage and all kinds of fish and other choice dishes. Vodka and wine were consumed in great quantities. I was especially overwhelmed by a party which I was not allowed to attend; I only caught a glimpse of it when I brought some papers to the host, my then boss at Altai Gold. It was a birthday party for the local chairman of the soviet and the entire provincial *nachalniks* (Nomenklatura) was in attendance. The tables were laden with mountains of cakes, *pelmeni* (traditional Russian dumplings), caviar, bottles of wine and vodka ... I remember thinking: 'Where, in heaven's name do they get the money for these goodies?' And, even more puzzling, 'Where do they get these things from?' These goods were then like a fata Morgana, and, I thought, 'So much for socialism, equality, and care for the working people.'

These matters were even more visible during some trips which I made as a student representative to conferences in Alma Ata, the capital of Kazakhstan and to Dzhambul, a major provincial centre. What struck me most were the great contrasts between the city centre of the Kazakh capital and some other parts of the city. In my eyes, coming from Semipalatinsk, the centre appeared magnificent. There were a number of imposing government buildings, but most impressive were the colonnaded, grand marble buildings of the Opera House and the Youth Theatre. The view of the centre was made even more impressive by the conical, snow-topped mountain in the background. During the several receptions at the celebratory opening and closing of the conference, which were attended by almost all republican nomenklatura, once again mountains of choice food and drink were consumed. The same took place at the Dzhambul conference. All this, while even black bread was strictly rationed, to say nothing of the other choice foods which were had never been seen by the ordinary citizen in years.

The same was the case with everything else: members of the elite were able to enter closed shops where they could get anything – meat, butter, cakes, coffee, sugar, flour, sweets, leather coats, boots, galoshes, furs – items of which ordinary Soviet comrades could only dream. While large families of workers lived in shacks and dark, wet basements, mostly several families in one flat, without heating, the elite were housed in comfortable separate (!) apartments with all modern amenities. It was truly a 'workers' paradise'. Not far from our college there was a 'Party House',

1. Family portrait in front of log house, Semipalatinsk, Northern
    Kazakhstan, 1943. From left to right, back row: brother, Moshe
    and father; front row: brother, Lemel, sister, Ruth, mother,
    Batya and Zev.

2. The Town Hall, Yaroslav, Poland: Zev revisits after 62 years
    with his wife Doris in 2002.

3. A student by day and porter by night in Semipalatinsk, 1943.

4. Author's B.Ed. diploma, from the State Pedagogical Institute, Kazakhan University, Semipalatinsk, 1946.

5. Zev (on the left) with his two brothers at the house in which they were born, Yaroslav, Poland, 1932.

6. Author's graduation class with professors at the Pedagogical Institute, Semipalatinsk, 1946 (Zevin, top row).

7. The author teaching Hebrew at Wetzlar DP Camp, Germany, 1947.

8. Youth Leader, Zionist Youth Movement, Wetzlar DP Camp, Germany, 1947; Zev, second on right.

9. Soldier of Israel, Anti-Tank Artillery, Jerusalem, 1948.

10. Class at Hebrew University, Terra Sancta Building, 1952: Professor Norman Bentwich is in the centre; the author is standing to his right in profile.

11. Zev and Doris Katz leaving the New West End Synagogue, London, after their wedding in May 1955.

12. Zev Katz interviewing Georgi Malenkov, then Prime Minister of the Soviet Union, on a visit to London in 1956.

13. Zev Katz at an election meeting in Tel Aviv, 1965, with Golda Meir (far left).

14. Author with Shimon Peres (third right), Jerusalem, 1975.

15. Author teaching Modern Jewish History, Eton College, UK, 1981.

16. Author attending a graduation ceremony at Glasgow University, 1968.

17. Author with Y. Yevtushenko, Russian poet and dissident, author of the poem 'Babi Yar', Moscow, 1994.

which included a rather comfortable library. In time, I discovered that with my student ticket they let me in there, supposedly to study Communist Party history. Once in the building, it was possible to enter the small buffet there. It was a real feast: for a ridiculously low price one could have a meal containing dishes totally unseen outside: steaks, fruit, ice cream, real coffee!!! On various occasions, we students were 'mobilized' to do some urgent work on the railway, in one of the factories or at the river port. On those occasions I had the chance to taste (!?) the food at the workers' canteens. A comparison of that fare with the food at Party elite places spoke volumes – more than the endless lessons on 'proletarian rule in the Soviet Union' to which we had to listen at college.

In May 1945 Soviet radio announced the entry of Soviet forces into Berlin. On 8 May we heard about the capitulation of Germany to the Western powers and on 9 May the surrender to the Soviet forces was signed. There was much celebration in Moscow and in many other places all over Russia – but nothing at all in our town of Semipalatinsk. I remember walking the main streets of our town looking for some signs of celebration – nothing. Some weeks later a grand victory parade took place in Moscow: a multitude of German military standards were thrown into a heap at the base of the Lenin Mausoleum in Red Square, on top of which stood the triumphant Stalin with a phalanx of his comrades-in-arms. During a grand reception at the Kremlin he gave a speech the content of which struck me deeply. Instead of speaking as a Soviet communist international leader, he spoke like a Russian nationalist–chauvinist: 'We have to give thanks to the Great Russian People who stood heroically in this great war and brought us victory.' He did mention the other peoples of the Soviet state, but the predominance of the 'elder Russian brother' was heavily stressed. Of course, this was not entirely new. It tallied with Stalin's speech shortly after the outbreak of the German war against the Soviet Union. Then he did not call the population for a revolutionary war to defend socialism; he called for a 'Fatherland War', for the defence of the 'Holy Motherland' from a cruel foreign invader, much like in 1812, during the war against the Napoleonic invasion. He did not rouse the people with the images of communist leaders or the heroes of the civil war (1918–1921), but with the names of the tzars and Russian generals – Alexander Nevsky, Minin and Pozharsky, Suvorov and Kutuzov. The core of Russian nationalism was there already; it became even stronger as a result of the war – and with it resurfaced its old companion – anti-Semitism.

We hoped that shortly after the end of the war we would be repatriated to Poland. Yet it was not to be. At the end of the war, the problem of Poland became the subject of a major conflict between the Western allies and Russia. Stalin cut off relations with the pro-Western Polish government in London, especially after the mysterious death of its leader, General Sikorsky. On entering Polish territory, Moscow established a pro-Soviet puppet government. Much of the strength of the pro-Western Polish underground *Armia Krajowa* was destroyed as a result of the ill-fated Warsaw uprising. The Soviet army, located on the other side of the Visla river, opposite burning Warsaw, waited patiently while the Germans systematically destroyed the Polish capital and with it the flower of the *Armia Krajowa*. Remnants of this underground movement continued to fight the Soviet-installed puppet government after the Russian forces drove the Germans out of Poland. A number of those active in the new pro-Soviet administration were Jews. This exacerbated the ancient anti-Semitism of the Polish Right. Anti-Jewish attacks were quite frequent, survivors of the camps and repatriates from Siberia were murdered, wounded and beaten.

The economic situation in 'liberated' Poland was also very difficult. However, we thought that the Polish authorities would be interested in speeding up repatriation of its citizens from Russia in order to settle the empty, formerly German, lands in the west, which had been transferred to Poland. However, months passed and we remained in Semipalatinsk. By the end of 1945, signals came from Moscow that we should be ready to leave within months. A long period of waiting, of 'sitting on our suitcases', followed. From time to time, rumours about our impending departure circulated; the appointed time came and nothing happened.

In the meantime, I had a personal problem. By the year 1945/46, I was completing my studies at the faculty of history of the college linked to the University of Kazakhstan. It was my fourth year. At the end of it, sometime in June 1946, the final exams were supposed to take place. Success in these exams would provide me with a diploma, the equivalent of a B.Ed. I was among the more outstanding students at this college, consistently receiving the highest marks in all courses. Early in 1946, we received an official letter from the Polish representative mission in Moscow to be ready for repatriation in the near future. The letter included an appeal to all Soviet authorities for all necessary assistance. I presented this letter to the dean's office and a period of confusion followed. The dean invited me to his office; he assured me that the college would like to do everything possible to assist me in this matter. Could I not stay on for some time until I passed the exams and gained the academic title I deserved? I explained that the papers for our leaving the Soviet Union as repatriates were not personal, but on a collective visa, under special escort and in a special train. No possibility of a private, personal repatriation existed. Actually, we had had a bad experience with the changes in Soviet–Polish relations in the past; we were afraid that if I did not leave together with my family and the other Poles, I might never be able to leave.

Weeks passed and it looked as if nothing could be done in this matter. Then suddenly, early in April, I was again called to the dean; he informed me: 'The Ministry of Higher Education of the Kazakh Republic has given us authorization to form a special state examination commission to examine one person – you. Provided you pass these final exams successfully you will be granted a diploma and the appropriate academic degree.' He explained that it would take some time to form such a special exam committee; and since in any case I needed some time to prepare for the exams, these would take place early in May.

A feverish period ensued. I had to attend my regular courses and review the material for the final diploma exams. At the same time, there were more indications that we would soon be leaving and I had to help with some of the preparations for the trip. All the time there was the threat that we would suddenly have to leave before the exam. In early May an unusual thing happened at the college: a special examination committee of three senior academics sat to examine one person – myself. For several days the strange ritual continued and after a week I was informed that I had passed the exams with top marks across the board. In the meantime a new difficulty had risen: there was no diploma scroll. The college received these from the ministry just before the final exams and they were strictly numbered. (I was not surprised: a member of our family was supplied with a matriculation certificate in exchange for a sack of wheat flour, a virtual fortune in war time.) In the end they did find an old diploma form and stuck new sheets into it with my name on.

At the end of May I was invited for a short ceremony at the dean's office: in the presence of the members of the special examination committee and some other senior academics I was

From the Gestapo to the Gulags

presented with the diploma scroll 'by the authority of the Ministry of Higher Education of the Soviet Republic of Kazakhstan'. I was proclaimed a graduate and congratulated all round. After the official part of the ceremony the dean invited me into his private office. There he gave me a serious lecture: 'You have been one of our best students. We have given you education and made a major effort to see that you graduate ... You will shortly return to Poland. A Polish citizen who graduated from a Soviet university, who studied Marxism–Leninism, is very important to us. I am sure that you will be able to make a meaningful contribution for the good of both our countries.' I was rather startled by this summation.

Little did he know that only a few weeks after repatriation, I was to leave Poland illegally on my long journey to the Land of Israel, and that I would become one of the leaders of a Zionist youth movement in Germany.

19 • Not So Welcome in Our Polish Patria

The day of our repatriation arrived at last. The day we hoped and suffered for. The thing we wanted most was to get out of the Soviet Union. Our overwhelming desire to return to Poland was also coloured by the idealized memories of our pre-war 'fine' living there. Also, we knew from various sources that despite the pro-Soviet government there, there was incomparably more freedom in Poland – and more possibilities for contact with 'the West', as well as with Palestine.

One week before the great day, we were already completely packed – and very nervous indeed. A consular representative from the Polish embassy arrived and announced that he would accompany our special train as far as the Polish border. When at last we arrived at Semipalatinsk railway station, a major disappointment awaited us. We had expected that the Soviet authorities would put at the disposal of repatriates, citizens of a 'friendly neighbouring country', a comfortable passenger train. Instead, we saw at the station a very long, primitive goods train, with much the same arrangements as the one that exiled us to Siberia years ago. We were again packed in, a number of families to each carriage. Of course, this time we were not locked up, there were no KGB guards and the food was adequate.

At last the locomotive whistled, the wheels started turning, we started cheering, and off we went on the long journey 'home'. This time we went on the Central Asian Railway, at first southwards and then to the north in order to circumvent the Caspian Sea. Then our train turned west, crossing to the south of the Ural mountains and through the great east European landscape. We passed near many great cities – Alma Ata, Tashkent, Sverdlovsk, Kiev and so on – but were not allowed to stop there and visit. It took us almost two weeks until the great moment – arriving at the Polish border.

I shall never forget that moment when our train stopped at the border control point. A Polish officer in a fine uniform, shiny boots and a four-cornered traditional Polish military hat was standing there on a little hill. He viewed our train with obvious disgust and from the corner of his mouth issued one single sentence: 'Well well, this is the last thing we need now.' Of course, he immediately recognizsed that many of the repatriates were Jews, like our family. This was our welcome to our 'loving *patria*' Poland, and it gave us a truthful indication of what awaited us in our beloved homeland.

Meantime, we were fascinated by what we saw on this side of the Polish border. It hit us: this is Europe! Despite much destruction during the war, things looked much better than in Soviet Russia. Shortly after the border, we passed a small town with a little park. We could see some shops with mannequins clad in suits and dresses in the windows. In the park well-dressed couples were walking; some ladies were pushing children in nicely decorated carriages. The entire atmosphere was that of European *Gemutlichkeit* (cosiness) – so different from the drab 'Asian' look of Russia (or at least so it appeared to us). At one of the first stations I bought some newspapers; how different they were from the Soviet ones … We were astonished to see the variety, and that they were published by different parties and groups, giving so much more information about the West. Private vendors came to our train to sell and buy from us whatever it might be.

As our train travelled deeper into Poland we wondered where we should go to live. We would not return to our home town of Yaroslav, from which we had been originally expelled by the Germans, without first learning about the situation there. We wanted therefore to remain for some time in central Poland. When we came to the major city of Lodz, not far from Warsaw, the authorities proposed that those who wanted to proceed and settle in the new lands to the west should remain on the train. Those intending to live in central Poland should disembark here and would be provided with some temporary lodgings. Lodz was the second largest city in Poland, and a major industrial centre. Whereas Warsaw had been totally destroyed, Lodz had remained largely intact.

We decided to stay in Lodz. Travelling by truck through the streets of this town we were surprised to see cafés, some of them with pre-war furniture, lamps and curtains, with people sitting there, smoking and reading newspapers – as if the war had never happened. Shop windows displayed all kinds of merchandise, the like of which we had not seen for years. Vegetable stalls were packed with many kinds of fruit, kiosks were selling ice cream and chocolates ... However, our high spirits soon fell when we turned off from the broad central boulevards into narrow sidestreets. These were lined by empty-looking shabby, buildings, often with gaping, unglazed windows and broken doors. The entire area had the appearance of neglect and a smell of decay. The truck stopped in front of one such building. We were told to take our things and marched to the second floor where we were shown into a middle-sized room with a window into the inner courtyard. 'This is your home now', said the accompanying official, and left.

We were stunned. There was no furniture whatsoever, just bare walls. There was a small alcove that could serve as a kitchenette and a run-down toilet. In one corner we noticed some loose sheets of paper and torn, written-on, yellowed books. Upon closer examination we discovered that they were in Hebrew. During our trip by truck, there had been some mention that this area in which we arrived had been the Lodz ghetto under the Germans. Now, on seeing the Hebrew papers, a horrible thought dawned upon us: 'These were prayer books and Bibles left behind by victims of the Holocaust taken from here to the gas chambers.'

The sun was setting and – in a sombre mood – we prepared for the night as best as we could. There was no electricity, so we had to hurry. We put on the floor whatever we could use for bedding, had a quick bite to eat and lay down. However, the moment it grew dark a new problem started: mice. They were running, scratching the walls, squeaking, searching for food. We could do nothing about them apart from hiding our food beneath us. At first it was impossible to sleep, but in the end tiredness overcame us. This was not the way we had imagined our first night in our Fatherland.

Next day the picture became clear. The Lodz ghetto had been one of the largest in German-occupied Poland and one of the last ones to be liquidated. There had still been some Jews there as late as 1944, just before the Soviet army fought its way in. In the interim period some Poles had come to live there illegally, but they were removed shortly before our arrival. So the Polish authorities settled Jews returning from exile in Russia in the abandoned houses of the Jewish victims of the Holocaust. To us it seemed as if the souls of our martyred brothers and sisters still haunted these rooms in which we were housed.

Soon, trouble arrived in a quite unexpected form. Around midday a strange visitor entered our small apartment; a rather small, muscular fellow, in warm clothes and shoes, and stinking of alcohol. 'So here you are, *Zhidki* (Yids) – I thought I would never see the likes of you again. Know that I am the warden of this block of houses, so I am at your service. I shall do for you whatever you need, of course, for a small, eh … consideration.' He sat down on the windowsill obviously waiting for some kind of 'gift'. This 'warden' became a kind of an overlord: he used to come unannounced at any time of day or evening, often drunk and demanding more drink and food. He used to tell us about his girlfriends, swamp us with opinions – church affairs, news about the mayor and his cronies, national affairs and the rise in prices of sausage and vodka. He often sat at the entrance to our courtyard, together with several other vile-looking men, making lurid suggestions to our passing women, cracking crude often anti-Semitic jokes, checking on the parcels which we carried. There was no way of getting rid of him – the police would do nothing about it, and we were afraid that if we tried forcibly to oppose him he would mobilize his gang and become violent. There were many rumours that Jews in Lodz and elsewhere were knifed, shot at and beaten to a pulp. He looked like a person who would not have any qualms about tossing a grenade into the rooms of anyone who might enrage him. So we had no choice but to accommodate him and suffer his insolent behaviour.

Once we got some beds and furniture and settled in a fashion in our temporary dwelling in Lodz, we had to tackle the most important problem: could we return to live in our pre-war home town of Yaroslav? Our family owned there considerable property: a shop close to the market-place, two houses and the contents of our apartment which was quite richly furnished and equipped. My mother dreamt about us returning 'home' and setting up business again. The omens were, however, not good at all. We enquired at the offices of the Jewish community in Lodz. It transpired that no Jews remained alive in our area and that it was extremely dangerous for any of us to be seen there. We decided therefore that mother and my younger, 'Aryan-looking' brother Moshe would travel there and assess the situation. Being blond and blue-eyed, Moshe, despite his obviously Jewish name, was not at all Jewish-looking. My mother, who might be 'suspected' of being Jewish, wrapped her face in a huge peasant-style kerchief – and off they went.

When they returned three days later, they related to us a tale of woe. One single woman and her child had somehow survived the

Holocaust in our town. She had returned to her previous home there and opened a small grocery shop. The local anti-Semites close to the pro-Western Polish underground warned her several times that she had to leave town since 'there is no place for Jews'. She answered that she was alone and had nowhere to go; she did not take these warnings seriously. One day, early at dawn while she and the child were sleeping, a grenade was tossed into her bedroom and killed them both. There was nobody to bury them until a local priest arranged for them to be buried at the Jewish cemetery. My mother was afraid in case she be recognised, she disguised herself like some kind of criminal, while walking in her home town where she had lived for many years as a highly respected citizen; and this was over two years after the Nazis had been driven out from there.

At last they arrived at the house of our non-Jewish pre-war friends, the Sternitsky family. They were customers at my parents' shop for many years. As time went on, they became personal friends, even towards the end of the 1930s, when anti-Semitism became rampant. Mr Sternitsky was a fireman, which meant that he had a steady income, took goods on credit and paid regularly on the first of each month – a thing rare at that time in Poland. She was an elegant lady, of Czech origin. I especially remembered that on Purim or Simhat Torah we used to borrow a fireman's outfit from him to masquerade in. Mrs Sternitsky, who opened the door, was shocked when she saw my mother alive at her doorstep. She quickly took them inside and closed the door so that nobody would notice that 'Jews were hiding there'. She received them in a very friendly way, gave them food, advice and information – but warned them immediately: 'You cannot sleep here overnight. It would be too dangerous – in case someone saw you coming.' So my mother and Moshe left before darkness for the nearest major city of Rzeszow where they found a place to sleep over – without of course revealing their identity.

Next morning, mother and Moshe returned to the Sternitsky house. Mother explained that she had some ownership papers for the two houses and that – in view of the situation in our town – she was willing to sell them. Additional copies of the papers could be obtained from the mayor's office, since Yaroslav had remained generally intact despite the fighting during the war. Mrs Sternitsky explained that under a pro-communist government the price of property was very low. While she did not know how to deal with this matter, she advised mother to put it in the hands of a lawyer she knew. Two weeks later our mother travelled again with Moshe to Yaroslav where they signed papers selling the houses for a ridiculously low price. (When my parents went to live in Israel three years later, they bought for this money a little kiosk shop which provided for their needs until considerable old age.) Before leaving our home town, they went to have a look at the house in which we had lived before the war. Some strange people were living there and the place was completely neglected. These people received them in a hostile way, especially when they tried to search the place for some caches which we had hidden there before being expelled by the Germans in 1939. They did nevertheless find one such hoard with some valuables; two more could not be found. As the behaviour of the Poles residing in our house became more and more threatening, mother decided to give up. Within an hour they left town – never to return again.

Our – and especially our parents' – dream about returning to our home town was shattered. What should we do? Where were we going to live? How would we support ourselves? A radical answer to these fateful questions was at hand as a result of the events of the next few weeks.

20 • Poland: A Zionist Education

Zionism was totally forbidden in the Soviet Union. There were no Jewish community offices, no representatives of international Jewish organizations, no contact with the Land of Israel or with the West. In Poland all this was different. It was one of the things that struck us most – there was a relatively intensive Jewish life there: communal, religious, Zionist and cultural. During our stay in pre-war Poland, we had all been immersed in a rich Jewish life. We, the youngsters, had had an intensive Jewish education and participated with our parents in Jewish religious rites and services. But the greatest influence on us had been exerted by the Zionist youth movement to which we belonged. It was a natural 'home' to us in the atmosphere of the rise of German Nazism and rampant anti-Semitism throughout eastern Europe, and in Poland especially.

Lodz, where we resided temporarily was at that time the centre of much of the Jewish activity in Poland. Warsaw was in ruins; Vilnius and Lvov were within the borders of the Soviet Union. There was some Jewish community in Cracow and in the newly acquired former German territories. Some tens of thousands of Polish Jews had survived somehow in hiding and in the concentration camps; but the bulk of Jews in post-war Poland were those who were repatriated from Russia; some had been in the Soviet army or among the partisans, some were evacuated or exiled to the east. Overall, the number of Jews in Poland in 1946 was estimated to amount to several hundred thousand – about one-tenth of the pre-war Jewish community.

On coming to Lodz we soon realized that we had no place there within the non-Jewish community: the right wing was extremely nationalist and anti-Semitic; the left was pro-communist and Soviet-oriented. We were neither one nor the other. We felt that we belonged within the Jewish framework. The Jewish community offices rendered support to repatriates and the Joint

Jewish–American charitable organisation supplied us with parcels of food and clothing. But the greatest influence exerted on us came from the Zionist youth movement activities.

A week or so after our arrival in Lodz we met at the Jewish community centre some young people whom we eagerly engaged in a conversation. It turned out that they had been in town almost a year, and knew much about Jewish and Palestinian affairs. We absorbed avidly all we learned from them since much of it was new to us after years in isolation in Russia. They explained that they worked at the centre, but they lived and belonged to a 'Zionist youth kibbutz who prepared themselves for *aliya* (emigration) to Eretz Israel'. We were in total shock; we did not know such a thing existed or was even allowed: 'A Zionist youth kibbutz here in Lodz – preparing to go to live in Israel?' They assured us that all this was for real: 'If you want to see for yourself come this evening to our place not far from here', they invited us.

That same evening we went to the address they gave us, and could not believe our eyes. A large room was filled with some 40–50 young Jewish boys and girls joyfully singing Hebrew and Yiddish songs. In the corner some of them were dancing; some were sitting around a long table, on the windowsills, in the adjoining corridor. The atmosphere was that of informality, camaraderie and youthful exuberance. We stood by the entrance stunned: the songs and the dances, and the atmosphere were identical with those of our own youth movement in pre-war times. The entire scene could have taken place during our teens in our home town of Yaroslav. The whole thing looked as if the Germans and the Holocaust, camps in Siberia, years in Central Asia had never happened – all those terrible, eventful years each of which seemed like an entire epoch. To us, just several days out of the Soviet Union it seemed as if we had miraculously travelled back through time into our past; or that we had travelled in space and reached another planet.

After about one hour of this kind of camaraderie, they divided into small study groups – some to learn Hebrew, others to listen to a lecture in Jewish history, and another group to study the geography of the Land of Israel. I knew Hebrew and could already converse in this language at 'home' in Yaroslav before the Second World War, so I joined the history group. Later in the evening, all gathered again in the large room. How great was our surprise when one of the fellows announced: 'This evening we have a special guest, Jacob Vardi, member of the kibbutz and fighter in the Jewish Brigade against the Nazis. He left Palestine only a week ago and can give us an up-to-date picture of the situation there.' A tall, sun-burned, white-shirted fellow stood up and began to talk in a low, slow, factual way. When he finished, many questions were asked. The session lasted late into the night; we were afraid that it might be difficult for us to return to our apartment that late, but we could not tear ourselves away from the place. In one evening, we learned more about Palestine, the Zionist youth movement and the situation of the Jewish people than we had learnt in all those years in Russia.

From that evening on, we became frequent visitors to this kibbutz. We did not come to live within the kibbutz; we lived with our parents, whereas many of its members did not have family and living together was an ideal solution for them. Our parents objected to our going to live separately from them. They argued: 'We have gone through all those years as one family and we should not break up now.' We accepted their point of view, but we often went to the kibbutz, especially for the Sabbath when tables were covered with white tablecloths and flowers. On Friday evenings there was a festive meal, with the lighting of candles and raising a glass of wine. Members were usually dressed in white, special Sabbath songs were sung until late into the night. There were special readings and short amateur performances by members. This was not a religious kibbutz, but its members believed in upholding Tradition, albeit in a non-religious way.

There were a number of such kibbutz groups and other public Zionist organizations in Lodz – left-oriented, religious or right wing. We did visit some of them and attended some of their activities. But we identified with the kibbutz and its movement which we came to know first. It turned out to be of the centrist, non - religious orientation, much like the one we had belonged to before the war. It also suited our own orientation. Through long and candid conversations with members of these groups, and from Jewish newspapers and books on Jewish themes, which were not to be had in Soviet Russia, we learned many things about which we had previously only a hazy idea. The most fascinating information was about the ways in which these young people were 'preparing to go to the Land of Israel'. Only some individuals were allowed to go there legally. The British Mandate authorities continued the anti-Jewish policies of the 'White Paper' of 1939, which allowed only very limited Jewish immigration – as if there had been no Second World War and no Holocaust.

Hundreds of thousands of Jewish survivors and repatriates who could not return to their pre-war homes were roaming central Europe with nowhere to go – no country in the whole world would accept them. Most of them only wanted to go to Palestine, but the British shut the borders of this country.

To fight this British policy, the Jewish community in Palestine and the Zionist movement, with the support of the entire world Jewry, engaged in an all-out struggle against the British Mandate. In Eretz Israel the Jewish military underground organizations – Haganah, Irgun and Lehi – were engaged in armed operations against the British (some of the operations of the latter two groups were regarded as 'terrorist' although they were directed against military and not civilian objects). Another form of struggle against the closing of the borders of Palestine was organising a mass illegal immigration movement – *'aliya* B' (as distinct from *aliya* A – legal immigration). Tens of thousands of Jewish refugees were moving across the borders of Europe to Mediterranean ports. There they boarded old freight ships which tried to break the British blockade of the shores of Palestine. Some of them succeeded in slipping through and landed secretly, but the great majority, especially the large ships, were caught by the British warships. The illegal immigrants were then taken forcibly from the ships and located in 'prison camps', at first in Palestine and then – when their number grew to tens of thousands – in Cyprus.

At the various kibbutz places and other Jewish centres in Lodz – as in many other cities in east-central Europe – groups of Jews with their bundles and suitcases were waiting for departure. We attended some such farewells – intensely moving occasions filled with tears and joy. They usually ended at a railway or bus station with kisses and embraces, singing the 'Hatikva', Jewish national anthem and shouts of *'lehitraot* ba'aretz' – see you in the Land of Israel! Actually it took years of wandering through Europe and the Mediterranean until those departing reached Israel.

Behind the entire operation, which embraced many countries in Europe and Israel itself, was a secret arm of the Hagana underground movement called 'Berikha' (escape). Members of this organization, mostly 'emissaries' from Israel, together with teams of local assistants, operated all over Europe. They directed the human traffic, organized the means of transportation, provided (and where necessary falsified) the official papers, opened (sometime by bribes) the borders and took care of food and sleeping quarters for the travellers. It was the Berikha agents who searched for old ships, bought them and secretly fitted them out for the transportation of people from Mediterranean ports to Palestine.

All of this became gradually known to us – things we had not known about at all several weeks ago, before leaving the USSR. As time went on, it became clear to us that we could not return to live in our pre-war home town and that there was hardly any place for us in Poland, and that leaving pro-Soviet Poland for Palestine – a thing we had regarded a fantasy – was an all too real possibility. We understood that it might take a long time to reach the destination – but we believed in getting there in the end. Yet, as a family we were not yet ready to leave Poland and start our long and hazardous journey – until 'Kielce'.

On a lovely July day, in the city of Kielce, a provincial centre not far from Warsaw, the underground anti-Semitic volcano active in post-war Poland, erupted. Buildings inhabited by Jews not far from the centre of town were attacked in the middle of the day by hate-possessed crowds. Jews – men, women and little children – were slaughtered in most brutal fashion, in front of police, army and government officers who did nothing to prevent it until it was too late. More than 40 Jews were killed, many were wounded; some survived in hiding. This pogrom appeared to us like a bolt from heaven. Some of the victims were survivors of the Holocaust; some of the women were raped and some of the children thrown to their death from upper-floor windows. In utter horror we pondered: 'How could such a thing happen in "liberated" Poland? A long time after the Holocaust? After that, can anyone guarantee that more of the same might not happen again in other places? Can we go on living in Poland?'

Kielce gave us the last push. We were ready to leave. And, along with thousands of other Jews, we left Poland, never to return again.*

---

* I did, however, return for a short visit in 2002, after 63 years.

21 • Leaving Poland Through the 'Green' Border

On the appointed morning we were taken to the railway station. We were leaving Lodz – and Poland, the land of our birth, the land in which our ancestors had been living for many generations. We were leaving without regret or sentiment, without looking back. We travelled in a large group of Jewish people accompanied by a 'guide' from Berikha. In the afternoon our train pulled in at a small station in the hills of former German and now Polish Silesia, near the Czech border. Trucks appeared from nowhere and took us to some wooden huts within an enclosure in the surrounding woods. There, some hot food was served and a young guide addressed us: 'We are waiting for a green light from our people at the border. You may be going tonight or may have to wait a day or two. In any case, you should be ready to leave any moment. As explained to you previously, you may have to walk at night through difficult terrain for up to an hour; so everybody should be in walking shoes and able to carry their luggage. Only one suitcase per person is allowed. The entire operation must be carried out quickly and in total silence. You must do exactly what your guides instruct you.' We were divided into groups of 20, each headed by an 'elder' who was to keep in touch with the Berikha instructors. There were more than 100 people in our place, but we were told that there were several such staging points in this area.

A room with some beds was assigned to us. We prepared to sleep there fully dressed in case we had to move during this night should a new major crisis develop, although the previous crisis was not due to an external cause. It came from within our own family. On this last night before leaving Poland, our mother had suddenly had a radical change of mind. After talking quietly in the corner with our father, she lay down on one of the beds and proclaimed in a determined voice: 'I am not getting up from here! I am not leaving for an uncertain future abroad! You are young people, strong and healthy – you will manage in Palestine. I and my husband, we are old and ill – how shall we live in this poor, desert country. You go, whereas your father and me, we shall somehow find a way to live in this country which we know and speak its language. In any case, I am not going over the border.'

We, my brothers and I, were thunderstruck. Our mother's outburst was totally unexpected. True, we knew our mother as a very proud and independent person. She often declared: 'I would rather be dead than have to depend on the charity of anyone – including my own children!' There were some sad cases in our own family. For example, my grandmother on my father's side was widowed when I was a child in our home town of Yaroslav. I remembered how she was ill-treated by their own elder son: she was ejected by her eldest son and heir from her own house and removed from our grandfather's business. She lived then in a small, dark, rented room and was dependent on the support of her children. Often, however, this was not forthcoming and she knew degrading poverty. Many a time on Friday afternoon my mother gave me a bag with some food and cakes baked for the Sabbath; father then produced a five zloty banknote (quite some money at that time). With these riches in hand I marched off and brought it to our grandmother. I remembered quite well her wrinkled face and dry hands as well as a tear in her eye when she kissed me and thanked for these much-needed goods. There were some other more serious cases; there were no old age pensions and no social welfare arrangements in pre-war Poland.

All our efforts to persuade our mother to go with us were of no avail. She stuck stubbornly to her statement that she would remain in Poland. The more we argued, the more intransigent she became: 'All through those terrible years of the war, of the Germans, Siberia, Central Asia we held fast together as one family – and now when we go to Israel we shall break up?', we asked. We promised to help, we argued that Palestine was not such a poor desert country, that as we had managed everywhere else we would manage there as well – nothing. Then a break came from an unexpected quarter: Ruthie, our little ten year old sister started crying – at first quietly in the corner then out loud. Nothing we did could stop her crying. All of us loved her, and my mother above all. Mother got up from the bed and said: 'Our sages said that God speaks through the mouth of little children. We shall ask Ruthie – what she says, we shall do.' While continuing to cry, Ruthie explained: 'I do not want to part with anyone, with my brothers ... I want us to go together.'

Within an hour we received the signal. We took our bundles and suitcases and lined up outside in the darkness and total silence. We were to begin our long journey of almost three years until we all gathered together in Israel.

This was a very lucky night. It was possible to bring one truck quite close to the border-crossing in the woody hills. So we did not have to carry our heavy luggage all the way. We walked in small groups very quietly, stopping and moving on until close to the border itself. There we recovered our luggage from the truck – not without some difficulty in the darkness. One elderly man dropped his suitcase; not only did it make a loud boom in the silent wood but he issued a huge yelp. Our group had to wait tensely for more than an hour until we got the signal to move again. Some people were arguing because they had mixed up their luggage in the darkness. After several hours, we arrived at last at a road along which we came to what seemed to us clearly to be a border post with a striped barrier in front. Inside some military people could be seen sitting and drinking with some civilians, among whom some of our Berikha people could be recognised. Quietly the guides passed the word: 'You passed the Polish border. These are Czech border police – not to worry. They have instructions to let you through.'

A collective sigh of relief could be heard. We knew that also on the Polish side instructions came down to the border authorities to close their eyes to the 'illegal' outflow of Jews. In addition, the guards themselves were heavily bribed. Yet, sometimes a local commander took a tough line: people were caught, held for some time, forced back into Poland and the Berikha guides were arrested. Our column passed without a hitch. We were out of Poland!

On the Czech side, police and authorities were friendly. We were led to a place where food and drinks were served and we were able to sleep a little after a sleepless night. Late in the afternoon, a long train arrived; this time it was an old passenger train and without guards on it. Our Berikha instructors briefed us again: 'You will now be going through Czechoslovakia, the Soviet zone of Austria and into the Soviet part of Vienna. These areas are packed with Russian troops who must not know who you are, especially about those of you who came out from the Soviet Union. All documents and photos, especially those with Russian markings or content, must be got rid of … You are travelling now with collective papers which testify that you are Greeks from eastern Europe being repatriated to Greece. The Soviets might make a search, and anything which could be found to be contrary to that, might endanger our entire train.'

'But', asked someone, 'if they talk to us, how shall we answer them?'

'You act like you don't understand Russian, or any other language, except for Greek', the Berikha man answered.

'But we do not know Greek!' said the same person in exasperation.

'Neither does any of the Soviet officers who might talk with you ... But you surely remember some of your Hebrew prayers. In Ashkenazic pronunciation it sounds very much like Greek, I assure you .'

The train started moving and the 'search and destroy' operation began: a tragedy after so many tragedies. With tears in her eyes an elderly woman was tearing up photos of her husband in the uniform of a Soviet general. 'He was a hero and fell at Stalingrad', she explained.

A bewildered middle-aged, intelligent-looking fellow argued: 'I have here my engineer's diploma from a technical university in Kiev. How shall I be able get work in my profession without a diploma?'

In our family we consulted quietly and decided to destroy those of our photos and papers that might be most compromising if discovered. The rest of the material, including my diploma so miraculously gained from Kazakhstan University and my younger brother's matriculation certificate, we packed into a little bag. We set up a constant watch at the window of our compartment. We reasoned that in such a way we would be forewarned about a possible search by Soviet officers. If we saw such a search coming, we would then dispose of the compromising bag. But why destroy it in advance? As it happened, there was no search, the important documents and photos remained with us. With these in hand we were later able to work as teachers and enter university studies in Israel.

Next day, disaster struck! Our train was parked at a small railway station already within the Soviet occupation zone of Austria. Our people were busy with their morning chores – washing, eating breakfast, talking to each other. Suddenly, a huge train pulled up just opposite us, on the next platform. Oh horror, the train was packed with Soviet soldiers and officers – no more than two metres from us. Two of the officers next to us looked at us for some time and then came to the opening of our carriage. One of them greeted us in Russian. We pretended not to understand and just made queer movements with our shoulders. The Soviets did not give up and talked to us again. Remembering our instructions, one in our carriage started spouting a well-known Hebrew prayer, kaddish: *'Yisgadal ve yiskadash ...'* Suddenly, the elder of the two Soviet officers opened up: *'shmei raba bealma'*. We were stunned – he continued to say the prayer with excitement. Then he said: 'You can't fool me. *Ihr zayt yidden* (You are Jews (in Yiddish))'. We could not pretend any more. We took them aside and told them the truth, including that we hoped to get to Palestine. 'Some of us are survivors from the camps, some survived in Russia ... As you are Jews, we beseech you by all that is holy to you not to divulge our secret', we begged them. By that time some other Russian military were walking close by. The two officers whispered: 'Godspeed! *Furt gezund und kumt dort gezund* (go in health and arrive there in good health)' – and they were gone. A great sigh of relief went up when our train moved out of the station without being molested at all. The Jewish Soviet officers kept our secret.

When I opened my eyes next morning, I saw massive fine buildings, squares with statues, huge elegant shops – our train had entered Vienna. This was the first time I had seen a major European city. Despite the war, Vienna remained largely intact. It had been the capital city of a major empire for centuries. Vienna held a special place in the hearts of our family. During their youth, both my parents lived in southern Poland which had then been under the Hapsburg Empire. My father spent the years of the First World War in Vienna. I visited Warsaw briefly when we lived in Lodz; it was in total ruin, and even before the war it could hardly compare with the major European capitals. Unfortunately, I was able only to have a glimpse of Vienna from the window of our train and when passing through its streets while moving from place to place. We had no individual papers and could not move freely around the city.

From the Soviet zone of Vienna we were quickly moved to the Rothschild Hospital in that part of the city which was then under American military administration. Here, for the first time in our lives, we encountered American military personnel. Compared with Soviet military we knew, they looked like people from another planet: even the ordinary soldiers wore fine military uniforms (only officers had such in the Soviet army). They had quality shoes, good-looking vehicles which did not stink of low - grade petrol. They were well-groomed and more relaxed. Little did we know at the time that, in the future, we were to have some far from pleasant encounters with the American military.

Within the fine, massive Rothschild building utter chaos reigned. The building was not able to cope with the major influx of Jewish refugees from the east. There were not enough rooms, beds, toilets or showers. People were lying with their bundles everywhere: in the corridors, entrance halls and even on the wide front steps. The rooms were packed beyond capacity. Huge queues were pushing and shoving in front of the various facilities – showers, toilets, administration offices, eating places. Some Berikha men and local administrators were moving around the groups trying in vain to bring some order into this chaos. People were milling around, searching for acquaintances, inquiring after lost relatives and friends. In some corners business was going on: people were exhibiting all kinds of goods for sale, valuables were being exchanged for US dollars and Austrian money, all kinds of tinned food was on offer. At all times of day and night, new groups of people were arriving and others were leaving. It was almost impossible to sleep amidst this constant commotion. At the same time we were not allowed to go freely out of the building; it was not safe, we had no papers and the whole operation was supposed to be kept under wraps, otherwise the coming out of other Jews from the East might be endangered.

After a few days in this madhouse our group was quite pleased to learn that were going to be moved somewhere else. Trucks arrived and we were driven through ever more hilly terrain and winding roads until we arrived at an empty barracks compound in the mountains next to a small lake. A tall officer came forward and announced: 'You are now under an American military administration, in the American zone of Austria'. At last, we were under American protection.

22 • From a Former Nazi Death Camp to an American Military Camp

During the first few days we were quite elated: after the constant din and bustle of the 'Rothchild Hospital', this quiet, small Ebensee camp in the mountains appeared a fine place indeed. We walked in the surrounding woods and meadows, enjoying the sunshine and the fresh mountain air. On one of these walks we found some rather strange-looking structures behind our barracks in the thickets in the wood. They looked like ovens – only the hole in the middle was not as wide as a normal bread baking oven, and the length of it was about that of a man. How great was our horror when we realized that these were actually incinerators for buring human bodies!

Our horrible suspicion was confirmed soon enough by the tales of the inhabitants of the closest village, so much so that the administrators of the camp had to formally admit that this 'beautiful mountain campus' had been a vicious Nazi extermination concentration camp. We immediately decided that we would not stay at this place of horror. When the American Military Administration did not respond to our demand to leave, we proclaimed a sit-in strike and threatened to begin a hunger strike. We sent word to the 'Berikha' people in Vienna about our situation, and they indicated that we should demand to be moved to the American zone of Germany where large numbers of Jewish refugees were being relocated. After several days of our strike, three people arrived at the camp at Ebensee: an officer representing the American Army, an American Military rabbi, and a representative of the JOINT (a Jewish-American Charitable Organisation). They promised that we would be transferred to the American zone in Germany.

A few days later a column of military trucks arrived – and we were off. After a drive of several hours, the trucks halted at a large, green field with rows of military tents on it. We were told to line up in front of a long, green tent which turned out to be the administration headquarters. An American officer addressed us briefly: 'You are now in the American Zone of Germany, near the town of Landshut. After registration here, you will receive some food and the necessary equipment and be directed to a tent. You will stay here for some time until proper accommodation can be found for you … I would like to warn you to keep order and hygiene at this place. Meanwhile, you have no papers and you must not go outside the perimeter of this camp. Any infringement of the rules will be severely punished.'

Trouble soon started. The Americans were not prepared for such a large number of people. They thought they could run a huge mass of civilians – including women, children and many ill and elderly – much like a military camp. The trucks stopped at a considerable distance from the administration headquarters and the tents allotedto us were far away. There was no assistance and no carts. Yet some of the families had heavy luggage with them. Registration took a long time and the food and equipment added weight to our luggage. The sun was hot and the field was partly wet and slippery. At the administration tent we were given American military canvas beds with wooden handles; they were heavy and difficult to put up. By the time we were set up in our tent, we were hot, sweaty and exhausted. We became very thirsty, – but the water tap was some distance from the tent, and the fluid in it was warm and brown. As it happened, we were still the lucky ones; those from the later trucks had to wait in the sun until some more tents had been put up, in some cases only in the evening. Some of the younger people soon organized voluntary help; yet the families with children, the elderly and the sick suffered badly.

After several days in this camp, the situation became impossible. More and more people arrived – all of them Jewish refugees like us. The queues everywhere became longer and longer – at the field kitchens which supplied us with one warm meal a day, at the supply tent which provided us with bread and canned food, at the administration tent, at the makeshift showers. Worst of all was the situation at the toilets: these were field latrines, with a hole in the ground. The smell and the flies were overwhelming. Sometimes one had to wait up to an hour to get in; due to overcrowding and lack of sanitation the place was often full of excrement. Rains came and turned much of the field into a bog. Strong winds damaged and in some cases blew over some of the tents; people in them and their few belongings got drenched. The electric field generators broke down from time to time due to over-loading, and we found ourselves in total darkness.

Again, some American army officers and military rabbis arrived and asked us to be patient since places were being made ready for us. But as the days passed the weather turned colder and the situation at the camp grew increasingly worse. Eventually, one day, huge crowds of embittered people were milling through the main field of the camp shouting abuse at the administration officers. The guards attempted to push back the crowd, some of them quite brutally. The same afternoon a general meeting was called and several thousands attended (by that time about 5,000 lived in the camp). A general hunger strike was declared and a delegation was elected to go to Munich to present our case before the US military authorities and before the Jewish Council of Germany located there. What enraged people most of all was the realization that many former Nazis went on living in great comfort in their fine houses, even in the vicinity of our camp and we, many of us Holocaust survivors and victims of Nazi persecution, had to stay in a boggy field, in tents, in the sun and rain with our infirm people and children.

Next morning, a large crowd gathered again at the administration tent shouting in unison the demand to be moved out of the camp. Suddenly, a column of jeeps appeared from behind the long tent. The jeeps drove directly into the crowd almost crushing some of the people who shouted angrily. Then out of the jeeps jumped huge police officers with white wooden batons in their hand and started to beat people right and left.

I could not believe my eyes. I was at the other end of the crowd but could see distinctly: American police were mercilessly beating Jews, civilian refugees, survivors of the Holocaust! And why? Just because they demanded to be moved out, away from the inhuman conditions of the camp. Surprising as it may appear, I had never witnessed large-scale violence. I had seen some incidents of cruel violence under the Germans – but these were against individuals. Soviet violence was usually covert and unseen. I was utterly shaken by the mass brutality of the military police. This was how AMERICANS treated us!? Not far away a tall, helmeted officer was flaying an elderly Jew who was running away. He slipped, fell into the boggy ground, his hat fell off and he shielded his head with his arms to ward off the blows.

That same afternoon we decided to leave this camp on our

own. Luck came our way. My elder brother, Lemmel, had a fiancée, Hannah, who was in another group of refugees. We learned from visitors to our camp that she and her family were in a permanent camp in Wetzlar near Frankfurt, to the north of us. Lemmel travelled there by train and returned after two days with a very positive report: 'The camp there is situated in a former German armoured forces campus. The buildings are of concrete, with large rooms; the roads are of asphalt. There are several thousand Jewish refugees there. But with the help of Hannah's family a large room with a window is being kept for us. The camp is on the outskirts of a fine town, not far from a railway station, and conditions there are entirely favourable. So we had better move immediately, in order not to lose the room.'

We were very eager to leave this hapless camp and its administration were glad to get rid of as many of us as possible. On receiving travel papers, we moved to the nearest railway station the next day. Towards the evening we arrived at the camp in Wetzlar. Here, however, a rather unpleasant surprise awaited us – the room which had supposedly been reserved for us had been occupied by a middle-aged couple with two small children. Hannah's family explained that when they arrived there the previous evening they found this family already there and nothing could be done about it. Bitterly disappointed and in a bleak mood we went to sleep there – our parents and little sister in the room of Hannah's family and we, the boys, in the corridor.

Next day, after much shouting, threats and yelling, the camp authorities made a classic Solomonic judgement: the large room was to be divided in the middle by a canvas partition. Fortunately, the entrance door had two wings so that it was possible to enter each part without having to pass through the other. The camp administration stressed that this was just a temporary measure and they would move us to a room of our own 'as soon as one became available'. They never did.

So we found ourselves again in a makeshift abode – the seventh in as many years since the beginning of the Second World War. It was a long, narrow space partitioned by the canvas through which we could hear our neighbours shouting at each other (they frequently enjoyed doing this) and the children's crying, night and day. On the right side we placed two beds against the partition; in one slept my mother and our little sister, in the other our father slept. We, the three boys, had each night to put up camp beds on which we slept. In another bloc we found a small, old table and some chairs and we triumphantly installed them in our 'room'. Toilets and washrooms were in the corridor, for the use of six families. Accommodation here was not much better than that which we had in Siberia, though there were fewer bugs. Actually, in Semipalatinsk in Central Asia we had had a small house to ourselves.

In other matters, however, there was no comparison. As we soon found out, the Displaced Persons' camp in Wetzlar was in fact something like a 'Jewish autonomy'. There was an administration building in which an American commanding officer was installed. He was rarely seen and kept a low profile. Real running of the affairs of the camp was very much in the hands of the UNRRA (United Nations Relief and Rehabilitation Administration) officer. The American army and UNRRA jointly supported the camp and supplied us with food rations and clothing. Then there was a representative of the Jewish Agency for Palestine, a body of the World Zionist Organization. They were usually Palestinian Jews, often from the veterans of the Jewish Brigade which fought against Nazi Germany as part of the British forces. Then there was an agent of the influential American–Jewish charitable organization 'Joint' which supplemented the meagre food and clothing rations supplied at the camp and took special care of the needs of the children, the sick and the elderly. Usually the Jewish Agency emissary (*shaliach* in Hebrew) was dressed in a uniform similar to the American military, with a Star of David on the arm and cap. To the camp inhabitants the emissary was closest, a whiff of the Land of Israel, a representative of the Haganah, the self-defence underground movement there.

To provide order and protection there was a unit of Camp Police in dark blue uniforms with the Star of David on their caps and breasts. It was entirely composed of our camp inmates and under a DP commandant appointed by the administration. The German police had no right to enter the camp without the permission of the administration. During public holidays, camp festivities and demonstrations, the police unit marched like a military unit with a Jewish flag and with commands in Hebrew.

On the DP side, there was a Representative Council with a chairman and other officers. The members were periodically elected, and there were quite edgy election contests between the various political groups in the camp. Because, in accordance with the hallowed Jewish tradition, there developed all kinds and shades of parties and groups in the camp from 'Hashomer

Hatzair' on the far left, through the social democratic 'Mapai-Dror', the general liberal 'Hanoar Hatzioni-Akiba' group, through to the right-wing 'Betar-Revisionist' movement. Apart from these, there were various religious, sport, women's, art and entertainment clubs and organizations. Our camp numbered some 4,500 Jews, and it had more than 45 of these groups. The camp had a very intensive political and social life.

Surprisingly, there were many children in the camp. We asked for permission and support to open a school. The administration gave useful support and within several weeks it started functioning. No division developed as to the character of the school – there were few ultra-orthodox or yiddishist Bundists in our camp. The school was of an obviously Hebrew, Zionist, traditional character. It soon turned out that among our camp dwellers there were a number of professional teachers and highly educated specialists who were able to teach. A former teacher at a Hebrew High school in Riga and his brother were appointed principal and his deputy. I had already a B.Ed. from a Soviet college and knew Hebrew from my childhood in Yaroslav. My younger brother, Moshe, and a few of the other former teachers also had some knowledge of Hebrew. It was, however, impossible to teach the other subjects in Hebrew – maths, geography, history, chemistry and so on. Neither the teachers nor the pupils knew enough of the language, so we had to compromise and teach in whatever was practical, mostly Russian and Polish.

'Salaries' were no problem. DPs did not work outside the camp. But the camp management and we ourselves were interested in inhabitants having some work within the camp. Practically all those who were willing to work found some employment. On the other side of the camp there were huge hangars which had been used by the German army for their armoured vehicles. They were turned into warehouses for the supplies for the camp. Some craftsmen – cobblers, tailors, seamstresses – opened their little shops there. Since there were no washing machines in the rooms, a huge laundry functioned in the camp. The management did not have funds to pay for work. But all those working – in the police, camp administration, school, health clinic, warehouses as well as the cleaners within the blocs and in the public areas of the camp – all of them received additional rations of food and clothing which aptly supplemented their meagre regular supplies.

My brother, Lemmel, was a professional driver in Russia and secured a driving licence from the authorities in Wetzlar. Soon he found worthwhile work as the driver of the UNRRA lady manager of the camp. But my father had nothing to do and all these combined 'salaries' still did not amount to much. Some of the camp inhabitants indulged in all kinds of 'non-kosher' activities. The black market was flourishing in post-war Germany: dollars, American cigarettes, gold, meat, coffee, butter, furs and other items were the objects in a lively 'unofficial' commerce. Our father would not have anything to do with this kind of activity. But he certainly needed some kind of 'business', something to do and earn some money so as not to live entirely off the sons' 'bounty'.

There were no shops whatsoever within the camp. Yet we noticed that there was a great interest in getting the newspapers and journals as well as in writing paper, envelopes, writing utensils and postage stamps. Apart from the newspapers in German and English which were then published in Germany, many publications in Yiddish appeared for the growing number of Jewish DPs there. They were in Hebrew script but mostly in Yiddish written in Roman script, since many did not know Hebrew and it was difficult after the Nazi period to find printing firms able to print the Hebrew characters . The leaders of the camp prohibited any commerce within its confines, but were interested that the inhabitants should have some reading material available. They were prepared therefore to tolerate something like a make-shift 'newspaper stand' inside the camp.

Our camp was actually composed of two parts. One contained almost all the housing blocs; in the other part the administration and warehouses were located. The two were connected by a narrow, covered passage, through which many pedestrians used to pass. It was there that from time to time groups of people congregated. There was not a single café, restaurant, bar or pub within the camp. One sunny morning my father and I marched from our bloc towards the passage carrying two benches and some bundles of newspapers. We put down the benches inside the passage, spread out the newspapers and were ready for business – we did not know how our venture would be received. It was a success from the start. Previously, a newspaper in German or English was available only in the centre of the nearby town of Wetzlar, some two kilometres from our camp. As for a Jewish one, it was possible to get it only in Frankfurt or Munich. Now all this was available inside the camp. Also, the publications were inexpensive, especially the Jewish ones. Within an hour and a half all our newspapers were sold out. Highly pleased with the result of our 'pilot' sales experiment we lifted our benches and went home.

From that day we continued with this informal newspaper stand until leaving the camp. We extended the business to include some glossy and more expensive journals and small books, writing pads and notebooks, maps, pencils and pens, and so on. The administration did not interfere: they only asked us not to put up our benches on days when some representative from the authorities was visiting. On the other hand they never agreed to give us a formal permit or to allow us to erect a permanent stand of any kind. As the business expanded, we could not get enough paper and stationery supplies in Wetzlar. So once every week or two we travelled by train to Frankfurt and lugged back a full, heavy rucksack containing these supplies. The 'newspaper stand' did not bring much profit; but it certainly gave our father something to do. He became well known in the camp; people used to buy papers, look at the headlines and discuss the latest news on the spot; and the 'stand' did supplement our income considerably.

Nobody was as happy about our 'newspaper business' as I. I had always been always fascinated by current affairs. When I was a child in Poland we did not have newspapers at home. So I used to stand in the street and read the front pages of the papers on the kiosks or go to the dentist a good hour before the appointed time and read the papers in his waiting room. While we lived in the camp, major events in the struggle around Eretz Israel were taking place. I followed these with immense interest, and here I had all these newspapers in my home – and they cost me nothing.

23 • At a DP Camp in Germany – A Zionist Youth Movement and the 'Hagana'

'Wider vi amool
hoin hyiant in Yisruel
arbet dos Yiddele
zeks tog in der wokh…
Di zyidelekh, di babelekh, di tatelekh, di mamelekh,
mit yingelekh un meideleekh,
lebn zikh shoin wider fryi.'*

A virtual spiritual revolution was shaking our innermost thoughts, feelings, our very identity. During the long and extremely intensive seven years when we had lived in the Soviet Union, we had been the object of a most concentrated Soviet-communist 'education'. It is difficult to fathom how thorough and intensive it was; sufficient to mention that it was at the height of the Stalin era, during the Second World War. The last years of our stay in Russia saw great Soviet victories which were of decisive importance for the fate of all mankind. These had a major impact on us, yet it took only a few months outside Russia for our convictions to change completely – we became ardently Jewish and Zionist.

Within me personally a far-reaching metamorphosis occurred over the course of only several months. In May of that year I was still an exemplary student of Marxism–Leninism in a Soviet communist college. By the end of the year, I was a teacher of Hebrew at a Jewish school and a leader in a Zionist youth movement.

---

*'Just like in ancient times already today in Israel the Jew works six days in a week … Grandfathers and grandmothers, daddies and mummies, with boys and girls, live free again.' (One of my mother's Yiddish songs.)

A more in-depth analysis shows a somewhat different picture.Before we found ourselves under Soviet rule, we were immersed in a Zionist youth organisation with which we fully identified: we sang the Hebrew songs, danced the *hora*, attended pro-Israel activities, parades, celebrations and a summer camp which had a profound impact on us. Furthermore – and what was, above all, decisive – we were never really taken in by the communist convictions. Outwardly we parroted the official line, since this was the only way to survive, or study, but inwardly we rejected it totally. Though it was dangerous, even in the Siberian camp we sang 'Zionist' songs (in Hebrew – we explained that they were Jewish folk songs). We even talked about a 'country of our own' within the family and with our closest friends. Finally, the several months of anti-Semitism in communist-ruled Poland and the fuller awareness of the Holocaust which hit us at that point – all this combined caused a transformation within us. After all, we fell back on our pre-war innermost selves. The entire formal Soviet communist shell fell off like a discarded shroud.

As mentioned in the previous chapter, Zionist youth groups soon sprouted in our DP camp in Wetzlar. One of those was a continuation of the youth movement to which we belonged before the war. It was called 'Hanoar Hatzioni-Akiva' (Zionist youth named after the great Jewish sage, martyr and supporter of the Bar Kochba revolt against the Romans in the second century CE). I and both my brothers joined this group, and as I knew Hebrew and was the 'educated' one I soon became the leader of this group in Wetzlar. Our group turned out to be one of the largest in the country; so I became a member of the movement's Supreme Council for all Germany located in Munich.

Our youth group, which numbered almost 100 youngsters, engaged in a full programme of activities. We had study circles on Jewish history, Hebrew, the geography of Eretz Israel, Zionism, and so forth. On the Sabbath and Jewish holidays we had a general 'parade', festive evenings with sing-songs and Israeli folk dancing (salon dancing was regarded as bourgeois and not allowed). As this was a period of major day-to-day dramatic events around the Palestine issue, we followed these develop-ments avidly. We held frequent demonstrations and marches with demands for 'free Jewish immigration to Palestine' and 'a Jewish state in Eretz Israel'. On 'national days' (like the Herzl day in July) and 'days of protest' (for example, upon the turning away of the illegal immigration ship *Exodus* from the shores of Palestine back to Germany) the entire camp population marched around and gathered for a mass meeting in front of the camp administration. At the head marched the Jewish Camp Police with a small orchestra, followed by the various youth groups and adult detachments – the school-teachers with their pupils, the war veterans, the fire brigade, the warehouse and camp employees, and so on.

Above each column the white and blue flag fluttered, with the Star of David in the centre. We carried huge slogans, sang and chanted in unison, and demanded that a member of the American camp administration come out and listen to our demands. We listened to some fiery speeches by our spokesmen: 'Free Jewish immigration to Palestine! End the British Mandate immediately! A State of Israel in the Land of Israel!'

Some months after our arrival at the Wetzlar camp, a national 'jamboree' of Zionist youth was announced. It was held at a huge DP camp at Landshut, near Munich. Several dozens of our group participated in it, and it was an unforgettable experience. There must have been more than 1,000 young people there. For several days we were in 'delirious heaven': we sang in huge choirs of hundreds of people, we sat around fires in the surrounding woods late into the night, we had addresses by some prominent people including 'emissaries' from the Land of Israel. We met again with young people we had known and made many new friends. The final parade made a great impression on us. Huge columns of our Zionist scouts were arranged around a large field. A small orchestra of bugles and drums played Israeli and Jewish tunes, and hundreds of us sang with it. At the sound of a single bugle, a huge white and blue Jewish flag was raised on a tall pole in the centre. After a brief address by the principal leader of our movement, a memorial service for those who had perished in the Holocaust and in Soviet camps and prisons was held. We also honoured the memory of those of our people who fell in Eretz in defence of the Yishuv. Finally, all of us stood to attention and sang the national anthem 'Hatikva'. This final parade ended with a march past a small stand with our leaders and prominent guests.

Less than one year ago I had been at a Soviet college all wrapped up in Marxism–Leninism, Revolution, the Red Flag … Zionism was regarded a state crime, Jewishness was completely suppressed. At this Zionist youth jamboree, more than anywhere else, I was filled with a sense of wonder and disbelief: 'What I see with my own eyes – is it true?' It was light years away from the world I had been in only several months back.

A few months later we ran a large summer camp for our youth organization in a forest to the north of our camp. It was again a significant formative experience for me. At this camp I was one of the scout masters responsible for the teaching programme. It was there that I became involved in a hitherto unknown activity – the Haganah, the 'underground' Israeli defence organization. The camp itself, with several hundred young Jews, had to have some form of defence in case of incident. We did not entirely trust the local German police and the American military would not provide us with a GI guard. As the fighting in Palestine was becoming more frequent and it looked as if an overall military conflict mightdevelop there, the Haganah intensified its preparatory work not only in Israel but abroad as well. In Germany alone there were many thousands of young Jews, many of them with previous military experience. The Haganah therefore sent some 'emissaries' of its own to Europe and especially to Germany. These 'emissaries' started their own training programme within the existing Jewish youth movements, schools, the camp police, and so forth. Gradually, an entire network of 'unofficial' Haganah groups developed.

The UN resolution on the partition of Palestine and creation of a Jewish state had a profound impact on the refugees in the DP camps. It was a great national Jewish victory, but to us it confirmed the promise of finally getting out of the DP camps and going 'home' to Israel. Our elation at this news was soon overshadowed by the sad news of Arab attacks on Jews in Palestine. As the numbers of Jewish victims mounted and the fighting spread, our Haganah activities increased in intensity. In early spring of 1948, when it became clear that the British were going to withdraw and that the Arab countries would make war on the fledgling Jewish state, the underground Haganah command in the DP camps in Europe decided on 'mobilization'. We 'proclaimed' that the 'Jewish people in Eretz Israel are in mortal danger, and that it is our duty to prevent another Holocaust from happening'.

On the practical side, a call for 'volunteers for Israel' was made, and groups of these volunteers were being taken to several training centres in southern Germany. Officially, these centres were run as 'youth colonies'. After a period of training, the groups moved under various covers towards the Mediterranean shores of France or Italy to await shipment to Palestine – legal or illegal. As the situation in Eretz became desperate, we devised measures to 'induce' more and more young people to become volunteers. At that time I was mostly in Munich, working as member of the command of the Zionist Youth in Germany. We accepted a ruling that from each family with young males at least one should go to Israel to join the Haganah. Bitter feelings arose between those families from which youngsters went to fight for Israel and those families with young people who did not enlist.

Much as in other camps, an unofficial 'mobilization command' was established. It included local leaders, war veterans, fathers of volunteers who had left for Israel and young people who had enlisted. Teams worked their way through the camp and brought in the youngsters who did not enlist for a 'chat' with members of the 'mobilization command'. Those who refused, or excessively prolonged their decision were then hauled from their rooms late at night to attend an 'investigation'. They were first blindfolded and then kept in a dark room in total silence for an hour or two. Thereafter they were led into a darkened room where members of the 'mobilization command' were seated behind a table covered with an Israeli flag. On the table a Bible and a revolver were placed. A reflector light was shone in the face of the unwilling visitor, but he could not see the faces of those sitting behind the table.

The 'visitor' was commanded to stand to attention and answer all questions truthfully and briefly: 'There are several young people in your family; why did not a single one enrol? ... The Jewish people in Eretz are fighting a life or death battle – are you just going to standby?' If the respondent argued that his parents would not let him or gave some other 'excuse', the members would counter 'My parents opposed my enrolment but I was determined and they gave me their blessing.' The veterans would recall the fighting against the Nazis; news about the latest onslaughts of the Arabs were read.

If the youngster declared himself willing to enrol, he was made to put one hand on the Bible, raise the other hand and say: 'I ... solemnly swear to enrol to fight for the Jewish people in the Land of Israel.' He then signed a personal enlistment declaration. If he refused, he was repeatedly harassed and labelled a 'shirker'. Ultimately, nothing more was done; he was left alone.

At our Zionist Youth command we all volunteered at the very beginning of 'mobilization'. However, the 'command' and the Haganah decided that we were not all allowed to leave at once: 'We have thousands of youngsters under 18 years old in the

Zionist Youth Movement and at Hebrew schools – all this will collapse if you all leave together ... We are not interested in mobilizing several dozen youth leaders – we need you to mobilize thousands of others.' It was therefore decided that we would leave gradually, one or two with each major group. My own enrolment was scheduled to be about six months later.

In our family, we were three sons. My elder brother was married already, and my younger brother was engaged to marry soon, so I was the obvious candidate for volunteering – in line with the demand 'one from each family'. Yet my immediate enrolment was forbidden by the 'command'. Due to the great pressure of work I was now living mainly in Munich, in an apartment rented by the movement. But as the weeks passed, a strange feeling developed within me, like an illness. I could not go on with our work, I was virtually incapacitated. Events around Eretz became increasingly dramatic. All around, volunteering and 'mobilization' was going on, with groups of young people moving through Munich on their way to the fighting in Israel. I felt like a 'shirker' when I had to explain that I could not leave yet because the 'command' would not release me. In the middle of April I returned to our DP camp in Wetzlar. The situation there was both elated and very tense. Everyone felt that in Palestine the time of decision was near; 'mobilization' was in full swing. The entire camp was taking leave from a major group of young men and women who volunteered, many of them from our Zionist Youth movement, my own pupils and trainees. A mass meeting was called at the central square of the camp to say goodbye to the departing volunteers. They stood there with their backpacks and coats in hand, ready to leave for the railway station. They were surrounded by members of their families, by friends and sweethearts. They were crying, shaking hands, hugging and kissing,. One of the camp leaders spoke, then one of the parents: 'We have gone through the Holocaust and Stalin's camps. Many of us fell while fighting the Nazis. Now we are called to fight for the Jewish people, for a state of our own – so that we shall never have a Holocaust and never be homeless again ... May God keep you and bless you and grant you victory.'

I felt that I could not hold back any more. I went up to the podium and announced there and then that I would be going with the next group of volunteers from our camp. I issued a call to my friends in the camp to join me so that a large number would be going.

My family was rather shaken by my decision, especially my mother, as I was her 'favourite', but nothing could change my resolution to go. I went to Munich and told our 'command' about my decision. Over a period of several days they tried to persuade me to delay my departure but eventually they gave in. I returned to Wetzlar elated, as if a heavy burden had been removed from my shoulders. No more procrastinating, no more 'explanations', no more delays – at last I was going to Israel!

24 • *To Israel – Like Thieves in the Night*

'Tam, tam, u Jerozolim bram
zakwitnie wolnos'c' nam.'*

I returned to Wetzlar. An intensive period of gathering a new group of volunteers started, and after several weeks a group was ready. The news from Eretz was ominous – the Jewish forces had had some successes – but the threat of an all-out war with the Arab countries became more real. We went through a round of tearful farewell meetings; a large crowd went to see us off at the railway station. When the train arrived we all sang 'Hatikva' at the top of our voices. German police and railway officials came running, not knowing what to make of it (all forms of public demonstration were then strictly forbidden in Germany). An explanation was given to them: 'We are singing because some Jews here are going to Palestine.'

We travelled to the south of Germany where we entered a Haganah training camp, which was officially presented as a recreation camp for young people from DP camps. The regime there was strict and quite spartan. We were woken at 5 o'clock in the morning to run in the surrounding woods and for an hour of physical exercise. It was often still dark and cold. Most of us were naked from the waist upward. The woods around reverberated from the running, singing and shouting of hundreds of us (there were more than 600 altogether). After washing with cold water and a quick breakfast we lined up for morning parade at 7 o'clock. During the day we engaged intermittently in marching, judo exercises, fighting with big sticks, physical combat, climbing, crawling and jumping through various barriers. Although it was absolutely forbidden, we had some weapons, mainly revolvers,

---

'There, there, at Jerusalem's gate, freedom will blossom for us.' (One of my mother's Polish songs.)

hidden in the camp. So we had some weapons instruction and practice – shooting in secluded places. All of this was mainly run and supervised by some Haganah and Berikha 'emissaries' (the latter were members of an underground branch of the Haganah which specialised in the illegal transfer of people through the borders of Europe). In the late afternoon and evenings we had educational programmes: Hebrew, history of the Jewish people, of the Zionist Movement and the Yishuv, geography of Israel, talks by our leaders and readings of the latest news. In the evening, fires were lit and we spent some time singing under the stars. At 8 p.m. we had to go to sleep, to be able to get up at 5 o'clock the next morning. All went to sleep apart from those on night duty; guards and patrols were posted around the camp, both for security and for training purposes.

From time to time we had some major celebration such as when a group was leaving for Eretz, or when some important visitors came. But all the time we were training, we were waiting for the signal to leave. Sometime in the middle of June it arrived. We were to move within a week. I was allowed to go to Wetzlar to bid farewell to my family. They were extremely pleased and quite surprised as they had not expected to see me after my departure for the training camp. It turned out that my father, because he suffered badly from asthma, had been provided by the Joint with a several week-long recuperative stay in the Bavarian mountain resort of Bad Reichenhall. I travelled there sitting at a window of the train, gazing out at the enchanting countryside, hills, woods, flowers, meadows, beautiful villages and townships … and wondering: 'So this is the area where Hitler had his headquarters. What did people here miss that they had to go to war and bring disaster to others and to themselves … And now we have to go far away to fight another war.' I shall never forget how, on saying goodbye to my father, there were large tears rolling down his cheeks. We had gone through all kinds of terrible times, but I had never before seen my father cry.

At last the day of our departure arrived, after some five weeks of waiting. We were taken by trucks to the railway station at Munich and boarded a special passenger train. However, something appeared to be wrong. We waited for hours, but still the train did not move. Then suddenly, a number of vehicles of the American Military Police parked alongside our train. A number of baton-wielding, white-helmeted MPs ran to our train shouting 'Out! Out!' When at first we did not move, they entered the carriages and started to push people from the train and beat them with their batons. It turned out that this was as a result of the UN Security Council restrictions imposed on the transportation of military reinforcements to 'both sides in the Palestine conflict'. The American Military administration in south Germany, under British pressure, had decided that we were such 'military reinforcements' and acted to prevent us from leaving.

We were shocked and bewildered: 'Can it be that we shall not be able to leave?' But soon our leaders were moving quietly from one carriage to another: 'Do not oppose the MPs. Leave the train in an orderly fashion. We shall wait for another opportunity to go.' The same night a long column of covered trucks lined up in front of the building in which we had been temporarily placed. In total silence, group after group boarded the trucks, the covers were put down so that from the outside there was no sign of their human cargo, and we moved off. We travelled in the dark, in total silence for several hours along bumpy sideroads. Then we stopped several times. Later it was explained that we had encountered some American military vehicles. Then we stopped at the check points of the French Occupation Zone of Germany and at the French border. A short time after that, the truck covers were raised, we were allowed to talk and even to sing quietly – we were inside France!

After several more hours of travel, the covers were once again drawn and total silence was enforced: we were nearing a camp outside Marseille where we were to stay until a ship became available to take us to Israel. Quietly, we left the trucks and entered the barracks of this camp. Though the state of Israel had already been proclaimed and recognised by many states including the great powers, and as such was fully entitled to decide upon immigration to it, there was a hitch. As mentioned above, the UN had imposed an embargo on the entry into Israel of people of military age. Therefore our going had to be kept as secret as possible. We were free to move around the camp, though not in large numbers, and we were not allowed to leave the camp, so as not to draw attention to ourselves. So we travelled through a major part of France and spent some time close to Marseille, without seeing anything at all.

After several days of subdued waiting, we were given the signal: 'A ship is waiting for you!' We could hardly restrain our elation. Late in the afternoon we were taken by truck to a small, nearby harbour. There we saw a long, grey ship rocking gently in the small bay. Long lines of mainly young people from our camp and from other places were moving quickly towards the gang-ways and onto the ship. 'Hoorray! In a few days we shall be in Israel!'

Our elation cooled once we entered the ship. It was obviously a cargo ship that was fitted out to carry people at the time of illegal *aliya*. We young men were taken down into the lower hold. It looked like some kind of slave ship; rows upon rows of bunks in several tiers filled the entire space. On the bunks, one could see hundreds of young people, half lying, half sitting. They could not sit straight because the bunks were only 30–40 centimetres high. There was little free space in the middle of the hold, so the 'passengers' had to stay mostly in their bunks. The air below was dense and the noise was overwhelming.

We were shown to our bunks. Mine was in the third tier, not far from the entrance. I could have fared worse, in the fifth tier and far from the entrance where there was no air. On the bunk I found sheets and a blanket, a package of food (with some fruit in it) and a full water flask. An instructor came by and gave us a briefing: 'We are not supposed to carry young people of military age. You are therefore not to be seen on the deck unless told that you are allowed to do so. We have here 800 Haganah volunteers, an entire regiment. Also, we have on the deck 300 women, some with children, some pregnant – for cover, in case of an inspection. On your bunk you find your food and drinking water for the next 24 hours. You will use your water for drinking only. Anyone who finishes his water before the next 'filling' will not receive an additional portion. Our supply of fresh water is quite limited. You will wash, shave and shower with seawater which is available on deck – when you are allowed to go there. During this trip you must maintain strict discipline – and let us hope we shall arrive there safely in seven to ten days … In case of storms or danger of discovery you will receive further instructions.'

I climbed onto my bunk. No sooner had I lain down and closed my eyes than I was asleep. I had not slept much the night before and was emotionally exhausted. I was very tired but somehow felt curiously secure and 'at home' on my bunk in the dark hold of the ship.

When I woke up, I realized that we were at sea. Soon a command summoned us onto deck for a morning wash and exercises. On the other side of the deck we could see rows of field beds where the women had been placed under a huge cover. We washed with cold seawater, ran around the deck, stretched our limbs, filled our water cans and returned to our bunks, to make place for the next batch of 'passengers.'

Thus we continued our passage across the Mediterranean. I have since crossed this sea many times, including on the Queen Elizabeth II – but this was the most momentous sailing of all. Since we avoided all land and the main shipping lanes, we saw almost nothing. Several times, when a ship or plane was spotted in our vicinity, we ran down from the deck in the middle of washing or exercise. The women and children were visibly spread out on the deck and the entrance below deck was covered with a tarpaulin. Then, when danger passed, we climbed up again to complete our morning or evening chores.

Despite the crowded conditions, we soon organized all kinds of activities – learning Hebrew, Israeli songs, some judo on the deck, readings, short performances. Since I had taught Hebrew before enlisting, I was quite busy here just like in the camp. There was a loudspeaker system on the ship through which instructions and music were broadcast. The ship radio constantly picked up news about the fighting in Israel. The news was then translated into several languages, since the passengers did not all understand Hebrew, and rebroadcast all over the ship. When this happened, a great silence reigned all over the ship. Announcements about casualties were received with great sadness; news about success of Israeli forces aroused cheerful exclamations.

I did sometimes participate in translating the news and this was my opportunity to get to know some of the Israelis who were running the ship. They were the 'captains', but behaved as if they were at summer camp: they were very young, scantily and simply dressed, and sat anywhere – on the table, on the floor, on the steps. They slept in the captain's quarters, but several in each cabin on field beds. They carried the same water canteen as we did – no privileges there. But what struck me the most was that they did not look the least bit Jewish!

On the seventh day it seemed that we were close to the shores of Israel. But we identified two ships on the horizon and had to change course in order to avoid them. Then we received a signal from the shore to delay a bit since conditions were not favourable. On the next night all was clear. It was difficult to describe our feelings. Towards dawn, when the ship was still far from the shore, the entire deck was full of people excitedly looking in the direction of the slowly emerging line of land on the far horizon. There, in the morning mist, was the land of our forefathers, the country which we had never seen but about which we had dreamt many times. There, in front of our eyes shining with tears of wonderment, happiness and hope was the land for which we had come from the ends of the earth – to fight for it, to defend it, if necessary to give our lives for it. As we were told that we should not be seen on the deck when the ship came into the harbour at Haifa, we had a brief ceremony then. A vast Jewish flag was raised on the top mast, a command 'attention' was heard and more than a thousand voices rose together in singing a mighty 'Hatikva'.

The briefing we received below deck was short and to the point: 'You are not to be seen on the deck when coming into the port of Haifa, only women and children. When we arrive at port, it is very important that you disembark as quickly as possible. At a given signal you will run from below to the deck and onto the gangways. So as not to be delayed by your luggage you will throw it onto a heap at the foot of the gangways. Your luggage will be taken care of and brought to your place of destination. There will be buses and trucks waiting for you close to the gangways. You will run to one of these and leave the port area as soon as the vehicle is full. If an inspection should occur – you are on excursion from your kibbutz.'

And so it was. We came up running to the deck and along the gangways. We barely had time to glance at the city of Haifa stretched beautifully around its picturesque bay. As soon as our bus was full it moved off at a high speed. We were on our way – we did not know where to, but what did it matter – we were in Israel at last!

Yet we could not refrain from some sad reflections: no welcome, no festivity of any kind, no relatives and friends coming to embrace us, not to mention such things as an orchestra or parade. It was 11 July 1948, almost two months after the proclamation of independence of the State of Israel. The main *raison d'être* for its existence was to be a place of refuge for Jewish refugees from all over the world. And here we were coming to our Homeland from DP camps in Germany, many of us Holocaust survivors. Yet we were not able to come like free people. We were made to come like thieves in the night. But what did it matter now – in our innermost souls we felt an almost mystical feeling of elation: we were in Israel at last.

25 • A Soldier of Israel

'On your walls, O Jerusalem,
I posted guardians
by day and by night.'

(Isaiah, 62:6)

Our bus was travelling slowly south ... How great was our curiosity to see this country at last – the land of our hopes and dreams. We travelled at first along the foothills of the picturesque Mount Carmel, past some banana plantations, vineyards and fish ponds. Not far away the white-crested waves and the blue waters of the Mediterranean sea could be seen. Here and there we saw some settlements, mostly flat-roofed and with white walls. Beyond the green agricultural areas, the countryside was rather brown and some of the houses looked somewhat neglected, not like the green and carefully cultivated areas of Europe to which our eyes had become accustomed during our lives there.

After more than half an hour, our bus turned off the main road. Soon we passed through a gate guarded by some military people. This was our first glimpse of an Israeli soldier; he looked rather bedraggled (we learned soon enough that this was partly because of lack of military dress and partly because this was the Israeli 'style'). We realized: we are within an Israeli military camp! Our bus stopped in front of a long warehouse where some other trucks and buses were parked. An officer came by and addressed us shortly: 'Shalom! This is a recruitment base of the Army of Israel. You will go into this building where you will find military attire. Take off your civilian dress and make a bundle of it. Go into the showers and then chose a suitable military shirt and trousers. Sorry, we have not received yet military shoes and caps, so keep your own for the time being. Then, after half an hour or so, form up in one line at the other side of the building!'

After a light breakfast we assembled in a long line on the other side of the huge warehouse. I looked around: only a few hours ago we were a bunch of civilian refugees packed into the dark hold of a decrepit ship. Now we practically formed a new regiment of the Israeli army.

A command sounded: 'Attention. You will proceed now to the enlistment area! Right turn! Forward march!' Though the command was in Hebrew, all understood and obeyed – we knew these commands from our training period in Europe. In a nearby field we were faced with a number of tables; each had a designation in Hebrew on it (later we could read them: 'Artillery', 'Brigade ...', 'Signals', 'Transportation', 'Anti-tank', 'Air Force', 'Engineers'). At first we were asked whether we had any previous military experience and of what kind. Those who had such previous training were immediately directed to the appropriate table.

I was together in the line with several fellows from our camp in Wetzlar. The directing officer looked at us and said: You look some burly, strong fellows. We need just such as you in the first regiment of our anti-tank artillery. Any objections?' Of course we had none, we had come to serve wherever we were needed. We were duly enlisted in the anti-tank artillery, some 80 of us. During our first briefing at the edge of the field we were told that the Israel army had no anti-tank regiment as yet, neither had it any such guns apart from several six-pounders that had been 'left' by the British army. Such guns would be arriving soon. In the meantime we would train and do any other fighting.

Meanwhile, it was announced that our luggage had arrived; I was very glad to see that my sack with personal goods had survived. After a few hours' rest in the warehouse we were given our military eating utensils (mess tins) and provided with our first proper meal – lunch. We came to Israel forewarned that it was a small, poor country blockaded on all sides and in the middle of a serious war. Consequently, we expected a poor food supply. We were therefore pleasantly surprised at the relatively rich fare given to us: white bread, meat, soup, fruit and vegetables. (This remained the case all through military service apart from the times when we ate dry 'battle' rations.)

We were allowed several hours' rest. In the afternoon, training started. All the time we listened to the news broadcasts through loudspeakers. It did not look good; there was fighting on several fronts. It was especially heavy around the Latrun fort which was held by a strong force of the Jordanian Arab Legion, and thus closed off the road to beleaguered Jewish Jerusalem. At sunset we were again formed in a line on the field by the warehouse. A youngish blond officer in short trousers and sandals stepped in front of us (later we learned that this was the 'official' attire of Palmach soldiers, an elite fighting unit mostly composed of Israeli -born youngsters). In a loud voice he addressed us: 'A major decisive battle is now going on at Latrun. The fate of Jerusalem it at stake. Also some of our units there are in a difficulty and need urgent reinforcements. We call now for volunteers with previous military experience. All such people who want to volunteer and join the battle forthwith – take two steps forward!'

A number of people stepped forward. To our great surprise we noticed that three people from our camp friends were among the volunteers. We were especially surprised to see among them our friend Chaim Lieberman, a fine-looking, bright young man, with curly black hair and a thin delicate body. He was a member of a family of Holocaust survivors, an only son. His mother tried in every way to prevent his going to war in Israel but in the end had to give in to her son's strong resolve. Within an hour trucks arrived and we gave a rousing farewell to the departing volunteers.

Next morning the terrible news spread like wildfire through the camp: our volunteers had been sent into battle last night; they encountered some crossfire from the Arab Legion and seven of them fell in battle. Among them was our Holocaust survivor friend, the ever-cheerful and smiling Chaim! We were deeply shocked and incredulous; here, in our camp, the sun was shining, it was so quiet and pastoral. And there, several dozen miles away, were the killing fields where many of our soldiers were dying, including our volunteers. Later in the day the entire camp marched in total silence in a funeral procession. In front of the huge column seven simple wooden caskets were carried aloft, each covered with a blue and white Israeli flag. On both sides of the caskets marched military guards with bayoneted rifles. The slow funeral procession moved up to the crossroads at the entrance of the camp. There the bodies were put in command cars with the military guards sitting on both sides and they drove off to be buried at the nearest military cemetery. In our hearts we said farewell to Chaim, our first fighter killed in battle on the night of his arrival in his land, a land which he never had the opportunity to see with his own eyes before he was gathered into its dust forever.

So we spent our first full day in Israel at a funeral and in mourning. We were in despair; who would find the heart to write to Chaim's mother about the death of her son? Could we allow it that she should learn about it in a cold, official letter? For several days we agonized over this matter until it was decided that two of his closest friends would write. Later we learned that the sad news about Chaim had travelled fast, and had reached the camp in Wetzlar before our letter or an official notification arrived there. A huge mass-mourning meeting took place at which Chaim's mother delivered a dignified patriotic speech. A call to arms in memory of Chaim was proclaimed and a number of new volunteers stepped forward. Far from being a deterrent, Chaim's memory became a catalyst for further mobilization for Israel.

The next day we were taken to the temporary camp of the First Anti-tank Regiment at Pardes Katz, not far from Tel Aviv. It was a small camp, consisting mainly of several rows of tents with a wooden barrack in the middle which served as a canteen and headquarters. At the end of the tents there was an exercise field with one non-functional anti-tank gun and several wooden stumps which 'impersonated' guns. Despite tiredness I could not sleep during this first night at my unit; packs of jackals howled in a nearby orange grove not far from our tent; mosquitoes buzzied next to my ears, there was considerable noise from the main road to Tel Aviv, and I was too excited by all that had happened during the past few days.

Next morning we had a pleasant surprise. From the moment of our arrival some of us had been requesting free time to go and visit our relatives and friends. Actually, we wanted to travel a little and see the country. Our commanding officer explained: 'We cannot give you a lot of time off. Fighting is going on and they have no anti-tank protection there. We are expecting to receive guns within several days. Then you must train to operate them as soon as possible and go to the front. Meanwhile, you have two precious days off.'

In my rucksack I had a little address book with details about my extensive family in Israel. The closest were the two Mannheim brothers, sons of a sister of my father who went to Palestine in the mid-1930s as *chalutzim* (pioneers). During the Second World War both had served as volunteers in the British Army and after the war the elder, Mati, settled in Netanya whereas Willy, the younger, lived in Tel Aviv. It was to the latter that I decided to go – especially to leave with him the luggage which I did not need in the army. With my luggage I walked to the road nearby and soon a passing car stopped and gave me a lift to Tel Aviv. Soon the driver started talking with me. As the car moved on we passed a long street with white, flat-roofed buildings several storeys high. I asked: 'Is this Tel Aviv already?'

'No, this is Bnei Berack',he answered.

A little later I asked the same again. 'No, this is Ramat Gan', he answered. 'What is the matter with you, have you never travelled to Tel Aviv?' he asked in a tone of surprise. He could not believe me when I told him 'I am only three days in the country. I am a new *oleh.*'

'But you speak excellent Hebrew and you are in military uniform. I thought you were one of our boys.'

At that time there could not have been a greater compliment in my eyes. I explained: 'I was a Hebrew teacher before coming here, and they enlisted us in the army on the day of our arrival.'

It turned out that my first cousin, Willy, lived in a small room which he rented opposite the Habima Theatre in the very centre of Tel Aviv. He was much surprised when a strange soldier came in and introduced himself as 'the son of his mother's brother'. After a light meal and a lot of talking about family and everything, I departed, relieved of my luggage, into the streets of Tel Aviv. I liked this city instantly. After weeks of travelling in isolation and days in the primitive conditions of the camps, Tel aviv looked like 'heaven'. Here and there one could see some sandbags at entrances and many people were in uniform. But otherwise, there was little to suggest that a war was going on not far from here. The streets were full of people strolling around at their leisure, the coffee houses were packed with many sitting at tables on the pavement and on terraces. The shops, though not as elegant as in Europe, appeared well stocked. Many of the main streets were lined with trees and had green areas with benches in the middle. The houses were mostly modern, white, flat-roofed and with extensive balconies.

The part of Tel Aviv which impressed me most was, of course, the sea front. When I arrived there on that warm July afternoon it was packed with people in bathing costumes enjoying a swim in the sea, playing games, relaxing in the rays of the setting sun. I was quite struck by the many lovely-shaped girls in rather reveal-ing bathing suits. Wow! This was a long way from our military camp! The sunset came – it was spectacular: at the shore white foaming lines of the waves, further on the deep blue and patches of shimmering green aquamarine, then far away the flaming orb of the red sun and the purple and yellow clouds (this had a great impact on me since had I never lived by the sea). When the sun disappeared, the shore became lit with street lamps and the many lights of the restaurants and coffee houses all along the coastline. In time, small orchestras started playing in some of them and couples started dancing. It was a very far cry from the dreary existence which I had led for so long. And yet, I felt suddenly sad and lonely. Here I was, with no close friends, girlfriend, money – I could not even go into any of the coffee houses. I could only sit on the side as an onlooker, and envy those who were inside.

The next evening I returned to our unit camp near Pardes Katz. How great was our excitement when several days later some real anti-tank guns were wheeled into our camp. At last the comical training with wooden stumps would be over. We would train with real guns even if they were out of commission! Little did we know that we would be going into battle with completely different weapons. Several days later we took down our tents, loaded our equipment onto trucks. To form at last the first regiment of the anti-tank forces, we were transferred to the south of Tel Aviv, to the greatest central military base in Israel, Sarafand.

26 • Teaching Soldiers at the Sarafand Camp

After the little tent camp at Pardes Katz, Sarafand (Tsrifin in Hebrew) looked more like a comfortable city. It was built by the British as one of their main military bases in the country. We were told that during the Second World War it housed some 10,000–20,000 soldiers. It had several entrance gates, many kilometres of roads flanked by compounds of warehouses, living barracks, depots and all kind of buildings. As befitted the British, it had in the centre an entire recreation area with a restaurant, officers' mess, swimming pool, some tennis courts and an open air cinema. When I was stationed there only a simple soldiers' canteen was in operation, where some toiletries, biscuits, sweets and ice cream could be bought, and sometimes films were screened in the evenings.

Our First Anti-tank Regiment was housed in a number of barracks with an exercise ground nearby. After a day of settling down, a period of intensive training ensued. We had to wake at 5 o'clock in the morning, put on the shoes and trousers only and do almost an hour of running and morning exercises. After washing and breakfast we engaged in all kinds of military training, with and without weapons. All the time new groups arrived to complete our regiment. At first, these were of European origin (from Bulgaria, Romania, the DP camps). Then a change occurred; the newcomers were from North Africa – Morocco and Algeria. At first we were shocked: while some of them were educated, urban people, many of them looked as if they came straight from the desert. They were dressed in long, Arab-style *ghalabiyas*, had crude sandals on their dark, hardened feet with thick black nails; their hair was long and wild. Worst of all, we could not communicate with them: they did not know Hebrew or any language known to us. A few of them spoke French, but then we did not know it. Many of them did not have European hygienic habits. One morning I found our sergeant-major standing in front of a line of such newcomers demonstrating to them in all earnestness how to use a toothbrush; at other times I saw him pushing some of them with his stick towards the shower head. We used to shower quite often, but some of these newcomers were not too keen on it. Originally, there was some talk that they were good at fighting with a knife but not with guns in modern warfare.

In time a complete change took place; with their hair and nails cut, dressed in military uniform, they looked human. They learnt Hebrew quite quickly and turned out to be good fighters. As it happened, our six-man gun crew was quite an international team; two of us were Ashkenazi from DP camps, one was Bulgarian, one Romanian and two Moroccan. And I was the only one with a good command of Hebrew.

Which brings me to what happened next. Some days after our arrival at Sarafand I was suddenly summoned by our training and education officer. When I arrived at his small office he came straight to the point: 'You are just what we need! I understand that you are a teacher of Hebrew and you were a Zionist youth leader. You have a university education. I appoint you herewith to be my assistant. Soon we shall be sending our soldiers here into battle. But how can they fight as a team when they can't talk to each other. Also, many of them know very little about the geography and history of the country for which they are risking life and limb … From now on, the afternoons will be devoted to the intensive study of Hebrew and to education in the history and geography of Israel. Find yourself some knowledgable helpers; I shall bring you some teaching material. Start your work tomorrow.'

Thus I became assistant education officer for our regiment. It was 'in formation' waiting for the arrival of anti-tank guns. Meanwhile the fighting stopped following another cease-fire agreement. As explained by the officer, mornings were taken up with all kinds of military training. After lunch, I had to fill the time with 'educational programmes'. Together with some others who had some knowledge of Hebrew and in Jewish studies we engaged in the teaching of Hebrew and of the history and geography of Israel. We taught the soldiers some songs, we explained to them some basic things about Jewish and Israeli history, we showed on a map the geography of our land. The greatest interest was aroused when we read out to the soldiers the latest news about events at the cease-fire lines and in the country. Most of them could not read the Hebrew papers and papers in other languages were not available at the camp.

One morning, in autumn 1948, we were notified by one of the officers of our regiment: 'Get ready, spick and span – you are to participate in a military "parade" of the Israeli Army. The Prime Minister himself will attend ...' We were especially stunned by this announcement since it was asserted that the IDF 'hates' such military displays.

We became busy: several anti-tank 'six-pounder' guns were mustered. We polished them thoroughly and attached them to command cars. We were issued new green uniforms; we polished our boots, put on military belts, black artillery berets and helmets. We were also presented with new Czech rifles. When we looked at each other we could not recognize ourselves – compared to the dishevelled hair and dirty, dusty appearance when we were 'in the field'. We looked rather 'neat and elegant'.

It turned out that the 'parade' would only be a 'march past' at the Tel Aviv Stadium near the former sea port. By the time we arrived we saw formations of many military units from the various services of the Israeli Army – armour, navy, air force, infantry and artillery, even communications and military ambulances. A military band was playing next to a flag-decorated podium where we could see a number of officers and civilians. When all units were properly placed, a white-haired civilian stepped forward and addressed us in a ringing voice.

'Look, Ben-Gurion ...', my neighbour in the command car nudged me.

For some inexplicable reason, I did not take well to Ben-Gurion's presentation. (A rebound from the 'cult of personality of Stalin' to which I was exposed during my time in Soviet Russia?) Anyway, he repeated in his presentation more or less the same as he said in his other frequent public speeches. At the end of his address, the various columns passed in front of the podium. We were lucky – we did not have to march since we were 'motorized'. All we had to do was to turn our heads to the 'right' and incline our rifles in the direction of the podium when passing by it. We then returned rather speedily to our base. What made an indelible impression on me were the orderly military formations with flags and weaponry. I felt there and then 'we are an army!'

One morning, great excitement gripped our compound: at last our weapons had arrived, and how different they were from what we had expected and were trained for. Instead of field anti-tank guns, each served by a team of five artillery men, we saw a long line of armoured cars. Each had an open top where a small 22-

millimetre Swiss rapid-fire gun was mounted. It could be easily swivelled around to shoot in all directions, including up into the air. It had therefore many advantages: it could serve as a kind of big machine-gun in support of troops in ordinary fighting and as an anti-tank and anti-aeroplane gun, provided that special armour-piercing ammunition was fed to it. Whereas a field-gun was usually stationary and difficult to move around if enemy armour attacked from a different direction, these armoured cars with their gun were fully manoeuvrable. The crew was protected inside from ordinary rifle fire. Each car had in addition a heavy machine-gun and was equipped with a two-way field radio. However, the 22-millimetre shells did not have the armour-piercing strength even of a six-pounder field-gun – not to mention the bigger ones. Each armoured car had a team of five; a driver, two soldiers operating the big gun, one behind the machine-gun and one in charge of the radio. Each team member had an ordinary rifle for personal use. One of the team, usually the senior gun operator, was commander of the car in constant radio contact with the company commander. Our regiment soldiers had had only several days to train when renewed fighting erupted in the Negev. Our forces there needed anti-tank cover and our cars were ordered into action. However, I was suddenly summoned by the Deputy Commander and ordered to stay in camp: 'Every day more groups will be joining our regiment and more weapons will be arriving. It is more important for you to teach many soldiers here … there, one soldier more will not make a difference.' Upon my insistence, he promised that this arrangement would be only temporary.

So I said farewell to my friends leaving for the front and stayed in the camp at Sarafand. All the time, more groups were coming to our regiment, and we had to train them intensively, make soldiers out of them in the shortest possible time, so that they could join our forces at the front. Many of them were *olim* (new immigrants); they did not know any Hebrew or anything much about Israel. Our small group of teachers had its work cut out and I felt that I was doing an important job.

However, as time went on I felt more and more 'uncomfortable'. Fighting was going on in the south, not far away from our camp. Some of our units were engaged in the battles; some of my friends were killed or wounded. It was during a visit to the hospital adjoining our camp in order to see one of our original group that I made up my mind: I was going to leave the sheltered life in the camp and join the fighting.

The next day I asked to see the commander of our Regiment 'on a matter of urgency'. Two days later I was standing to attention in front of him in his simple office. I said: 'Much as I appreciate the trust you have in me and the importance of the work entrusted to me, I ask to be relieved of it. I did not come to Israel as a volunteer to stay behind the front in a comfortable camp. I cannot stay here any more when my friends are fighting there. I ask therefore urgently that you assign me to a fighting unit at the front.' He tried to persuade me to stay, at least several weeks until a replacement could be found. I felt that somehow the 'several weeks' might turnout to be months and that the entire fighting might have stopped soon before I would be able to join in. I asked therefore that he accept my resignation forthwith and send me to a front unit.

For several days thereafter things were as usual, as if I had not met with the commanding officer. Then one of our junior officers informed me that a new unit was being sent to the front and I had been assigned to it. Therefore I should leave my teaching and education work and join the intensive military training of the new group. Unfortunately, I knew only a few who were my pupils at Hebrew classes; the others were complete strangers to me.

Meanwhile a new cease-fire was proclaimed. Our going to the front was delayed, allowing some time for in-depth training. It turned out that the most urgent need was for radio operators. The problem was that they had to be fluent Hebrew speakers, and these were rather scarce. I was a natural candidate and so I found myself on an intensive three-week communications course in another part of our sprawling camp. As a trained communications operator I was returned to our regiment. It was just in time, because the 'new company' was about to leave for the front. At the central front at Rosh Haayin, just to the east of Petach Tikva, only ten miles north of Tel Aviv, considerable Iraqi armoured units had been spotted. Fighting could flare up at any moment, and the Israeli forces in the area had no anti-tank defences there. Reinforcements were urgently needed and we were therefore dispatched forthwith.

After a small farewell party, at which the regimental education officer expressed appreciation for my work at the camp, we finally moved on. Our 'grand reinforcement' of the central front opposite the Iraqi forces consisted of four armored cars with the 22-millimetre guns, several command cars and jeeps and finally trucks with ammunition tents and equipment. In those times, it looked an impressive column and force. It was a pleasant, sunny autumn morning. On the way to Petach Tikva we had to pass through some of the main streets of Tel Aviv. Traffic had to stop to let us through and many strollers in the streets stopped to greet us enthusiastically and search for a familiar face. One of the soldiers in a truck in front of us jumped off the slow-moving vehicle to embrace an elderly passerby – his father. On a balcony above us a woman was blessing the passing soldiers. From a synagogue on our route a group of men came out in their prayer shawls lifting high an open Torah scroll.

Less than an hour after we left Sarafand we were approaching a line of hills behind Rosh Haayin – the front line.

27 • At the Front Line

'Jerusalim my nye sdadim
ye vreuskuyu stolitsu
vsekh vragov my perebyom
staniem na granitsu.'*

Several miles to the northeast of Petach Tikva, on a hill overlooking the springs of the Yarkon river there is a small fort. It was named Antipater after a son of Herod and it served as a military outpost for the Crusaders, the Mamluks and the Turks. The British in turn built there a military camp during the Second World War. The place was of great importance to the fledgling State of Israel, since it controlled the Yarkon from which water was pumped as far as Jerusalem. It was immediately occupied by Israeli forces upon independence. However, the Jordanians and their Iraqi allies were intent on attacking this area of Rosh Haayin ('Head of the Spring'). The Israeli command decided to prevent such a dangerous development which would give the enemy an important strategic advantage, and of course deny Israel a significant water resource.

It was in order to strengthen this position that our company was sent there. We arrived there on a sunny autumn morning and parked our armoured cars by the high stone walls of the inner square of the fort, in front of the local command. The local force received us with great enthusiasm, especially as there were some reports about a concentration of enemy armour not far from there.

So for some time our company was integrated into the life of this section of the front. Stretched out to the north and east from the central position of the fort was a major line of forward Israeli

---

*'We shall not abandon you, Jerusalem, the capital of the Jews, we shall finish off all your enemies and shall stand on the border.' (Sung by Russian volunteers during the War of Independence, 1948.)

posts. These were mostly in abandoned stone buildings and dugouts. They were usually approached and supplied at night since many were quite close to enemy positions which opened fire immediately an Israeli target was available. Some of our soldiers were wounded as a result of such firing. From time to time the enemy launched sudden attacks on our posts, albeit without success. If enemy armour suddenly appeared we would have to confront it either from behind the walls of the fortress or in the open – depending on conditions. We kept to a training schedule and held our armour and guns in battle-ready condition. We did not drive our armoured cars on patrols on the other side of the fort which was visible to the Iraqis since their presence was to be kept as a surprise in case of military action.

We were, however, active in manning the posts and in the local exchanges of fire at the forward front line. At each post we constantly observed through field binoculars the movements at the enemy posts and roads. One afternoon we noticed unusual comings and goings on several enemy roads near us. It was decided to send a reconnaissance party as close as possible to the forward positions of the enemy in the hope of capturing a prisoner who could give us some information. At least we hoped to overhear something of value. Soon I was assigned to my first front action. We slept in the afternoon, to be ready not to sleep throughout the night. Late in the evening we blackened our faces, put on shoes with rubber soles, checked all our equipment and dress for any shiny surfaces that might give us away. In total darkness we marched at first along a winding path. From time to time we stopped and a forward patrol checked the way ahead. At some point the word was passed back: 'Crouch, we are close to enemy front position.' We moved on soundlessly until we were practically able to hear the Iraqis talking and moving around. Our orders were not to open fire since we might ourselves be caught in crossfire from other enemy positions. Our task was to obtain information. Those among us who understood Arabic crawled forward as close as possible. As it turned out, not much could be learned from listening to those enemy soldiers, only that they expected more reinforcements. Before dawn, we crawled back; twice the Iraqis fired some rocket flares. Somehow, they had a hunch about our presence there; but they did not discover us and we returned to our fort safely. Another reconnoissance group was not so lucky: they stumbled on an enemy dugout, a brief exchange of fire followed in which some Iraqi military were killed but several of our soldiers were wounded. From time to time, enemy artillery opened fire on our camp but without serious results.

Our great entertainment at this time was walking to the plantations near the river to pick bananas or some other fruit. But above all, it was to go to nearby Petach Tikva. This small town seemed to us the height of luxury. It was almost unbelievable that only several miles from the front life was going on as if there was no war in the world: shops and cafés were open, buses were cruising around, people were strolling around or sitting on benches. To me the most important place was the local public library, where it was possible to read some of the latest papers and borrow some books. These were a precious gift, alleviating the boredom of camp life.

After several weeks of stay at the Antipater fort, participating in some fighting during night patrols and repelling one Iraqi attack on the fort, we were suddenly ordered to move to another part of the front where heavy fighting was going on. It was at the Beit G'obrin area to the southwest of Jerusalem. The Israeli military operation was aimed at pushing back some of the Arab forces from this area thus ensuring a link between the Jerusalem area and the Israeli forces in the south.

Coming closer to the fighting area I experienced for the first time real visions of war: the rattling of machine guns, the explosion of artillery shells from both sides, heavy, black smoke covering much of the area. At the side of the road, lines of soldiers were marching towards the front, and some vehicles were driving in the opposite direction with soldiers with bandages on their heads or other parts of their bodies. As we came closer to the fighting our armoured cars were directed off the main road and drove uphill through such narrow mountain tracks that it seemed we were falling off into the abyss below. Twice our truck stalled, we had to get out and push. At last we succeeded in getting to the top of a high hill. Actually, our position was at the side of the enemy; we opened rapid fire at enemy positions, hitting one of the tanks. The Arab forces did not expect fire from that direction; our four armoured cars were hidden behind the ridge so that the Arabs could only see their upper part. The enemy could not see us well; they might have thought that we were tanks. Whatever the case, after discharging several volleys in our direction, slightly hitting one of our cars, they withdrew to the south.

We set up our quarters in an abandoned stone house not far from Beit G'obrin. Day after day we drove out along impossible hill roads to fight some of the enemy forces in the hill area. One day while this fighting was going on, it dawned on us that the next day was Yom Kippur. On that sacred day our team went in the morning for a patrol in the vicinity. Then we arrived at the headquarters and asked whether we could join prayers some-where. We were directed towards a half-destroyed building. In a room inside we found some two dozen soldiers in prayer shawls singing and swaying in prayer. There was no Holy Ark, no Torah scroll, no prayer books. One elderly soldier, however, held the special prayer book for Yom Kippur in one of his hands and a *shofar* in the other. He slowly pronounced the prayers and the 'congrega-tion' followed him. From time to time he blew the *shofar* but quietly, since we were not that far from enemy positions. As we prayed, some groups were coming in to join us, with smoke-blackened faces from the fighting. Just as we were at the silent prayers of the 'Eighteen Blessings' an officer came in shouting and ordered his unit to run out immediately to a place where the enemy were trying to break through. Then a group of wounded soldiers came in, some of them with bloodied bandages. The prayers and the sound of the *shofar* were accompanied by the constant clunk of weapons and some nearby shooting. Before we were able to finish our service two officers rushed in shouting: 'All must return immediately to their units ... the enemy has launched an attack!'

Some days later a new cease-fire was announced. We stayed on in the Beit G'obrin area to clear some remaining enemy troops. Then we were quartered again in Sarafand for a further period of training and regrouping. We were formed into the First Anti-tank Regiment of the Israeli Defence Forces. Not only more young people were inducted but, for the first time, proper anti-tank guns and bazookas arrived. Our passage from a small partisan-like force to a large regiment was marked by something most unusual in the Israeli military: a parade and a form of a swearing-in ceremony. We were issued with a single style of uniform (until then soldiers in our unit had been dressed in all kinds of what passed for military uniforms). For the first time we polished our shoes, belts and buttons (anyone who polished his shoes when we were at the front was laughed at and warned never to do it again – the idea being that in the desert a polished surface might reflect light and reveal our hidden position to the enemy). We did one more thing which was taboo to us – we learned to march and turn in unison ... and to salute.

Here a small digression about the 'character' of the Israeli army is in order. Basically, two contrary traditions influenced it from the outset: the 'British' and that of the 'Hagana–Palmach', the under-ground Jewish forces during the Mandate period. The Palmach units were mostly composed of youngsters from the Zionist, mostly socialist, youth movements, the majority of them from kibbutzim and other settlements. They were a vanguard fighting force and much of the military successes of Israel were due to them. Their style and manners can best be described as 'anti-military' – no saluting, no formal chain of command, no parades or drill. They went into battle in shorts, open-necked shirts, hatless or with woollen caps (putting on a helmet was contemptible). There were then no official military ranks in the IDF; an officer simply had a band on his arm: 'regiment comman-der', 'brigade commander', and so on. There was no differentia-tion between officer and ordinary soldiers whatsoever: they ate, slept and lived with their men. Often they were from the same youth group, their 'subordinates' were their friends. Whenever not fighting they spent their evenings sitting around a fire, sipping a Turkish coffee, singing Israeli songs and telling tales. Girls were equal members, fighting alongside men. During one of the battles in which I participated, I saw a girl fighter in a nearby jeep furiously firing a heavy machine-gun. There were strict, almost puritanical, relations between women and men; women slept alongside the men and washed nearby.

The 'Palmach–Haganah' tradition related also to strategy and tactics. It engaged in small-scale surprise – mostly night – fighting, informal elastic planning and improvisation. The Palmach hated long, elaborate written and rigid battle plans, 'fighting by the book'. It relied very much on the commander in the field; he was entitled fully to change the original plan, even without the autho-rization of his superior when this was not possible. All was settled by a word or two between Yoram and Dudu (David) … There was no formal discipline, no military police or court. If a fighter was guilty of a serious breach of discipline – for example, he left the unit for some days without permission – he was tried at a meeting of his unit. The most severe punishment was transfer from the elite Palmach force to an ordinary army unit or suspension of his participation in the next battle.

As Palmach units were in need of anti-tank protection, we were attached to them in some battles. They invariably treated us – city people, new *olim* and 'inexperienced' in fighting – with an air of superiority. However, after several encounters with the enemy in which our armoured trucks proved to be of crucial importance, they became very friendly. As a result, I spent quite an evening sitting with them around a fire – especially since I was able to speak Hebrew and sing along with them. I remember one evening when I gathered some wood for the fire together with a brigadier; as a rule high officers did menial work along with ordinary soldiers, including washing dishes and their clothes. One day we were approaching a front line. Suddenly, several jeeps passed us swiftly; some soldiers jumped out and ran to the head of next hill. In front we saw a young man in shorts and an Arab-style *kefieh* on his neck. The wind rustled his long hair on his forehead. Those behind him carried some big maps and binoculars. I asked an officer near us: 'Who is it?'.

'Yigal Allon, the commander of the southern front', was the answer. He was then 30 years old.

The other tradition was the 'British' one or that of a regular, formal army: drills, saluting, polishing boots, buttons, weapons, barking orders, breaking the 'civilian spirit' and making a man a soldier. The basis of this tradition is a hierarchical differentiation between soldier and officer and within the officer corps itself. Strategically it means fighting by the book – formal, detailed, written battle plans which have to be strictly implemented. Many of the commanders – not in Palmach but in the Israeli army in general had served in the British or in some other regular army (Soviet, Polish and so on). Naturally, they brought with them the 'British' way. (The Palmach was disbanded in autumn 1949 by Ben Gurion who wanted a uniform Israeli army. Ultimately, however, this army has successfully integrated both traditions up to the present day).

Anyway, here we were at our first regimental parade: we were marching more-or-less in step, saluting, and listening to a brief address by our commander. A small military band was playing, flags were flying – both of Israel and of our newly constituted anti-tank artillery. We felt that we were an army, at last. Little did we know that soon we were to encounter a major battle in which the crew of our truck would be severely hit.

A MAJOR MILITARY OPERATION INTO SINAI

After the fighting at the Beit G'obrin area and the south we were again returned to quarters – this time near Ramleh. I was given a brief spell of leave and decided to go this time to Jerusalem. I had been raised in a religious household; naturally, I was quite moved when travelling uphill along the winding road – for the first time – to the ancient Jewish capital and holy city. All along the road, signs of the recent fighting were quite visible: red and black burned-out trucks and armoured cars, buildings pockmarked by shells and bullets, big holes in the ground from mortar and gun shells. At the entrance to Jerusalem itself there were several barriers with barbed wire and anti-tank concrete boulders. Armed guards manned these roadblocks and checked the identity of those coming and going. In all, the Jerusalem that I encountered then was anything but a city of peace, heavenly beauty and serenity. It was more like a beleaguered fortress: concrete walls had been erected in many central places in the city to guard against Jordanian snipers who manned the top of the wall of the old city and some tall buildings in the eastern part of the city taken by the Jordanian army. From time to time a burst of firing on both sides was heard with explosions of mortar and gun shells. Few civilians were seen in the streets; in some places they had to walk bending their heads because of intermittent firing, or run for shelter. Few shops were open; those open were poorly stocked and mostly empty. Strict rationing had been introduced not only of food but also of most goods (clothing, soap, toiletries and so forth). In several places queues were seen – for ice blocks, for petrol, for food, for water …

There was no possibility whatsoever of visiting the Jewish holy places (the Western Wall) in the old city. I remember standing behind a concrete wall in King George street in the very centre, raising my head from time to time during a break in the shooting and looking toward the old city walls. I was thinking: 'This is the city where kings David and Solomon walked, where the great prophets Isaiah and Jeremiah preached, where the Hasmonean priests and kings ruled thousands of years ago … And now we cannot even enter that area .'

When darkness fell, Jerusalem became a totally dead city: a kind of curfew enveloped the entire place, no street light or any other for that matter was to be seen for fear of drawing enemy fire. Only in some inner places, mainly in basements, was there light by which one could see people – mostly soldiers – drinking, eating and even singing. By around 9 o'clock in the evening it was dark and completely quiet. Anyway, this visit, my first to Jerusalem, a city in which I was later to live for many decades, was a far from elating experience.

How different was Jerusalem from Tel Aviv where I used to go whenever I was given leave. This city was a marvel. Its main streets and tree-flanked boulevards were packed with people until the small hours of the night. The shops, hotels, cafés and restaurants were brightly lit with multicoloured advertisements, full of people at any time. The Mediterranean sea front was packed with people in swimming suits. In the warm evenings, the cafés along the front had small orchestras playing. Waiters in white jackets served ice creams and cakes, young couples danced … Was there a bloody war, young people dying, being maimed every day? We would watch the whole scene with mixed feelings, also because we did not have the money to frequent these restaurants and cafés; neither did we – especially the *olim* – have our sweethearts to dance with. We felt sharp pangs of envy and, at the same time, pleasure at the music and the scene.

Towards the middle of December we suddenly received an order to move quietly at night to Beersheba. Beersheva was then a forlorn Bedouin town with one major street which ran from the mosque and police station in the north towards a *wadi* (river gully)to the south. It had been recently captured by Israeli troops and abandoned by its Arab population. Much like other units, we were quartered in an abandoned Arab house, where we were able at least to have a shower and sleep on proper beds (though the mattresses had been removed for fear of vermin). More and more units were arriving and a period of tense waiting ensued, filled with rumours of a major operation. After several days of waiting we were ordered to get fully battle-ready, load as much ammunition as possible and move southeast into the desert near the Halutza settlement. On arriving there we were astonished: as far as the eye could see there were army camps, artillery and armour. More and more were arriving. We realized that most of the fighting units of the Army of Israel were concentrating in this desert area. Two days later, the various units were called to order; a small column of command cars arrived. On one of the cars a head was seen – bald in the middle, with protruding hair on both sides. 'Ben Gurion' – a murmur went around the troops. He stood up and spoke briefly. We could barely hear him so our officers gave us the gist of his address: 'Soldiers of Israel! We are going into a decisive battle to remove the Arab military occupiers from our holy homeland. We shall move along an ancient Roman road in the desert discovered by our archaeologists and recently made passable by our Engineering Corps. We shall come upon the enemy from a direction he does not expect and surprise him. Hit the enemy with all your might and be victorious. The future of the state and people of Israel is in your hands.'

When darkness fell, the huge operation started. A seemingly endless column of armoured cars, light tanks and artillery was moving along the narrow desert track which sometimes allowed the passage of a single file of vehicles only. On both sides of the column and in front of it, light jeeps and command cars which could function in the desert were moving, scounting the area ahead and on both sides. Behind the front column the main corps of armoured buses and trucks were carrying the main body of troops, ammunition and supplies. From time to time a vehicle got stuck in the sand and stones of the track; other vehicles would push it off the road and the people and their loads were reapportioned to other trucks. The element of surprise was crucial; there was no time to lose.

For the first few hours we drove with lights on. Then an order came: 'Switch off the lights and keep quiet. We are approaching enemy positions. We shall go around and attack from the south where they do not expect us.' There was some moonlight in the sky and we moved in semi-darkness. The jeeps and command cars opened fire in front of us – and then the command came: 'All lights on.' There were a few bursts of fire from the position on the hill in our direction. We returned fire as heavily as we could. In a short time the fight was over. The enemy stronghold was manned by a small number of Egyptian soldiers. They were shocked when they saw the immense column, with lights blazing , emerging from the desert from the direction of Egypt. A few of the Egyptians were hit; the others scattered into the desert night. Our first battle was an easy one with only a few lightly wounded.

The main body of our column remained around this position. The light fighting units (jeeps, light trucks, some armoured cars) went ahead to clear the way for further advance towards Abu Ageila, the main big Egyptian stronghold, on the main road from Egypt to Beersheva and on the border between Egypt and Palestine.

This battle came the next night, and was nothing like the one the night before. The element of surprise had largely gone; the enemy positions here were well fortified and defended by a large contingent of troops including some black Sudanese troops renowned for their ferocious fighting. When darkness fell we advanced with our armoured truck behind a ridge close to the main enemy position. We opened fire several times in the general direction of enemy targets, but the main attack was launched by commando troops trained in night fighting. I could see in front of us columns of fighters with blackened faces and shoes swathed with woollen socks. At first they were walked in total silence behind the ridge, invisible to the enemy. Then they fell to the ground and pressed forward crawling on their bellies. After about a tense half hour the whole place turned into hell: explosions, machine-gun fire, grenades, shells, rocket flares … Soon the first wounded and shell-shocked arrived. One of them next to me was shaking violently; from time to time he let out an animal scream. A military medic tried to give him an injection, but it was possible only when two soldiers held him down. We moved our armoured truck towards the top of the ridge and opened fire from our rapid firing 20-millimetre gun towards the sources of enemy fire. After several hours of fighting the sound of battle subsided and we moved back behind the ridge.

One of the lightly wounded sat on a stone not far from us. From him we heard about the terrible things that happened during the nearby fighting that night. The main troop was attacking the heavily fortified enemy positions; but on the left flank a company of French volunteers plunged forwards. They crawled undetected to within about 20 metres of the enemy trenches. Then they threw grenades into the trenches below, rose up with a war cry and jumped into the trenches. From then on it was hand-to-hand fighting; within an hour of intense fighting this part of the Egyptian entrenchment was cleared. But in another section of the Egyptian fortifications a group of the French got caught in crossfire by an overwhelming force and fell into Egyptian (apparently Sudanese) hands; these tortured them, clobbered them to death, cut off their penises and put them in the mouths. The French who took this position and found their dead friends thus went berserk and massacred some Egyptians. A Palmach officer who tried to prevent them and threatened them with a court martial was almost killed by them. Only when they were ordered to withdraw did they leave, carrying their mutilated dead and crying openly all the way back.

We slept a little, until after sunrise we were woken by an order through our radio (I was the operator): 'Egyptian tanks are counter-attacking from the south.' We moved immediately southwards since we were there specifically as an anti-tank unit. On our way, in front of our eyes a true panorama of battle was unfolding. Long columns of fighters were moving to and from the front.

Those returning had mostly blackened faces – from smoke and a special paste as camouflage for night fighting; some had bandaged arms or heads, others were carried on stretchers or leaning on crutches. As the sun rose and painted the desert red and yellow we could see that the entire area was full of trenches, burned and overturned vehicles, strewn with all kinds of equipment, clothing and even shoes that had been left behind by fleeing Egyptians. In some places our soldiers were sitting in a circle, eating breakfast, cleaning and loading their weapons. Further on a group of Egyptian prisoners were crouching on the ground, guarded by armed Israeli soldiers.

As we moved on, the enemy tanks came into sight. There were five of them, of the light class. Yet they outclassed us in every way: they had a proper gun whereas ours was actually a kind of heavy machine-gun. They had proper, thick armour when ours was rather thin. Yet we had special armour-piercing ammunition. Also their range was far greater than ours. When they came closer, they started to shoot at us but the shells fell far in front of us. As they moved closer and closer our situation became dangerous. Our commander was a courageous but inexperienced former Haganah officer. He was about to command us to open fire and move closer to the enemy tanks when Boris intervened and saved us and the day. Boris was the commander of our armoured car. He grabbed the mike of our radio and screamed in his broken Hebrew: 'There, behind the abandoned railway track! It will give us protection against the enemy while we shall be able to shoot at them.' And he commanded our car to move there as quickly as we could. The other cars followed. We positioned our cars behind the railway track so that only our turret was above it. When the Egyptians came quite close we suddenly opened fire aiming especially at the opening in the armour in front of the driver's seat. They opened heavy fire in our direction but we were behind the track and the shells fell behind us or hit the earth wall in front. After several exchanges fire was seen in one of their tanks and smoke rose from another. The Egyptian tanks moved back to a distance where we could not hit them. They continued to fire in our direction for some time, then they quickly withdrew. Our battle with Egyptian armour was over with no casualties whatsoever. They did not bother us any more. The way was clear for the further advance of our forces along this sector of the front.

A small digression is in order here about Boris and the crew of our armoured truck. It was a virtual 'international'. Our driver was an Israeli *sabra'* a big fellow from a Tel Aviv merchant family. He was a quiet, slightly slow fellow and felt himself the odd one out in our crew. The gun operator was a Rumanian *oleh*, the best soldier in our truck, who saved us in a battle by opening intense fire during a sudden Egyptian attack. Two of our crew were rather uncouth but strong new immigrants from Morocco. They did not know much Hebrew but proved to be sturdy fighters. I was of Polish–Russian background. In our truck I served as the radio operator and manned the machine-gun which we had as well as our main 20-millimetre gun. Boris was the commander of our unit. He liked to go around in a black beret with a pair of binoculars hanging on his chest. He was quite a character, as it turned out a tragic one. During the long dark evenings he used to regale us – and sometime the Palmach fellows who listened with awe – with stories about the fighting on the Soviet–German front, huge battles in which he participated. He had commanded an armoured brigade and encountered some anti-Semitism in his unit. He passed through Poland and learned there about the horrors of the Holocaust. After the war he was stationed with his brigade in Soviet-occupied East Germany where he was outraged by the anti-Semitic remarks from his own troops. He asked leave as if to visit his family in Moscow. On his way, he stepped off the train and went straight to the offices of the Jewish community in Cracow. The people at the office were astonished to see a Soviet 'general' in his full regalia – medals, gold braid and all – march into their humble place. They were even more stunned when he demanded to talk immediately in private with the head of the community. They thought that some calamity was about to occur … the KGB … The head was crestfallen when the door closed behind them in the inner office: the Soviet 'general' started up in Yiddish saying 'I am a Jew, you see it in my documents. I have been spilling my blood fighting the Nazis and serving the Red Army. But I have done with serving others who are also anti-Semites. There is a life-and-death war being fought for the Jewish people in Palestine and I have made up my mind to go there. From now on I shall fight for my Jewish people only.' He demanded there and then that the head supply him with civilian clothing and put him in touch with people who could assist him in getting to Israel. The head of the community was virtually shaking with fear: 'You know what punishment awaits us if we assist a senior Soviet officer in desertion from his army … even for not reporting you. I beg you, please leave.' He suspected that it might be some kind of provocation of the Soviet security services.

Boris started rapidly to take off his clothing; within a minute he stood there naked and declared: 'If you do not do as I say I shall report that you tried to kidnap me.' In the end the chairman had no choice but to provide him with proper civilian attire and give him the address of a Zionist group in Cracow. After some months of travelling – legally and illegally – he arrived in Israel. He volunteered and was immediately enlisted and sent to our unit. The commander of some 160 tanks was now a commander of one armoured truck in the Israeli Army.

As long as the war went on and he served in the army, he was all right. But after demobilization tragedy struck. He did not know Hebrew well and had no profession apart from army service. His wife and children remained behind in Moscow – there was no way then for him to go there or for them to come to Israel. He changed jobs a number of times but could not keep any. Beyond all that – he liked to drink. As his situation deteriorated, melancholy set in, he drank more and more. Despite the help he received from some of us, his army friends, his situation became increasingly worse. After some years of this kind of 'living' he died. I heard about it only some months later and was not able even to find where he had been buried.

28 • A Surprise Egyptian Attack and an End to the Fighting

The following afternoon we were camped beneath an Egyptian hill-position which had been taken during the night before. The general mood was good. 'Operation Ayin', of which we were a part, the largest and most daring campaign of the Israeli army so far, was doing very well. We hit the enemy forcefully from an unexpected direction, through the desert. By now we were close to Abu Ageila, on the Egyptian side of the previous international border. Many soldiers were catching up on sleep; others were preparing for the next night-battle – cleaning and oiling their guns, loading ammunition. Two of our crew – the Moroccans – were sleeping behind the truck. Boris and our driver wandered around. Our Rumanian dismounted our gun, cleaning and oiling its parts with my help. It was a tranquil scene indeed.

Suddenly, from behind the turning at the road below the hill a column of military trucks and cars appeared. At first we could not determine whether they were ours or enemy's. But as they came closer they suddenly opened intensive fire on us. From the large trucks behind soldiers were jumping out and forming a line. While running they fired at us from close range. We were in total-shock, our large gun, which could have saved us in this situation, was dismantled and we could not use it. Meanwhile I could see the Egyptians coming closer and closer until I was able to see their faces and the colour of their eyes. Crouching inside our armoured truck and trying to shoot at the approaching enemy I thought that this was it – any moment now a grenade would be tossed into our car or an Egyptian would open fire on it.

All of a sudden the battle situation turned. The Egyptians attacked us successfully below the hill but did not know that another unit was located on top of it. When that Israeli force realized what was going on below, they opened fire on the attacking enemy below with everything they had. As the Egyptians ducked under fire, our Rumanian, with my assistance, succeeded in getting our machine-gun in working order. He fired at close range with devastating results for the Egyptians. Until then I had always simply shot in the general direction of the enemy, here I could see them face to face. Not far from us a soldier was running. Our fire hit him in his right leg but he continued running while dragging his leg. The Rumanian hit him again in the stomach and he fell not far from us. Further on, by the roadside, a black Sudanese officer was stretched out on his back; his face turned grey and a small hole could clearly be seen in his forehead.

The whole thing lasted not more than ten minutes, but it took us an hour or two to come out of the shock. We realized that had we been alone, without the other unit on the hill, we would have been lying around dead, much like the Egyptians. We looked around: the entire Egyptian column was routed, some of them at the rear of the column were able to turn their vehicles and flee into the desert. All the others were dead. In the officers' cars at the front of the column we found some valuable maps and documents as well as a radio with some codes. These 'treasures' were immediately sent by jeep to our intelligence command unit.

Our column continued its movement to the southwest. The next night we were camped again in the midst of a large concentration of our forces. Late in the evening we were gathered in a natural amphitheatre. On a huge rock facing us we could see a commander with loose hair dressed in a simple khaki outfit and sandals. My neighbour whispered: 'Allon, the front commander.' He addressed us briefly: 'Soldiers, we are now on Egyptian soil. We have no claim on this territory beyond the international border of Eretz Israel. Our aim is to free our own land from the invading Egyptian forces which rained fire and death on our people. We have had great success in this battle. We are now not far from the sea. Our forward reconnaissance units have reached the airfield and outskirts of El Arish. If we take it and cross the seacoast road we shall practically cut off the enemy forces in Palestine from Egypt. They will be surrounded and will have to withdraw. Victory will be ours … We haven't much time, only hours, since the Security Council in New York and the Great Powers demand from us that we accept a cease-fire immediately and withdraw back beyond the border. So let us go onward soldiers of Israel!'

Within hours, without rest, our column started moving again. Here and there we encountered some resistance and there were brief skirmishes. We moved persistently ahead on a sunny morning with a clear sky above. Suddenly something happened that actually ended my fighting career. From the other side of a nearby hill several huge aeroplanes appeared. They were flying low so as to avoid early detection and started firing at our column. Before we had time to aim and fire our weapons, bullets started flying all around us. We had no time to run and hide. I crouched inside the truck in the opposite direction from the fire of the planes and covered my head with my arms. Suddenly our driver's voice shouted: 'Help! I have been hit.' Luckily, our truck was not moving at that time. Then two more shouts were heard. I felt some fluid dripping on my coat, I had a look – blood. But I was not hit anywhere, so it dawned on me that it was from one of the Moroccans who had been hit while crouching next to me.

The planes made two more turns and fired at our column but on another part of it. Then they disappeared as quickly as they came. The silence was ominous. I looked around. Three of our crew of six were wounded, but only one seriously, the driver. We called loudly for stretcher bearers; they came and took them away. We were ordered to stay with our truck. I examined my kit-bag which lay next to me in the truck where I was crouching; there was a bullet hole in it. In a piece of soap inside I found a bullet. I found two more in my mess tin which was hanging over my head … Miracles, if the shot had gone a bit lower …

Soon it became clear that the motor had been hit and our armoured car would not be able to participate in the fighting although the car could move slowly on its tracks. So they ordered us to drive it back to Sarafand for urgent repairs.

As we were driving back slowly to the north we heard on the radio that the Israeli forces halted their offensive close to El Arish in the Sinai and then withdrew to Israeli territory. Later we learned that the British effectively threatened to actively enter the military conflict if Israel did not withdraw, arguing that they had a treaty with Egypt about mutual defence against an attack; in any case, Israeli forces were coming close to the Suez Canal which was then in British hands. The United States supported the British in this and demanded that Israel agree to a cease-fire. Since the forces of Israel were so close to a total rout of the Egyptian army, Allon and many of the military heads asked Ben Gurion to stall some more so that they could complete the operation. However, the old man replied that although he could 'fight the Arabs, all Arabs', he could not fight the great powers, and he gave an order to withdraw forthwith. He allowed an Israeli attempt to cut off the Egyptians by breaking through the Gaza–Cairo road in the south of the Gaza strip. In fierce fighting the Israeli forces did capture hills in the area from which they were able to shell the road; but then time ran out and Israel had to stop its operation on the verge of success. By early January the fighting had stopped and several weeks later an armistice agreement was signed by Israel and Egypt.

Meanwhile we were driving our damaged armoured truck to the north for repairs. We stopped over at Beersheva for one night where we had a shower and a hot meal for the first time since the start of the campaign. We drove slowly to the north to Sarafand, but the truck stalled twice on the way. By the time we arrived at the gates of Sarafand it was evening. We reckoned that in any case they would not start working on the truck that late; and we did not know when we would be given leave once inside the camp again. All of us had been dreaming about another evening in Tel Aviv – we had family there and friends – so we drove on to Tel Aviv, after arranging to meet early next morning to bring the truck to its destination in Sarafand.

When I arrived at Tel Aviv beach the side of my coat was still covered with blood and the skin on my knuckles was torn from falling against the steel wall of our truck during the firing. Yet we could not believe our eyes: in the cafés along the sea-front lit with multi-coloured lights, couples were dancing to the sound of the waltzes of Strauss and Argentinian tangos, young people were promenading – as if there was no war at all.

I slept the night at some friends who were shocked to see me in the coat full of dried blood. Next morning we returned with our truck to Sarafand. By the time it was repaired and ready for action again, a cease-fire was in force and our anti-tank regiment was relocated to a camp near Ramle. We received bigger guns and continued our training; from time to time we were sent on patrol duty, otherwise we were kept in readiness in case the negotiations with the Arab countries failed.

In the meantime, at our camp we had a problem: mornings were devoted to training with the guns arms and cleaning. But what to do in the afternoon? Again a programme was arranged: Hebrew classes for the newcomers, lectures on various topics for the old-timers. In the evenings films were shown or an entertainer was brought in. Arranging these afternoon programmes and entertainment was the function of the regimental education officer and his staff. These activities demanded a lot of work with teachers, lecturers, entertainers, musicians, cinema technicians and so on. However, our education officer was often ill or attending all kinds of meetings outside the camp; he was also often absent for various 'family reasons'. I was frequently approached about going on an officer's course; but this meant undertaking a military career for several years at least. My paramount interest, however, was to enrol as soon as possible for further studies at the Hebrew University of Jerusalem. And that meant not prolonging my military service beyond the obligatory period. I did not agree therefore to attend an officer's course and served in the meantime as an 'education officer' de facto, even though I only held the army rank of sergeant. Such ad hoc arrangements were quite common in the Israeli Army at that time. Thus I found myself dealing with teachers, travelling to Tel Aviv to contact entertainers and collect films for projection at the camp, and so on. Part of the education programme at the camp was related to religious activities such as Friday evening prayers and festive meals.

During this period I was granted leave to go to Jerusalem to register for studies at the university there. At first it looked as if there was no way for me to renew my studies at the university and even less for me to be able to attend. The military activities were not entirely over and the university was exiled from its Mount Scopus campus. However, towards early autumn the situation change drastically: cease-fire agreements were signed between Israel and the neighbouring Arab states. The Israeli authorities requisitioned a number of buildings in Jerusalem and put them at the disposal of the university. One day in September I received at the army camp an envelope with the official university logo. I was thrilled to find inside it a formal letter of enrolment into the Hebrew University and a second letter addressed to the army authorities asking that they release me from army service for studies in accordance with a decision of the government of Israel.

Sometime in November 1949 I found myself in civilian dress sitting on a bench in the Terra Sancta building attending the opening lecture in philosophy. I was a student at the Hebrew University.

Epilogue: 1949–2000

1949–1969

1949–54: AT THE HEBREW UNIVERSITY IN JERUSALEM

I was accepted at the Hebrew University of Jerusalem in the autumn of 1949. By then Israel had signed cease-fire agreements with Egypt, Jordan and Syria and the fighting at the front had stopped. I was released from the army and started to attend lectures. This became possible through a lucky turn of events – my parents and younger sister had 'settled' in Jerusalem.

They had at last had been able to come to Israel in April 1949, together with my sister and two brothers and their families. I was still in the army and met them at Haifa port in full regalia. There was great excitement, embraces and tears. Soon, however, stark reality took over: they were sent to the large and primitive 'immigrant camp' where they were 'housed' in a military tent along with several other immigrant families. Simple iron beds practically filled the tent – leaving barely any place to put their few belongings or to sit down. So one had to 'live on the bed'.

The situation was appalling: long queues in front of the food distribution barracks and the wooden latrines at the edge of the camp, a crowd in front of the administration building. This was still the rainy season so strong winds were tearing the tent walls and rain poured into the tent. The paths between the tents became quagmires. The electric bulbs inside swung dimly and the electricity failed from time to time, leaving people in total darkness. And many *olim* were there with little children.

Fortunately, my parents did not even have to spend a single night in this miserable 'absorption centre'. I learned about these conditions before their coming, so I went into the abandoned area of Haifa and rented there for a small price a house not far from the centre of town. It was red-roofed and consisted of one large room only, with a recess in one corner which could serve as some kind of a kitchen. It was a rather drab place, but a palace in comparison with the tent. We brought over our bedding and some of our things and slept there in relative comfort, blessing our lucky stars, as it had started to rain heavily.

Slowly we cleaned the place and furnished it; my brothers found similar rented accommodation nearby. We kept up a presence at the tent at the 'absorption centre' and officially we all continued to live there since otherwise we would lose our rights for support and housing (in the unknown future). Every day two of our family would join the queue for hot food and supplies for all of us. They carried it to 'our house' in Wadi Nisnas (this was the name of the area) where our mother added some good ingredients (fat, meat, and so on) and we were able to have a decent meal.

I returned to the army camp satisfied that I had been able to help my family, but soon I received alarming news – my father had been taken seriously ill. His asthma was badly affected by the damp, heavy air of Haifa, and his condition was deteriorating with each passing day.

We were desperate. Then an idea occurred to me: why not try Jerusalem? As a soldier's father and due to his health condition he was granted a one-week stay at a 'pension' in the centre of Jerusalem – to see if the clear, dry mountain air there agreed with him. I accompanied him on this journey. I shall never forget how he stepped off the bus, stretched out his arms, breathed deeply and said; 'Wine – this air is like a clear wine to me.'

Within two weeks my parents and Ruthie, my younger sister, moved from Haifa to an 'immigrant camp'on the outskirts of Jerusalem. My brothers and their families remained in Haifa where the prospects for work and housing were better. At that time there was no university in Haifa; the only university in the country was in Jerusalem. I was quite pleased about my parents moving to this city even though it meant that, after so many decades of sticking together through adversity, we were separated from my brothers in Haifa.

My parents moved to Jerusalem, but our problems had only just started. At first they were given one room in an 'immigrant absorption centre' in an abandoned former Arab area. Conditions there were not as bad as in Haifa, yet it was certainly not a place where they could spend any length of time. However, the housing officer in the camp declared that we would have to wait until some housing became available – perhaps in a year or two.

Luckily, we heard through the grapevine that some houses close to no-man's land near the old city were empty of inhabitants.

In my soldier's uniform I had access to the area and after some reconnoitring found a house in the area of Musrara – in quite good condition and uninhabited. But when I approached the housing officer, she would not hear of it: 'We cannot hand out housing in a partisan manner. You have to wait until the area is surveyed.'

We brought the matter to the attention of the camp manager, invoked my rights as a war veteran and my fathers illness – all to no avail. Finally, I took leave from the army and proclaimed a 'sit in strike' in the office of the housing officer. After several days, she agreed to go with me and see the house. Two weeks later we were given a paper from the administration of abandoned property assigning to us two rooms in this house for a reasonable rent. Three years after leaving Poland on our tortuous journey we at last had a home in Israel.

We had a home – barely adequate but ours–yet now that we had left the immigrant centre we no longer had meals and supplies. How were we to live? My parents had already thought about it when they were at the DP camp in Germany. With the little money which they saved there and the little which remained from selling our two houses in communist Poland they bought a large wooden kiosk. When it arrived in Haifa port we had it transported to Jerusalem. Then a long bureaucratic wrangle started – much more difficult and protracted than that regarding living space for us. The city engineer decided that a kiosk was a 'structure', and therefore had to be approved by the 'appropriate planning and building authorities' of the Jerusalem municipality – which usually took a year or two. I decided to use the same tactics as with housing: I found a suitable place to erect the kiosk and persuaded two of the officials to go and see it. We found an 'in' at the municipal council when we learned that one of its members was from our original town of Yaroslav in Poland and he had known our family there. Within two months we received the city planners' permit and one month later the kiosk was ready for business.

We did not know whether the kiosk would be a success. It was situated on the corner of a street sloping down from the centre of town, but it was not far from a wall bordering on no man's land. Not that many people walked in the area, even though it was not far from the King David Hotel. The kiosk, however, offered a wide range of much needed goods in that time of shortages – cigarettes, cold drinks, newspapers, sweets and chocolates (when assigned to us), bagels, ice cream and as a special treat, freshly pressed orange or grapefruit juice. It looked at first as though not many customers would come to our establishment, but as the day progressed the situation improved. I shall never forget the light which shone in my parents' eyes when, at the close of the first day of business, they counted the takings and concluded with pride: 'It's going to be all right – we earned our keep today!'

LIFE IN ISRAEL AT THAT TIME

Life in Israel at that time was a paradox. Material conditions were very harsh. During the period of Turkish rule (until 1917) and during the British Mandate period (until May 1948), Palestine was an integral part of the Middle East, with open borders, travel and trade. After the establishment of Israel, it was cut off from its neighbouring countries, surrounded by a ring of hostility and an object of Arab economic boycott. The War of Independence gave Israel a great victory, but it brought great destruction, exhaustion and needs. Hundreds of thousands of Jews were pouring into the Jewish state which had no resources to provide for their needs in food, housing, work, health, education, and so on. We therefore lived in conditions where almost everything was strictly rationed: two or three eggs per week, a small ration of sausage and rarely meat, a little fat and other basic foods. From time to time, even oranges and vegetables were in short supply. Sugar, coffee and tea were rare. We had vouchers for two simple shirts a year, one pair of khaki trousers, two pairs of underwear and socks ... It was especially difficult for the new immigrants, who had no accumulated reserves or friends and family to assist them.

Despite all difficulties, we managed. Somehow, we were able to get hold of additional eggs, fat, sausage and chicken. What was abundantly available was white fish 'fillet' which, although tasteless and often smelly on its own, could be made much more palatable by adding some spices to it. So we had a meal which made one forget its origins (we had had long experience in Russia and in post-war Germany of this kind of 'cooking'). Especially difficult were periods of shortages, without electricity, water or blocks of ice for the ice box (obviously we had no refrigerator at that time).

The security situation was very grave indeed. Though the neighbouring Arab countries signed cease-fire agreements with

Israel, they constantly threatened to go to war again. They supported armed incursions of Palestinian infiltrators into Israeli territory, and although the situation was dangerous everywhere, it was more so in Jerusalem. Not far from our home in the Musrara area, and not far from our kiosk near the King David Hotel, there was a high wall which divided the Israeli part of Jerusalem from the Arab part. From time to time, the Arab Legionnaires (Jordanian soldiers) who manned the walls of the Old City and the partition wall in the middle of Jerusalem, would open fire, sniping at people in Israeli Jerusalem. This was especially the case when a convoy was proceeding to Mount Scopus (seat of the Hebrew University of Jerusalem). The Mount area remained in Israeli hands according to the cease-fire agreement with Jordan – but passage to it was through Arab-held territory.

Although I had been released from active service in the Israeli army, I remained on reserve duty like all young Israelis. Quite often, I heard a knock on the window of my room, during day or night, and a voice called 'mobilization'. I had an army uniform and rifle at home, so within 20 minutes or so I was on my way to my unit's mobilization point. I remained in an anti-tank artillery unit. At hidden places within Jerusalem and around we had some guns at the ready. We wheeled them out to prepared positions ready to open fire if the Jordanians attacked the convoy to Mount Scopus or West Jerusalem in general. From time to time I was called up to man positions and ambushes on the roads to Jerusalem in order to intercept Arab infiltrators.

While studying at the Hebrew University, I was among the founders of a student organization called the 'Volunteers Corps'. At that time, in the mountains to the west of Jerusalem, there were small isolated settlements in which mostly oriental Jewish immigrants lived. The security situation was so bad that these settlements were often Israeli by day, but infiltrated by the Palestinians at night. Each settlement had a few guards, but the majority of the settlers had no military experience, which often left them helpless when attacked. Also, neither the adults nor the children knew Hebrew. They could not communicate with the security guards or help their children in preparing their homework. The 'Volunteer Corps' organized students to help the immigrant settlements. With assistance from the authorities, we travelled by truck to those settlements, where we taught the parents and children some Hebrew, Israeli songs, dances and games. Sometimes, we had to instruct the adults and children alike in some basic rules of hygiene and household matters such as taking a shower, cleaning one's teeth, dressing in pyjamas for sleep or how to operate a kerosene stove or heater. Often, we stayed overnight and reinforced the guards so that the settlers would feel more secure.

STUDENT LIFE

Student life at that time in Jerusalem was far from the 'golden college years' experience: no student balls or dances, no major college sport events, no student meals in restaurants, no frolicking in pubs or bars. Life was very austere. Most of the students were engaged in some form of job to earn money – like myself, working in the kiosk of my parents. Our professors were mostly of the 'old school', some of them survivors of the Holocaust, people who had lost their families in it, and the escapees from Nazi Europe. Not surprisingly they regarded the very idea of a student ball at the university as anathema. Yet, life was not entirely without its brighter side. In time, I became acquainted with some of the students, mostly of a similar background to mine. Our group arranged regular private dance evenings at various homes and student rooms. Sometimes, we went together on Saturday evenings to the Talpiot Gardens in Jerusalem where the dance floor overlooked from afar, the Dead Sea area on a moonlit night. Despite its isolation, Jerusalem was a centre for political events, international gatherings and conferences. Concerts were held by the Israel Philharmonic Orchestra and other international activities also took place. There was no hall or theatre in Jerusalem at that time, so even the Philharmonic performed in the Edison Cinema Hall where the accoustics and arrangements were far from ideal, to say the least. A number of cinemas were active in the centre of town; but again, they were mostly of a low standard. In one of the major cinemas in the centre, the toilets were under the screen!

From Jerusalem, we travelled from time to time to other parts of the country, especially to the coast, for example to Tel Aviv, Netanya or Haifa. There we were able to swim in the Mediterranean and enjoy the many restaurants and nightclubs. Whenever we went down from Jerusalem by public transport (we had no car of course at that time) we realized again and again that Jerusalem was 'like another planet' compared to the Tel Aviv area.

Of all my trips around the country, one remains especially alive in my memory. It was a student trip to the Dead Sea and Masada in the early 1950s. We travelled by truck through Beersheba and down the steep slope to the Dead Sea. It was like a moon landscape, stony desert covered with sand and dust. It was spring time and we stopped at some of the *wadis* which had water in their river beds, and what a delight it was, when covered with dust from the desert, to swim in the cool waters of those *wadis*! At Masada, we got up before sunrise and climbed the mountain, starting off on the so-called 'snake path'. The last portion, near the top of the mountain, we had to climb using ropes since there was no other way to reach the summit. The view from the top of Masada at sunrise was spectacular, mystical and unforgettable. Although we had no trouble climbing up on the ropes, climbing down was quite frightening and we had to tie some of our companions to the ropes in order to get them down.

True, we lived in very difficult material and security conditions, but the mood of the country and our personal spirits were high, very much up-beat. We lived in the euphoria that followed the establishment of the 'Jewish State' and the victories of the Israeli army in the War of Independence. The dream had become a reality. A State of Israel in the 'Land of Israel' had become a fact. Israel was able to defend itself successfully against a number of Arab armies and hordes of infiltrators. Despite the border incidents and the occasional incursions, we felt secure and strong. Many thousands of *olim* (Jewish immigrants) were constantly arriving in the country despite the difficult circumstances. Especially memorable were the Independence Day military parades. In the brightly lit streets of Jerusalem, masses of people would dance through the night.

Having been accepted as a student at the Hebrew University, as a demobilized war veteran and a new immigrant I was exempt from paying tuition and even received at first a small scholarship. I also earned my keep by helping at the kiosk, especially by getting hold of supplies: sacks of oranges, blocks of ice, packets of cigarettes. Both our home and the kiosk were within walking distance of the university lecture halls, so I commuted between them. The road to the university campus on Mount Scopus was cut off by Jordanian forces so studies were conducted mainly at the Terra Sancta and other monastery buildings around town. As for teaching staff, I was lucky since at that time the Hebrew University was home to some outstanding Jewish scholars from the major universities of Europe (mainly Germany) and even the

United States. Most famous among these was Martin (Mordechai) Buber. I attended some of his lectures, for example, when he read to us some Sanskrit documents. His teaching was all right – until someone asked him a pertinent question. He then sat down at a desk opposite the student and engaged in a lively discussion with him, for a good half an hour, as if the rest of the class was not there. I knew Buber in his last years, when I worked at the *Ha'aretz* newspaper. He was always interested in 'what was going on' especially with regard to Israeli–Arab affairs and we had long discussions on this subject.

I took some lectures in philosophy from professors Leo Roth (brother of historian Cecil), Hugo Bergman and Nathan Rotenstreich. I studied political thought with Professor Benjamin Akzin, economics under Professor Dan Patinkin, modern history with Professor Jacob Talmon and other distinguished teachers. During the last year of my studies I was recommended by my university to the newly established Higher School of Political Science at the Prime Minister's Office in Jerusalem as lecturer in social studies.

One day, Colonel Dov Harari came to see me at the university. He was one of the leading parachute commanders then in the Israeli army. He explained that a 'Prime Minister's School' was to give concentrated higher studies to selected military, security and police officers who had been promoted in their career without ever having had the chance of higher education. There were to be three instructors – one for military strategic affairs, one for Middle East studies (David Kimche, who later became a top diplomat and intelligence officer) and one for socio-political studies (myself). Guest lecturers were to be among the most distinguished specialists in their field, mostly academic. The students were middle-aged people who received salaried leave for one year from their jobs in the army and police. During studies, they would live in the former British army Allenby Barracks in Jerusalem, returning home for weekends. Some of them had formidable knowledge about the Middle East in general, and Arab countries in particular. One of them, for example, was a specialist on Iraq. He was said to know by heart the wavelength of Iraqi broadcastings, as well as the timetable of trains in Baghdad. Another student disappeared from time to time during studies. Upon his return it was rumoured that he made regular trips to Saudi Arabia. My job was to make arrangements for the lecturers, give additional lectures and exercises in political and social studies and advise students on their independent work and reading. Some of them prepared 'overall strategic assessments' of Arab and Middle Eastern countries.

This year at the school provided me with some teaching experience. It also had a positive financial aspect: for the first time in my life I received a regular and relatively high salary. The board of the school gave a very positive recommendation about my work there.

While teaching there I was preparing for my final MA exams. To my great surprise Professor Norman Bentwich, one of my teachers, suddenly asked me in the spring of that year: 'Would you like to go to the University of London for one year on a scholarship from our university to do your doctoral studies?'

1954–57: DOCTORAL STUDIES AND MARRIAGE IN LONDON

My mother, saddened by my imminent departure, but otherwise proud about my selection for a scholarship, took me to a high-quality tailor shop and ordered for me a 'fine suit'. 'You don't even have one proper jacket,' she said. 'You cannot go like this to England.' At that time, in the middle of the 1950s, it was very expensive to travel by plane, so I went by a ship from Haifa to Naples and from there through Rome, Florence, Geneva and across the English Channel to London. The journey through Europe and London made an indelible impression on me. Especially since at that time Israel was in a period of strict rationing, mass immigration of Holocaust survivors and of poor oriental Jews, as well as in the aftermath of the War of Independence. Put simply – a poor and struggling country. Europe and England appeared rich and highly developed in comparison.

Soon after my arrival the pre-Christmas season started. When I rode on the top of a double-decker bus through Oxford Street and Regent Street with their elegant shops and imposing buildings, I was elated. I was enrolled as a doctoral student at the London School of Economics and the School of Slavonic Studies of London University. The academic standard impressed me immensely. I worked on my doctorate at these institutions for three years and had the priviledge of studying with some leading scholars. Among these were Karl Popper, Robert McKenzie, Leonard Schapiro, Michael Oakeshott; and among guest lecturers were

Isaiah Berlin and E.H. Carr. After some searching for a suitable subject for my doctoral dissertation I settled upon a 'History of Party-Political Education in the Soviet Union'.

Both E.H. Carr and Schapiro were internationally recognized major scholars of the USSR – but their positions were diametrically opposed to one another. Schapiro published very critical and realistic works on the Soviet Union and its leadership, Stalin especially. E.H. Carr wrote a multi-volume history of the Russian Revolution and of the Soviet Union which was relatively 'sympathetic'. His work was based mainly on official Soviet material, which was obviously subjective without confronting it with living evidence from 'anti-Soviet' émigrés and sources. And there was I, a doctoral student, who came some years ago from Russia and had been educated there. I was, therefore, able to tell him about the inside reality and what it was like living in the USSR. Furthermore, I did my doctorate from 1954–57 when, after the death of Stalin, the Soviets gradually started releasing material previously prohibited or secret. In my research, I unearthed some new materials of this kind and passed information about it to Carr. He sent me some of his newly written chapters and I returned them to him with my remarks.

I was also privileged in developing a personal relationship with Leonard Schapiro, then the leading historian and Sovietologist in Britain. This relationship continued into my later years of teaching in Britain at the end of the 1960s and early 1980s.

In the meantime, a major change occurred in my personal life. One Saturday evening I went to a Jewish student dance at one of the colleges. At first it looked to me uninteresting and I was about to leave. Just then I noticed Doris – a lovely young girl with a brilliant smile, fine face and figure. I summoned up my courage, invited her to dance and we danced and talked for the entire evening. We met on a number of further occasions, going together to the theatre, dances and on country outings. It turned out that she was highly interested in and knowledgable about music, opera and art. After going out together for a few months, we decided to get married. She knew it would mean leaving England and her family for Israel after I finished my doctorate – not an easy decision in those days. Our wedding encountered a major problem: I flatly refused to wear an evening suit and top hat. Doris cleverly invited me to another wedding at the synagogue. One look at it was enough to make me realize that I had to give in – even if my Israeli guests would laugh at me.

Shortly after our wedding I went from London for my first post-war visit to the Soviet Union, on an Israeli passport, which was unprecedented at that time. I visited Moscow, Leningrad and surrounding areas. Again, I was lucky: since I knew Russian and Yiddish and dressed like a Russian I was able to meet and talk with some residents of these cities and was even invited by some of them to their homes – a thing that did not happen to any other of our tourists from London. I attended Sabbath prayers at the Great Synagogue in Moscow and when the rabbis there realised that I was Israeli they invited me to address the congregation – which I did both in Russian and Yiddish. I returned to London with much inside information, especially about the youth and the Jewish people of Russia. The London weekly *Observer* published four articles of mine under the pen name William C. Just – for obvious reasons. I also published several articles in the London *Jewish Chronicle* as well as in the Israeli *Ha'aretz*.

The Hebrew University extended my scholarship for two additional years so that I was able to complete my doctoral dissertation – which I did by the end of summer of 1957, with the help of my wife who edited my manuscript.

In the autumn of 1956 our first daughter, Nina, was born. We lived in very modest student conditions – I received a scholarship of ten pounds a month, but my wife worked at the MGM Film Studios in Elstree in the publicity department of Ealing Films until the birth of our daughter. I especially remember one occasion when Professor Rotenstreich from Jerusalem visited us in London just after we married. We lived then in Swiss Cottage in a one-room studio apartment with a bed which had to be raised to the wall during the daytime and a tiny kitchenette in the corridor. Our visitor did not bat an eyelid, he had supper with us and we indulged in a profound discussion.

In October 1957 I returned to Israel. As my wife and daughter had the status of new immigrants and I was a 'returning Israeli' the cost of our travel to Israel was covered by the Jewish Agency. A relative of mine who lived not far from us in London came to take us to Victoria railway station for the start of our journey. 'You are travelling with your wife and small child – how much money do you have?' 'Five pounds', I answered. He gave us five pounds more – and it was with this money that we went through Paris to Marseille and from there by ship to Haifa.

1957–67: FOREIGN EDITOR AND DIPLOMATIC CORRESPONDENT AT *HA'ARETZ*

After a warm reception from my family in Haifa (both my brothers worked with the port police and they came out in a boat to meet our ship), we travelled to Jerusalem where my parents lived and where I was supposed to work as a lecturer at the Hebrew University. It soon became clear that we had a problem. My parents' flat, though centrally situated (a few blocks from the King David Hotel), was in an old house, simply furnished, and too small to accommodate us for more than a few weeks. The walls of the Old City were not far away and at that time Jordanian soldiers would occasionally snipe from them. Jerusalem was then divided and gave the impression of a poor, backward, beleaguered city, dark and empty in the evenings. To both of us coming from London it was difficult to envisage our living there. Also the position at the university was not exactly as I had expected.

The birth of our second daughter, Odette, briefly after our arrival accentuated the harsh conditions that then existed in Jerusalem. Labour started early Friday evening, that is, on the Sabbath. We were then staying with my parents at their flat in the centre of Jerusalem. On that dark Friday evening there was barely any traffic. Of course, we had no car or telephone, and no taxi rank answered my call from a public phone box. In some panic, I ran to the local station of Magen David Adom (the equivalent of the Red Cross) to get an ambulance. 'We have only two ambulances on Shabbat and both are currently in the field', said the officer on duty, 'so we cannot provide an ambulance for your wife.' Only after I threatened him with my press card (I was already working at the *Ha'aretz* newspaper) did he find an ambulance. At that time, the well-equipped Hadassah Hospital on Mount Scopus was cut off from West Jerusalem, and the new Hadassah Hospital in Ein Karem was still being built, so Doris was brought by the ambulance to the makeshift maternity ward at the Beit HaDegel Monastery near the centre. Compared to the modern, first-class maternity hospital at University College London where Doris had given birth to our first daughter, Nina, the situation at Beit HaDegel was cramped and primitive in the extreme. The front door of the ward was shut in my face; there was no arrangement for prospective fathers to stay inside, never mind being allowed to attend the birth, hold the mother's hand. I sat for some time on the bench by the entrance in the drizzle. At last a nurse came out, assured me that it would still take hours, at least until the late morning and advised me to go home. When I arrived in the morning, it turned out that the birth had occurred shortly after my departure! Both of us were very upset and even then they did not allow me to enter the ward. It was full of women of oriental or religious background, many of whom had had no preparation or advice on giving birth. The only way I could see my wife was when they allowed her to come outside for a short while to see me. I could not see the baby until Doris was allowed to leave the hospital. As it happened, she was so disturbed by the whole atmosphere that she asked to be released after a couple of days; how happy we were nevertheless to have a healthy baby and to be back at my parents' home.

To my great surprise, one day I suddenly received an invitation from Gershom Schocken, the editor and owner of *Ha'aretz*, to become Foreign Editor and Diplomatic Correspondent of the paper. It meant moving to Tel Aviv and a good salary. When I took Doris for a trip to Tel Aviv with its boulevards full of cafés and elegant shops, and its seashore full of people brown from the sun, she was visibly impressed and relieved. I accepted the position and started work. We moved to Tel Aviv several weeks later after the birth of our second daughter, Odette. As an 'immigrant family' we were allotted an apartment at reduced cost in a then new northern suburb of Tel Aviv called Ramat Aviv.

My work at *Ha'aretz* turned out to be most interesting and challenging. Five times a week, I wrote the leading article on foreign affairs which was sometimes a risky affair since from the time of writing it – usually late in the afternoon – until its appearance in the paper next morning situations sometimes changed significantly. As diplomatic correspondent I was invited to various receptions and celebrations where I met with some of the top people in the country – Golda Meir, Levi Eshkol, Abba Eban … I was also befriended by some of the leading foreign diplomats. Since I knew Polish and Russian I was often invited to drink vodka with representatives of those countries (they once tried to make me drunk but I refused more drink, stood up and left). Doris and I enjoyed these parties but there was a hitch, our apartment and budget did not allow us to reciprocate. Our children were small, so Doris could not undertake any formal work; yet she found a satisfactory way to supplement our income by teaching English in our home to groups of people, some diplomats and academics among them.

In the autumn of 1959 I received an invitation signed by the then Secretary of State for a three-month visit to the United States on a 'Young Leaders Programme'. It meant leaving Doris alone with the children for several months, but the possible benefits of the trip outweighed the difficulties. As it happened, I arrived in Washington just when Khrushchev came there for his first visit. My press accreditation allowed me entrance to some functions and to observe the Soviet leader close up. He answered journalists' questions pleasantly and with self-assurance. But when he was asked about anti-Semitism in the USSR and the right of Soviet Jews for family reunification in Israel he became irritable and went red in the neck. Half of my visit to the United States was to be spent in a place of my choosing; I chose Savannah, Georgia where I tried to understand the socio-political developments in the South and the situation of the black community. When I asked to meet some black leaders it turned out that it was possible only as a clandestine affair in the backroom of a Jewish furniture shop. Then I travelled around the country. One highlight of the trip was a visit to the town of Independence where I met with Harry Truman. It was my first visit to America and it made a forceful impression on me. The trip also had a financial advantage: I received a rather generous travel allowance much of which I was able to save. So on my way back to Israel (this time by plane) I was able to stop over in London and buy my first car – a blue Morris Oxford – which was shipped to Haifa.

One of my diplomat friends was the ambassador of Cuba, a Jewish millionnaire who had helped Castro when he was still an outlaw in the mountains. One day he invited me to his sumptious villa in Herzliya on the Sea and handed me an invitation to go to Cuba to attend the national day celebrations there. So in the summer of 1962 I travelled through Prague, Reykjavik and Newfoundland to Havana. I was then taken to attend a major rally with hundreds of thousands of *paisanos* at Santiago de Cuba, the main feature of which was a six-hour speech by Castro. Together with other 'delegates' I was then taken on a round trip of the island. I was quite impressed by the high spirit in the country but also by its poverty and ideological indoctrination with some frivolity. We were received for press conferences with the leadership of the country and for an elegant 'strip show' at the 'Copa Cabana' with beautiful dancing women. Upon return to Israel I wrote a series of articles entitled 'Communism With Cha Cha Cha.'

I had relatively good contacts with the head of some members of the Soviet embassy, and in the summer of 1964 they granted me a visa for a trip to Russia. As there was no direct way then to go there from Israel, I and the other Israelis flew first to Istanbul, where we boarded a Soviet passenger ship to Odessa. As it happened, the ship was coming from Alexandria by way of the Syrian port of Latakia. It was packed with Soviet 'advisers' from Arab countries on their way home or on holiday. As I speak Russian fluently and dressed like one, I was able to listen to their conversations and so get some idea about their attitudes to the Arab countries in which they were stationed. These were not very flattering. In some cases I did tell them that I was Israeli; almost all of them were very interested to hear about Israel. In the USSR we travelled to Kiev, Kishinev (in a small shaking plane without air conditioning), Moscow and Leningrad. Everywhere we had the same picture: on our tourist bus and at our table at any of the hotels small Israeli flags with the Star of David were placed linked with a red Soviet flag with the hammer and sicle. Almost every-where it attracted Jewish people: some walked around, some tried to talk with us; others were bold enough to come as if to shake hands but slipped a little note with an address of a relative in Israel or with an application for *aliya* to Israel. In Kiev they took us to a summer camp of the Young Comunist League where an offical march past took place with the youngsters waving Soviet and Israeli flags and shouting slogans for peace and Israeli–Soviet friendship. Despite the opposition of Soviet officials, I went in Kiev to Babi Yar – the place of mass execution of the Jews.

In Moscow I visited the Great Synagogue where I was asked again to address the congregation. Most interesting was my meeting with the Soviet poet-dissident Yevgeni Yevtushenko who wrote that famous poem 'There is no memorial stone at Babi Yari'. His talk with me was in the presence of some officials of the official Writers Union, and naturally he denied the existence of anti-Semitism in the USSR. Also memorable were my meetings with the families of Jews condemned to death for 'economic crimes' during Khrushchev's 'economic purges'. Before boarding the ship in Odessa for our return journey to Israel we were subjected to a meticulous search; some women had even to strip and walk on a floor with light reflectors beneath it. Upon my return I wrote a series of articles in *Ha'aretz*. While comparing favourably the material situation in Russia with what I had found on a previous visit some eight years ago, the articles presented a grim picture of the situation of the Jews and documented the burning desire of many of them to leave for Israel.

Meanwhile, dramatic things were going on in Israel. Ben Gurion resigned and was followed by the mild, humorous and peace-oriented Levi Eshkol. I disliked the harsh, somewhat arrogant and authoritarian inclinations of the 'old man' and his group which then included Moshe Dayan, Shimon Peres and others. Eshkol and his group seemed to me a chance for a peaceful resolution of the Israel–Arab conflict. I was drawn into active participation in politics. However, my 'Soviet experience' did not allow me to join the party of Eshkol which was a socialist party. So I became active in a newly united Liberal Party, where I found a 'Young Liberal' group and became its chairman. As such I was even put on the list of candidates for the Knesset, though in an unrealistic place. However, shortly afterwards the United Liberal Party split with the majority joining in a bloc with the then very rightist Herut Party of Menachem Begin. I did not agree with this and left party politics.

In the following election, however, a major confrontation was looming between the Eshkol alliance and the new Israel Workers' Party (RAFI) headed by Ben Gurion. I proposed then forming a non-party, voluntary, voters support group. I was invited to meet Eshkol himself and the group, 'Citizens for Eshkol' was duly created. I took leave from work and campaigned all over the country. Local chapters of the support group were created and contributed significantly to a resounding Eshkol victory.

As time went on I began to feel slightly restless with my work at *Ha'aretz*. It provided me with a prestigious and interesting position; I was invited to lecture on Israeli national radio and at various kibbutzim and public bodies. Yet it was very demanding and I was able to deal only with day-to-day events. There was no possibility of dealing in greater depth with the topics of history, politics and social thought which were of interest to me. From time to time I was invited to lecture at academic institutions and I felt drawn to this kind of milieu. Early in 1967 I received an invitation from a colleague, Professor Alec Nove who was then at the University of Glasgow to teach there for one year. It appeared a good prospect for me to re-enter academic work and I accepted. We agreed with the editor of *Ha'aretz* that I would work until July when I would leave.

THE SIX DAY WAR

In the meantime, a war crisis arose between Israel, Egypt and other Arab countries in late May/early June of 1967 – the Six Day War. I had not been called to serve in 1956 in the Sinai/Suez war since I was working on my doctorate then in England and the war ended in several days. In 1967 I was no longer in a fighting reserve unit but in the Education Division of the Israeli army. As such we were sent to various regiments and camps to address the units and to brief and accompany VIPs and foreign journalists. I remember vividly one such a case. Together with other journalists I was taken by military escort to a huge airbase 'somewhere in the south'. In a huge hangar packed with planes some 2,000 Air Force people were assembled. When question time came many asked: 'What is the government waiting for … we are faced with Arab acts of war and with every day of inaction the danger is becoming more acute … 'We answered as best as we could; I suggested that maybe we were waiting for an understanding with the United States. When the meeting ended we were invited to the office of the commander of the base. 'How can I convince you – and the government – that we can destroy the entire Egyptian airforce in a few hours … We don't need any Amecian cover …' I could not sleep that night after we returned from this meeting: 'Our military are too cocky, I thought, and this is dangerous.'

Two days later, at the start of the war, the Israeli Air Force did exactly what its commanders promised. We lived then in a rented villa in Herzliya Beach north of Tel Aviv. There was no bomb-shelter there so we made a ditch in a sand dune nearby, following official instructions. Every time the air-raid siren was heard – day or night – we ran, with emergency supplies, to hide in the ditch. Fortunately, nobody was hit.

The swift and decisive victory of the Israeli army over the Arab armies came as a total surprise – an almost miraculous event. Paradoxically, it was, to some degree, a considerable surprise for me personally. On the one hand I had more information about the great might of the army of Israel as a result of visits to army bases like the one described above and other information available to journalists. On the other hand, I was constantly reading material in the foreign press and despatches of the major news agencies. I also had frequent contacts with foreign diplomats. As the conflict unfolded, the press and the diplomats presented news items which were frightening indeed: 'Arab Armies mobilized for a concerted attack on Israel', 'Israel isolated and surrounded', and so on. Actually, as a premeditated policy, the Israeli press and Israeli radio, which was at that time government-owned, projected a similar picture of an imminent Arab all-out onslaught on Israel.

This line was also maintained during the first few days of the war. They did not immediately inform the Israeli public about the decisive victories of the Israeli Air Force and Armoured Divisions during the first hours of the war. Only following the third day did the Israelis and the entire world learn about the destruction of the Egyptian, Syrian and Jordanian air forces at the beginning of the fighting. The announcements about reaching the Suez Canal, about the liberation of the Old City of Jerusalem and about taking the Golan Heights came with some delay, one after the other, with stunning effect.

I was one of the few people in Israel who had information about what was truly happening only several hours after the start of fighting. Upon arriving in my office at *Ha'aretz* – on the morning of 6 June 1967 – I had a look at the teleprinters of the major international news agencies. At first, it looked incomprehensible: they were printing material like mad and the content was the same: 'Israel air force attacked all Egyptian air force bases simultaneously', 'Arab air forces totally destroyed by Israel', 'Israeli armour nearing the Suez Canal', and so on.

The Israeli media reported only that fighting had started. At first, there were even reports about Egyptian army attacks over the cease-fire lines with Israel. One of the reports said that the Jordanian forces started bombarding West Jerusalem and that the Jordanian army units had crossed the lines in Jerusalem and were advancing towards the centre.

I remember that from my office in Tel Aviv I phoned my parents in Jerusalem who had their kiosk and apartment close to the dividing wall. It turned out that they knew nothing and had opened the kiosk as if nothing unusual was going on. I shouted over the phone: 'Close the kiosk immediately, for heaven's sake … take a few of your belongings from your flat, and close it! Move over to Ruth's place.' My sister Ruth lived in an apartment in a safer part of Jerusalem, far from the border line.

At first my parents argued with me: 'No need to panic … it is quiet here', they argued.

'It is going to begin any moment', I shouted, 'and you are close to the border … you should leave without delay, it is an emergency,' I insisted. As they started walking uphill towards Ruth's apartment, the Jordan artillery bombardment and shooting erupted. They managed to get to her apartment safely.

1967–73: TEACHING AND RESEARCH ABROAD

At the end of July we travelled with our childen by ship to Venice then across Europe to London and to Glasgow to teach political science and Soviet studies at the university there. We spent a pleasant year in Scotland and upon receiving an invitation from the University of Essex we moved to London where I lectured during 1968/69. During my work at Glasgow and Essex I wrote some research papers on sociology and society in the USSR and sent them to a number of research centres. I was more than pleasantly surprised to receive a letter from the Russian Research Centre at Harvard granting me a generous research scholarship and an invitation to teach there.

AT HARVARD AND MIT

At the end of August 1969 we arrived in Belmont near Cambridge, Massachusetts, to do research and teach at Harvard. We were pleasantly surprised: the Russian Research Center at Harvard, to which I was attached, found us a lovely small house on a hill in a tree-lined street. At the Center, at the seminars and at the faculty club, I was able to mingle with some leading personalities and scholars, many of whom were then at Harvard, and soon also at MIT. Among them were Talcott Parsons, Richard Pipes, Daniel Bell, Merle Fainsod, Robert Nozick, Adam Ulam, Seymour Lipsett and others. I was proud to work in such a distinquished scholarly company. When, for the first time, I arrived at Harvard Yard I walked around looking at the buldings, the students and lecturers hurrying to their classes, I thought: 'Am I really at Harvard?'

I worked during the first two years on Soviet society and sociology producing a series of six major papers on these topics. I also did some teaching at Harvard on 'Soviet Jewry – a Case of a National Minority'. This was the first time such a course has been taught at the Sociology Department at Harvard and students from other colleges in the area (especially Brandeis) registered for it. Some of the Harvard management did not like it but the course was a success, especially since I invited some prominent guest lecturers such as Richard Pipes, Nathan Glazer and others.

Towards the end of my second year at Harvard, a US government agency, the United States Information Agency (USIA),
expressed its interest in an in-depth research project on Soviet
nationalities. Harvard was unwilling to accept government
funding for this project as there was much criticism at that time
(the early 1970s) of co-operation with (serving) the government.
The International Centre at MIT was only too willing to take up
this proposal. I remained a Fellow at the Russian Research Center
at Harvard and for the next two years worked there and at the
International Center of MIT on the nationalities project with
professors Ithiel De Sola Pool and William Griffith. It resulted in
my book, *Major Soviet Nationalities*, published by the Free Press in
1975.   During those four years we were able to do much travelling across North America. The owners of the house which we had
rented had a cottage in Saint Petersburg Beach, Florida. During
the summer they wished to stay at their former home in Belmont,
so we swapped places and travelled in our car through New York,
Washington, Atlanta and Savannah to Saint Petersburg. We spent
a fascinating summer there going out sea-fishing with friends of
the owners of our house, travelling along the Gulf of Mexico and
then through the Everglades and Miami back to Boston. We also
travelled to Montreal, Quebec and Toronto. I was invited to
address meetings for Soviet Jewry in Cincinnati and other places
and participated in the World Congress on behalf of Soviet Jewry
in Brussels, in the spring of 1971. I was also able to attend a
number of scholarly conferences in the United States and abroad,
for example, at Salzburg in Austria and Varna in Bulgaria.

1973–2000: BACK IN ISRAEL

In early 1973 I received an invitation from the head of the
Department of Russian and Slavonic Studies at the Hebrew
University of Jerusalem to come and join the staff. My research on
Soviet nationalities was coming to an end and though I had some
other proposals in the United States I accepted the offer to return
to Israel, to the Hebrew University. So towards the end of
September 1973 we went to New York where we boarded the
Canberra on a transatlantic voyage to Cherbourg, France and then
by train to Paris. It was while sightseeing by taxi in Paris that we
heard on its radio that the (Yom Kippur) war had broken out. We

were stranded in Paris since our booking to proceed to Israel by ship from Genova was cancelled and no air travel was possible. We were told to go to Rome where we fought for an early place on an El Al plane which was the only one then flying to Israel. We arrived in Jerusalem just after the cease-fire. The city was in a state of shock – much like the whole country. The university was closed and nobody knew whether the academic year would begin and, if so, when. All new appointments were frozen. However by early 1974 things cleared up: I started teaching both in Russian Studies and at the School for Overseas Students at the Hebrew University. My teaching was interesting since I taught Israeli students about Russian history and society and overseas (mainly American) students about the history and society of Israel.

In the summer of 1980 I was suddenly invited to see Abe Harman, the president of our university and former Israeli ambassador to the United States. He was English-born and had been a Zionist leader there before coming to Israel. He said: 'The Oxford and Cambridge Education Board has recently approved Modern Jewish History as an elective subject for matriculation. It is of great importance that young people in England should be able to study Jewish History. So it can be done now at some foremost British schools such as Eton. However, there are no properly trained teachers in this field. Our university would like to help in this matter. Actually, Mr Robin Spiro, who was instrumental in this matter, is now here in Jerusalem and would like to talk to you.'

Next day I was sitting on the terrace of the King David Hotel and listening to tapes produced by Mr Spiro with voices of students at Eton who had taken some preliminary lectures in Jewish History. One of them was from the family of a maharaja; another was the son of a British general, and so on. At first I had many misgivings about the whole thing: my courses for the next academic year were already listed. It meant teaching at some secondary schools and preparing a curriculum for training teachers in very hurried conditions. Mr Spiro proposed that I come 'for a few months only', and it was the tapes that ultimately decided it. I agreed. I thought that it was for a few months, but after I arrived I soon realised that I would have to stay longer if anything substantial were to be achieved. I stayed more than two years.

I had some misgivings about teaching at Eton. Established as an elitist royal college, its reputation was somewhat frightening for an Israeli-Jewish person, an outsider like me. But Robin Spiro, the founder of the Institute for Modern Jewish History, who was largely instrumental in persuading the Oxford and Cambridge Board of Education to include Modern Jewish History as an elective subject for 'A' Level examinations, took me there in his car. He introduced me to some of the leading people at the college. It turned out that as I was a guest lecturer, I was not expected to wear the black academic gown or attend services and functions in the chapel.

I had some 17 students who registered for the course. I was quite impressed when they stood up upon my entering the class and waited until I said 'Good morning, boys.' They answered in unison 'Good morning, sir.' (No such luck at the Hebrew University!) In time I was able to get to know them somewhat. It turned out that the students were of a most varied background. Some were from 'military families'. As one of them put it: 'My father comes from a family who served in the army for genera-tions. He said to me "to understand modern warfare, one has to learn what the Jews have done in the Six Day War. So take this course on Jewish History".' He really impressed me when he submitted an extensive and well-documented paper on the Israeli Army. Another boy was of Indian background from a family of merchants of maharajahan descent. Another boy had heard about the Holocaust; he was interested to learn about it since he could not understand 'how such a thing could have happened'.

I was naturally expecting that some of my students would be Jewish. But despite my enquiries, I did not at first find even one among them. Until, at one point, an American boy answered my questions about previous knowledge of Judaism. 'Yes', he said 'during my Bar Mitzvah ... '. He came from an Atlanta Jewish family; it was his grandfather who financed his studies at Eton. Before leaving for England, the grandfather said to him: 'You are a Jew, and if they are teaching something about Jewish affairs, you should take it and learn about your people.'

The delightful thing about Eton was that it was situated near Windsor Castle which was reached by a bridge over the Thames. My wife Doris would sometimes join me there after a lecture and we would take a leisurely walk along the Thames. The area was full of quaint restaurants where we could sit down for a fine lunch.

Parallel to my teaching at Eton, I gave a course in Modern Jewish History at the City of London School. Its building was then situated on the Thames close to the City. Supported by a number of Jewish merchants, the school had a large body of Jewish students. As at any English public school, the curriculum at the school included Christian religious services, led by Anglican priests. There was a problem with what should be done about the Jewish students. At first some Jewish religious instruction by rabbis was introduced, but the mostly non-religious boys did not take to it. The school was therefore only too willing to try a course of Modern Jewish History given at the same time as the Christian boys had their religious instruction.

The courses I was teaching at Eton and the City of London School were supposed to be 'experimental'. We had to check whether the curriculum proposed was suitable for the English youngster, both Jewish and non-Jewish. The main thrust of my work in London was to locate and train potential teachers for Modern Jewish History in a number of colleges in England. Also, we had to persuade these colleges to accept such a course. A group of teachers and other intelligent people were enrolled by the Spiro Institute as possible teachers. One evening each week, we gathered at the hospitable home of the Spiros in Hampstead, texts in hand. At first I gave the lectures, but in time, some of the participants were already able to present a paper themselves. In time, the group expanded, other lecturers were introduced, and we moved to a larger venue. The general atmosphere was of considerable enthusiasm; more and more courses were given at various places in England. I, for example, travelled each Sunday to Liverpool, where I gave lectures at the King David School.

When it was felt that a good beginning had been made and a number of trained teachers were available and able to carry on, I returned to teach at the Hebrew University in Jerusalem. The Spiro Institute continued its expansion. It moved to an impressive building in Hampstead and became in time an Institute for Jewish History and Culture.

Towards the end of my stay in London I noticed an advert in the *Jewish Chronicle*: 'You do not have to be religious to be Jewish – you can be a secular humanistic Jew.' It gave a telephone number in Detroit in the United States. I phoned them and was amazed: there was an entire organization with services, rabbis and lay leaders which had developed a secular kind of Judaism. Upon my return to Jerusalem I received from them an invitation to visit their headquarters in Detroit and to participate in the annual conference of the American Society for Secular Humanistic Judaism (SHJ) in Miami in the spring of 1983. On arriving in Detroit I found a congregation with a fine synagogue and the founder and leader of SHJ, Rabbi Sherwin Wine. Then in Miami I met with leaders of dozens of congregations and groups from many cities in North America. I also learned that parallel to the SHJ there was a Congress of Secular Jewish Organizations (CJSO) composed of former Yiddishists, followers of Chaim Zhitlowsky, and that arrangements for a common framework for the two movements were being discussed. I was deeply impressed and atonished: the ideas of the two movements were practically identical with my own, but I had not known a thing about it. I made up my mind to make an effort to establish a similar group in Israel.

Upon my return to Jerusalem I learned that Professor Yehuda Bauer, a distinguished scholar of the Holocaust at our university was similarily interested. An Israel Association for Secular Humanistic Judaism was duly established with Bauer as chairman and me as vice chairman. Together with the SHJ and the CJSO in the United States and similar groups in other countries we founded an International Federation of Secular Jews and an International Institute for Secular Humanistic Judaism. At various times I served as dean of the institute and vice chairman of the federation. I also attended their international conferences in Brussels, Detroit, Jerusalem, Moscow, Paris and Chicago. Presently I am a member of the Board and Education Committee of the Institute (now renamed as the Institute for Judaism as Culture) and of the Board of the Israel Association for Secular Humanistic Judaism. As part of the work with the Institute I edited – together with Renee Kogel – a book of sources *Judaism in a Secular Age – An Anthology of Secular Humanistic Thought* (Ktav and Milan Press, New York and Detroit, 1995).

For many years I have followed developments in the USSR and especially the situation of the Jews there. When, under Gorbachev, towards the end of the 1980s, at last the gates of the Soviet Union were flung open I became active both in the absorbtion of the many thousands of newcomers from the Former Soviet Union to Israel and in the efforts to revive Jewish life and education there. I attended the founding conference of the first representative body of Soviet Jewry – the 'Vaad' – at the end of 1989 and travelled to Moscow, Saint Petersburg, Kiev and other places. On the afternoon of 18 August 1991 my wife and I were walking in the gardens of the Kremlin. Suddenly a large column of military trucks entered through one of the gates. Doris asked me suspiciously: 'What is the meaning of this?'

'It must be a routine changing of the guard of the Kremlin', I answered. The next day the putsch against Gorbachev and Yeltsin took place. It must have been a real change of the guard in the Kremlin.

When we looked through the window of our hotel the next morning we saw lines of tanks moving slowly to the centre of Moscow. At first we wondered whether we should go out. But later in the day the tanks came to a standstill; we saw people gathering around them and talking to the soldiers. We ventured outside and as I had a press ticket we were able to get in front of the White House where tens of thousands had gathered to defend Yeltsin inside. By that time huge crowds gathered around along the Moscow river. Young people – girls especially – climbed on the immobilized tanks, gave flowers to the soldiers and waved the Russian flag in support of Yeltsin. The next day the putsch collapsed. We witnessed history in front of our eyes.

I travelled to the Former Soviet Union many times lecturing to secular Jewish groups as well as to the Institute of Sociology of the Russian Academy of Science. From one visit to another I found major changes there; it was like a different country.

Postscript: Why I Did not Become a Communist, But Did Become Involved in Humanistic Judaism

Before ending this memoir it seems to me necessary to dwell some more on two issues: my relationship with communism and with Judaism. Why did I not become a communist? Or even why did I not become a member of the Union of Communist Youth (the Komsomol) to which each student in the USSR had to belong? In a wider sense – why did I not become overwhelmed by 'Marxism' in its Soviet rendering? I was exposed to it day and night with great intensity from the age of 15 for more than six years. It was fed to me by every means: radio, lectures, newspapers, books, journals, films, speeches, and so forth. Also, what enabled me to free myself so readily from the entire communist ideology, the 'Soviet spirit'? And, finally, what made me accept so readily, only a few months after leaving the USSR, the Jewish Zionist ideology?

There are a number of answers to these questions. Before I came under the Soviet influence, I had had the previous 'Polish Jewish' experience. The Soviet influence came to me only when I was 15 – a relatively adult stage. Until then I lived in a typical Polish–Jewish *shtetl* – Yaroslav. In the mornings I attended a strict Polish *Gymnasium* (secondary school) where I experienced Polish patriotism and acute anti-Semitism. In the afternoons, I studied Torah and Talmud with a rabbi. During some of the evenings and at the weekends, I attended a Zionist youth group. We talked about Eretz Israel, the new Jewish settlements there and the struggle against Arab attacks. We sang Hebrew Zionist songs and danced Israeli dances. Just before the outbreak of the Second World War, I attended a summer camp of the Zionist Movement in the Carpathian Mountains, an event which had a great impact on me.

Moreover, I was raised in a traditional Jewish family. My father led us – the three sons – to the synagogue each Saturday. On High Holidays (Rosh Hashanah and Yom Kippur) the three of us acted as a choir for the cantor during prayers at our synagogue. We celebrated all Jewish holidays with considerable decorum. We were a comfortably well-to-do merchant family, though hard-working. We had a good standard of living. We employed a live-in cook and a daily cleaning and laundry maid.

Our *shtetl* had some 7,000 Jews in a population of some 30,000. The Jews lived in a special area in town. It encompassed almost the entire spectrum of Jewish beliefs and organizations. There was a Burial Society, a Jewish primary school and a deeply orthodox Talmud Torah. It had a Chassidic Belz group as well as small Czortkow *shtibel* (small prayer room). It also boasted a Jewish Library, Theatre Hall and Great Synagogue. There were socialist Zionists, Bundists, general Zionists and Revisionists.

We had constant contact with the United States and western Europe: through films, journals, visitors, books, family, and so forth. We were, therefore, quite well informed about life in the West. The picture in our eyes was quite rosy. We were able to compare what we knew about the West with the Soviet horror stories about the 'oppressed proletariat in the capitalist countries'.

The brief encounter with the German Forces also had a shattering impact. They were an enemy of the Jews but they were well-dressed, clean, well-organized and motorized. Compared with the retreating Polish Forces and even more so with the Soviet Forces, they looked modern, superior. The Soviet Army looked Asiatic, shabby, unclean, backward, with out-dated trucks and tanks. Many of the Soviet soldiers were on foot or on horse.

Shortly after establishing their administration in the Western Ukraine, the Soviets proclaimed 'elections'. These were obviously rigged. Ninety-nine per cent of the voters supported the 'accession' to the USSR. So, from the beginning we saw that the Soviet system was founded on a constant and perpetual lie. This was our experience all through being under the Soviet regime. As I studied Marxism–Leninism at college, I learned to declaim the appropriate Communist formulae with sufficient conviction, but without ever believing in them.

To all this one has to add the total experience of Soviet reality. When we were exiled to Siberia, when we lived in Kazakhstan for several years, we witnessed the real conditions in Soviet society. All talk about equality, Soviet democracy, and so on, was so obviously untrue, a huge fraud. Many of the Communist Party bosses, the managers, police officers and state officials lived a very comfortable life at the expense of the general population, many of whom lived beneath the poverty line. Many of them were corrupt and dishonest. They lived privileged lives, receiving housing, scarce foods, goods and alcohol, as well as fashionable clothing and had access to so-called 'distribution centres' – closed shops only 'open' to the privileged. Workers in the USSR were living in extremely harsh conditions – before the war and even more so during it. And every one was stealing and transgressing the law, because otherwise it was impossible to live, to fulfil the production 'plan'. Almost all the people that I knew were cheating the state and stealing from it in one way or the other. An acquaintance of mine, a tailor who worked in a shop producing khaki uniforms for the army (during wartime almost no other textile was produced) cut the material in such a way as to save some of it and take it out of the shop. Then he handed it over to a person who sold it on the '*kolkhoz* market' for a price many times higher than that which was fixed by the state. He and the middle-man divided the spoils. Those who produced nails stole nails. Those who worked at a meat-packing factory stole tins of beef. Those who worked in shops, restaurants, cafeterias, and so on, stole some of the food and goods. And everyone who could cheat on reporting on their output sales did so.

Under these circumstances how could I have become a communist?

On the other hand, I was born into a deeply orthodox family of Belzer Chassids which is one of the 'fundamentalist' branches of religious Jews. So how did I become a non-religious, 'secular' person?

My grandfathers on both sides wore beards and side locks (*payot*). They were dressed in black gabardine coats and wore black felt hats. My mother's father was some kind of *Dayan* (religious judge). My father's brother was a religious official in Berlin, of all places. My grandmother on my mother's side had her head shaved and wore a *stern tiche* (a traditional scarf).

The point was that we were not entirely closed to the impact of modernity. The main influence in this direction was none other than my mother. My father had only a religious orthodox education and spent the First World War years hiding from Austrian army service in Vienna. My mother was different. Even as a girl, she was deeply interested in studying and reading. Her orthodox father died when she was a small girl and her mother did not prevent her from attending the regular school. During the First World War their family was evacuated to Moravia (a Czech area) where she was able to experience a 'Western' way of life. As a result, she was at home with both German and Polish culture – with Goethe, Schiller, Heine, Mickiewicz, and so on. She hummed the operettas of composers such as Strauss, Kalman and Lehar. It was under the influence of my mother that my father moved me and my brothers from a strict orthodox 'Talmud Torah' (religious Bible School) to an afternoon religious Yavneh School which was modern and taught Hebrew. This arrangement made it possible for us to attend government school in the morning. My mother's ambition for me was to be accepted into a government *Gymnasium*. She was enormously proud when I received excellent marks in the entrance examination without the aid of a tutor.

One could, of course, think that the process of 'secularization' or of becoming free of the orthodox indoctrination was a result of the shattering of the entire traditional religious beliefs and way of life following our expulsion from Yaroslav, our birth place. I was exposed to the influence of Soviet occupation and education, exile to Siberia, studies at a Soviet College and the impact of the Holocaust, amongst other things. But this was not the case. I had already become a non-believer in Yaroslav, at the age of 14 before the outbreak of the Second World War. I lived in two cultures. At the *Gymnasium*, studies started each morning with Catholic prayers and religious songs, during which we, the several Jewish students in my class, stood, but were excused from saying the Christian devotions.

It did not take me long to come to the conclusion that the Christian-Catholic religion was not to be taken at face value. From this it was a small step for me to make a comparative study of Judaism and Christianity. From a critical negation of one religion – Christianity – I moved on towards a critical examination of any religion, including Judaism. This was especially so since I suffered because of my religion. Studies at the *Gymnasium* were then conducted also on Saturdays. Attendance was obligatory. My parents – after discussions and family consultations – agreed that I should attend school on the Sabbath – since walking and study-ing are not forbidden on that day. But I was not allowed to write in class, since that was 'forbidden'. So, during my first year at school, I did not write on the Sabbath, despite anti-Semitic incidents and difficulties that were caused by it. In the second year I started to write on the Sabbath. I remember, when walking from school on that first Sabbath, I thought that at any moment lightning from Heaven would strike me for this horrible transgression of the holiness of the Sabbath. Nothing happened.

At the same time, I was able to examine the clash between religious beliefs and science. Religion offered the Creationist Theory of the beginning of the Universe in Six Days. We had a good physics teacher and were offered a comprehensive rendering of Darwin's Theory of Evolution (though without mentioning his name). I remember one day, when I was 14 years of age – after a lecture on the structure of the Universe – I was looking at the blue, cloudless sky when suddenly I was struck by the thought that there was no sky, only blue endless space. There was no Supernatural Entity there ... the Universe was empty.

One would think that our exile to Siberia and then our life in communist Russia would further break the hold of religious tradition on us and make us give up the religious ways even more. Strangely, the opposite happened; as the Soviets tried to coerce us into acting contrary to our custom, we reacted by upholding it in clandestine ways. On our first Friday evening in Siberia, the 'Soviet Boss' came into our small room, blew out the candles which my mother had lit in honour of the Sabbath, warning us 'not to indulge any more in foolish activities'. We did not stop lighting candles on Friday evening, but one of us was always on guard outside our door on the lookout for any approaching official. We held prayers on Yom Kippur in a hidden place in the woods – also with some of us serving as guards. When we lived in Kazakhstan, we found out where, on High Holidays and the Sabbath, prayers were conducted in private homes, not far from us. Before Passover, we baked Matzot at our home and even invited some friends to participate.

It was more after coming to Israel that I became outraged by the behaviour and especially by the politics of the orthodox religionists. Though they were a small minority, who did not serve in the army, or work, they tried to impose their total control on life in the country. And they often succeeded, despite opposition, especially in matters of marriage and divorce, kosher food, Sabbath behaviour and Jewish Holidays, burials, and so forth. Sometimes, when passing through the orthodox parts of Jerusalem, I often think how right were the early leaders of Zionism when they said: 'It is easier to get the Jew out of the *Galut* (Diaspora) than to get the *Galut* out of the Jew.'

While not satisfied with the Orthodox – or even the Conservative or Reform versions of Judaism – I was constantly in search of an enlightened, non-Supernatural, Humanistic interpretation of Judaism. I was constantly returning to the study of the Bible, Talmud, and modern Jewish thinkers – religious and secular. It was, therefore, quite natural for me to become excited when I 'discovered' the existence of the Society of Humanistic Judaism and Congress of Secular Jewish Organizations in North America. It was also why I became, together with Professor Yehuda Bauer, a Founder of the Israel Movement for Humanistic Judaism. I served as vice chairman of the movement and dean of its international institute as well as vice president of the International Federation of Secular Jews. I am active in this movement at present, as well as being active in Meitar – College for Judaism as Culture – which is an educational institution connected with this movement.

Nevertheless, while being secular, I believe in upholding positive Jewish religious traditions, customs and holidays, as well as learning and knowing Jewish religious sources in a humanistic and modern interpretation.

So we come to the end of my story so far. As explained at the beginning of these memoirs, our family was unique in several ways. We were a family of six at the start of the Second World War and that same nuclear family of six was still together at the end of it. We survived a period under the Gestapo, a harsh period under Soviet rule in Western Ukraine and the imprisonment of my father; exile to Siberia and a grim period of life in Northern Kazakhstan. Shortly after being repatriated to Poland we crossed the border to Germany illegally and lived there in DP camps. Our entire family settled in Israel and established our families there. We went through all the wars of Israel without casualties in our immediate family. I was able not only to do my MA studies at the Hebrew University of Jerusalem but was sent by this university to do my doctoral studies in England. During my years as foreign editor at *Ha'aretz* I was in a position to mingle and get acquainted with some of the elite people in Israel. Again, during my research and teaching at a number of major British and American universities as well as at the Hebrew University I was privileged to know some outstanding personalities and scholars in these countries. Through my activities at the Jewish humanistic organizations I came to know some top people active in this field.

I was able to establish a family of my own with my wife Doris and two daughters, Nina and Odette and have now four grand-children.

A unique Jewish life indeed.